Defendants in the criminal process

International Library of Social Policy

General Editor Kathleen Jones
Professor of Social Administration
University of York

Arbor Scientiæ
Arbor Vitæ

A catalogue of the books available in the **International Library of Social Policy** and other series of Social Science books published by Routledge & Kegan Paul will be found at the end of this volume

Defendants in the criminal process

A. E. Bottoms
and
J. D. McClean
Faculty of Law,
University of Sheffield
assisted by
Isobel Todd

Routledge & Kegan Paul
London, Henley and Boston

First published in 1976
by Routledge & Kegan Paul Ltd
76 Carter Lane,
London EC4V 5EL,
Reading Road,
Henley-on-Thames,
Oxon RG9 1EN and
9 Park Street,
Boston, Mass. 02108, USA
Set in 10 pt English on a 12pt body
and printed in Great Britain at
The Lavenham Press Limited, Lavenham, Suffolk, England

ISBN 0 7100 8274 6

Contents

Tables

Statutes

Cases

Preface

This book is concerned with the defendant's participation in the processes of the English criminal courts, and with the quality of justice in those courts as it is experienced and assessed by the defendants themselves. To each defendant, his case is of special importance, whether the charges are grave or petty, so we examine a wide spectrum of cases, guilty pleas as well as contested trials, the daily round of the magistrates' court as well as the occasional Crown Court drama. The defendant experiences, as no one else does, the whole criminal process, from the first questions of the investigating policeman through to trial, sentence and possible appeal. An account of the court system based on the defendant's experience of it shows how the various parts of the process knit together, and how decisions taken at an early stage, long before the case even reaches court, can shape the development of the whole.

The complexity of the legal system bewilders many of those who come into contact with it for the first time or infrequently. Yet those accused of crime have crucial decisions to take, for example as to legal representation, plea and choice of court. If these decisions are ill-informed or haphazard, not only may individual defendants be placed at an unnecessary disadvantage but the criminal justice system will suffer from criticism and resentment which could in the long term affect public confidence in the courts. Knowledge of the problems faced by the accused, of the extent and quality of advice available and of the factors influencing decisions is an essential prerequisite for sound development of the judicial system.

Much of the material needed to develop such knowledge is straightforwardly factual, but an essential additional feature will be consideration of the opinions of defendants, their attitude to the process and their reactions to its operation. The reasonableness or otherwise of such opinions may be impossible to judge; but even if an opinion is based on ignorance or prejudice, the fact that it is held is important in its own right, especially if it provides a basis for decision.

The result we present is thus a detailed account of the practical workings of the criminal court system as we found them during one period of time in one English city, setting out in particular the thoughts and reactions of the defendants who passed through the system. We must make it clear that we do not necessarily endorse the criticisms of the system made by the defendants, except where this is made explicit in the text. Our own comments are also often critical, but it is important to realise we have not essayed a full assessment of English criminal justice. Because we are primarily concerned with how matters appear to the defendant, we do not detail in the text many aspects of the system, and of the work done by judges, magistrates and lawyers in less than ideal conditions, for which we personally have great admiration and respect. We raise issues and questions which we believe need to be faced by all those involved in the administration of justice; we hope that it is clear that in doing so we are offering constructive criticisms within a system whose broad parameters we endorse, and not the destructive assaults of cynics or revolutionaries.

Our research took place in Sheffield, but our concern was not with the courts which sit in that city so much as with the general organisation and administration of the English criminal justice system. We do not imagine that the main outline of the picture would have been any different if we had been located in any other industrial city using the system of lay magistrates. In fact Sheffield once had a stipendiary magistrate: indeed Charlie Peace was committed for trial by the Sheffield stipendiary. But the office lapsed in 1915, and it was only in 1975, after this book was complete, that a stipendiary was again appointed to ease the flow of business. A more obvious problem at the time of our research was that of space. Despite its size and industrial importance, Sheffield has never been, as have Leeds or Manchester or Birmingham, a regional capital; it only became an Assize town in 1955. One of the results has been an acute shortage of court accommodation, which creates quite special problems in maintaining the smooth administration of the courts. As our research was in progress a deep hole was being dug alongside the Courthouse, and new courts will one day give much needed relief. It is right to record these local factors, but many of the tensions within and the pressures upon the court system are found in every locality. This is true in particular of the tension between the lawyers' civil-rights rhetoric and the demands of speedy and efficient administration, which tension we identify as a central feature of the English criminal court system.

Despite the very real local pressures and difficulties we have just mentioned, every help and facility was made available to us by official agencies in the Sheffield area. We gladly express our sincere gratitude for the co-operation and interest of the Crown Court Administrator, the Magistrates' Courts' Committee and the Clerk to the Justices, the police, the Probation and After-care Service, and the Prison Department. We received particular help from the members of the various bodies whose daily work was in the magistrates' 'lock-up court', and from the staff of the Observation and Classification Unit at Leeds Prison. We owe a fundamental and far-reaching debt to the Home Office, which suggested the study (see chapter 1), financed it, and subsequently was very patient with our delays in completing it: in particular we should like to thank Mr I. J. Croft, now Head of the Home Office Research Unit, who was concerned with the study from beginning to end. We were glad to be able to repay something of this debt by giving evidence to the Interdepartmental Committee on the Distribution of Business in the Criminal Courts (the James Committee). We are only sorry that at the time of our going to press the report of a subsequent survey of the London courts commissioned by the James Committee from the Government's Office of Population Censuses and Surveys, is not available for public comment, though we are gratified that its results are substantially similar to our own.

Our final debt is of course to the defendants, without whose co-operation the whole research would have been impossible. Their interest and concern with the issues we raised was often considerable, and we only hope that, in seeking to present the defendant's perspective, we have not distorted it.

More parochially we must thank our research colleagues, which we do with deep gratitude, for we were fortunate in having an exceptional team. Isobel Todd, as principal research assistant, was with the project from first drafts of the interview schedule to coding much of the final material; in particular, she was in charge of the fieldwork programme and its successful completion owes an enormous amount to her efficiency and verve. Elizabeth Elston was an enthusiastic and excellent interviewer who worked in the closest harmony with Isobel Todd. Dariel Merrills helped us out of a difficult situation by agreeing to undertake much of the drudgery of court observation in the later stages; we are also grateful to the various law students who assisted in this respect. Monica Walker, now Research Fellow in the Faculty of Law, gave us the benefit of her statistical expertise as well as putting in many hours of coding and analysis; we are greatly indebted to her. She and Professor John Wood also found time to read the final report in draft form and to suggest many useful amendments. The typing of the manuscript was performed with exemplary efficiency and speed by Mrs Patricia Groves and Mrs Joyce Keen; the University of Sheffield Research Fund kindly provided a small grant to cover typing and other ancillary expenses in the late stages of the work. Last but by no means least, we would wish to place on record our appreciation of the constant support and encouragement of our wives.

A.E.B.
J.D.McC.

1 Birth of a research project

A certain shop in the city of Sheffield has a policy of prosecuting all suspected shoplifters, and strongly encourages its sales staff to report customers acting suspiciously. Inevitably, this policy results in certain persons being brought before the courts while strongly protesting their innocence, on the grounds that they had taken the article in question out of the shop by mistake, and not through any intent to steal.

The formal legal position is clear. If the mistake is genuine, the defendant is not guilty, for 'theft' occurs only where a person 'dishonestly appropriates property belonging to another with the intention of permanently depriving the other of it' (Theft Act 1968, s.1). But if someone has been apprehended in possession of goods which he has not paid, for, how is he to show his innocent intent—or even, to couch the position in the correct legal formality, to raise a reasonable doubt against the prosecution's allegations of dishonesty?

Our legal system is deliberately designed to permit such a person a considerable freedom of choice in the protection of his rights. In the first place, of course, he may choose to plead not guilty, so forcing the prosecution to prove its case beyond a reasonable doubt. Next, he may decide to have his trial either before a bench of magistrates, or before a judge and jury in the Crown Court, where 'twelve good men and true' will be the final arbiters of his guilt or innocence. Whichever of these alternatives he thinks the more likely to secure acquittal, he may choose it. Third, he may if he wishes engage a solicitor to help present his case, and in many instances the State through its legal aid scheme will pay to help him do so. Finally, even if he is convicted at the court he has chosen, he has the chance of an appeal against conviction and against sentence, either to the Crown Court (if tried and sentenced before the magistrates) or to the Court of Appeal (in other cases).

Let us follow through the court system two defendants apprehended at the shop in question within a couple of months of each other:

Case 1049 R, a man in his late 50s, was caught outside the shop in possession of some electric light bulbs, valued at 40p. He claimed that not paying for them was a complete mistake. He was an upper working-class man, living with his wife in a very respectable area of the city, and although he had a minor previous conviction, this had occurred more than twenty years before. He suffered from hypertension, and had been told by his doctor to avoid stressful and worrying situations: he was thus terribly upset when he was suddenly faced with the prospect of a court appearance and possible conviction for dishonesty. In his anxiety, he called in at a probation office near his home for some advice. The probation officer was extremely helpful to him, and gave him useful advice about contacting a solicitor. He also arranged to write a probation officer's report on R to present to the court, although this is very unusual in routine shoplifting cases in the Sheffield area. R contacted a solicitor, who was very helpful and explained that he could and should plead not guilty, but that (because of the way court business was handled) this would mean an adjournment of the case for 6-8 weeks and a second court appearance before the magistrates. R decided that he could not stand this; his hypertension was such that he must get it over and done with. He determined on a guilty plea, while still asserting his complete innocence. His solicitor tried hard to persuade him otherwise, but with no success; his wife, who had also wanted him to plead not guilty, did not press the matter because she realised it would worry R too much. So R went to the magistrates' court, asked to be tried there at once, and pleaded guilty. His solicitor told the bench: 'I have been into the question of plea in some detail. It is his decision to plead: he feels any adjournment will make him very ill indeed.' The magistrates accepted the plea, listened to a plea in mitigation from the solicitor, read the probation officer's report, and read also three letters submitted by the defendant—one from himself, one from his doctor, and one from his employer testifying to his good character. An order of conditional discharge for 1 year was then imposed.

Case 5013 B, another respectable upper working-class man, also with a single previous conviction many years before, was caught outside the shop in possession of some glasspaper valued at 10p. He too said it was a completely genuine mistake. He decided from the outset that he would fight the case from start to finish, and would most certainly plead not guilty. In the CID office it was discovered that he had a previous conviction, and, he said, 'from that point on I was treated as a criminal'. He was advised by the CID officer to plead guilty, but resisted. He went to see a solicitor whom friends had recommended: this solicitor told him about the legal aid scheme, and gave him a form to complete, which B did. The solicitor agreed to fight the case, and told B this would mean jury trial in the Crown Court—B did not realise until after the case was over that he could have opted to plead not guilty before the magistrates. A barrister was duly engaged (solicitors may not appear in the Crown Court for this kind of case), and B eventually had his full jury trial. He was convicted. A fine of £10 was imposed, and B was also ordered to pay £50 towards the prosecution's costs in bringing the case. After the case B, incensed at the injustice of the result (as he saw it), consulted his solicitor about an appeal. The solicitor advised against this: it would, he said, 'get you nowhere at great expense'.[1] At this point the solicitor also told B that he (the solicitor) had not submitted B's legal aid application to the legal aid office, because the application disclosed that B had savings such as to debar him from entitlement to aid. The solicitor's bill eventually arrived, asking for £65; thus B's total financial loss in the case was £125 for a 10p theft. Not surprisingly, B was not very enthusiastic about either his solicitor or the legal system in general: 'I now realise I had no chance against the police: it cost me a lot of money and I have totally wasted all that money. I believed before in English justice, but not now. I did do the receiving the time I was up before, and admitted that: this time I fight it and there is a grave injustice.' He said the whole family had been very upset by the case.

From these two cases, we see clearly that it is not enough for lawyers simply to point out the existence of safeguards, and of ways of asserting rights, in our formal legal system. Obviously, if these defendants' stories were true, we have here two wrongful convictions. But even if they were in fact guilty, both men were entitled to claim that the administration of the legal system had in a real sense been unjust to them. In R's case, the way the courts were administered simply did not permit a plea of not guilty to be disposed of in one court appearance, and that was the only right that was of any importance to him. In B's case, he had apparently been very badly served by his solicitor, both in the lack of adequate information about choosing the court of trial, and in the failure to make clear at an early stage that B would have to meet all legal costs himself. But more than this, B had been penalised by the legal system to the extent of £50 for asserting his undoubted right to a trial by jury—prosecution costs are rarely awarded in lower court shoplifting cases, and even on occasions when they are, the amount is very small.

All this seems very unfair. Yet from a different point of view, one can defend the system that led to these apparent injustices. If there is to be a contested trial, the prosecution must produce all its witnesses on the right day. This is complex and costly to arrange: it is imperative that it should only be arranged where it is strictly necessary, i.e. where the defendant really is going to plead not guilty. It makes good administrative sense, then, to have a preliminary arraignment at which a plea is taken—if the plea is guilty, the case may proceed; if not, it can be put back to another court. Furthermore, even if one is certain that a particular defendant will plead not guilty, to mix his case up with a lot of guilty pleas, remands before trial, etc. makes little administrative sense—for contested trials take much longer to dispose of, and therefore create unnecessary waiting for a lot of people unless they are deliberately siphoned off to a special court. As to the administrative issues in B's case: it costs much more for the prosecution to prepare papers and brief a barrister for a Crown Court trial, so if B deliberately chose that form of trial and was convicted, why should the public, and not he, pay for it? In any case, if significantly more defendants opted for Crown Court trial, the administration of the Crown Court would collapse through overwork, so it is legitimate to have some safeguard against this in the form of a 'costs penalty'.

A similar argument can be developed on the question of plea: not guilty pleas are much more costly to handle, and take up significantly more of precious court time, so it is right that the judicial system should encourage guilty pleas by allowing some reduction of sentence or costs in respect of them.

These are administrators' arguments, and they do not marry easily with lawyers' rhetoric about the rights of the accused. The tension between the two points of view is one of the central themes of this book.

Approaching the research

The currently fashionable phenomenological sociology stresses the importance of researchers making explicit in considerable detail the nature of the research act which leads to the findings; for only in the light of detailed knowledge of the research act, including the background expectancies brought to the situation by the observer, exactly how he interacted with the research subject, and so on, can the reader make adequate sense of what is presented to him as research evidence (see generally Phillipson, 1972).

We are not phenomenologists, and it is not our intention to provide precisely this kind of account. But there is advantage in conventional social scientists being prepared to state, more openly and honestly than they sometimes have, exactly how certain research came to be done, and how it came to be done in certain ways.

The research reported in this book is a study of the English criminal justice system from the point of view of the defendant. It came into existence in a rather unorthodox way, almost by accident.

In the summer of 1969, one of the authors approached the Home Office with a request for financial assistance for another research project. The request was declined (it no longer matters why), but it was suggested by the Home Office that discussions might still be held about financing other research. Such suggestions are not to be ignored, and a meeting was arranged. The upshot was that the Home Office had noted the implantation of criminologists within the Faculty of Law at Sheffield, and had wondered whether, with this combination of legal and criminological interest, the Faculty would be interested in pursuing research into the administration of the criminal justice system. For internal reasons, the Home Office was anxious to expand funded research in this area: some was being conducted by the Home Office Research Unit itself, but more was needed from universities.

We must stress that no attempt was made by the Home Office to make us conduct any particular project; we were simply invited to consider whether we wished to propose research in this field. Equally, the Home Office was naturally not committed in advance to accept anything which we might propose, but had simply opened a dialogue. We thought, and still think, that this was a most helpful method of exploring the mutual interests of administrators and of outside academics.

Faced with this invitation, we considered a number of possibilities. While we were doing so, it struck us forcibly that, as we put it in our original research proposal, 'the pattern of the administration of criminal justice in this country is largely determined by the outcome of decisions taken at certain key stages by defendants in individual cases'. In recent years, the administration of English criminal justice has been increasingly stretched by the growing numbers of cases coming before the courts. Yet if such defendants had not pleaded guilty in the vast majority of cases, the system could have collapsed administratively. Similarly, higher court caseloads (twice officially considered in the 1960s, by the Streatfeild Committee and the Beeching Commission) would certainly be overwhelmed if significantly more defendants exercised their right to choose trial by jury instead of summary trial before the magistrates. Similarly again, the appeal courts could only function if the number of appeals were kept down to a reasonable level.

So, the smooth administration of justice essentially depended on the co-operation of the mass of defendants. Yet no systematic study had been made of why defendants exercised these choices in the way that they did. This administrative interest was the first reason for our concentration on the defendant's perspective.

A second reason, also important from the outset, was based on a civil rights or libertarian viewpoint. We suspected that investigation might show that all was not well with the system. As we put it in our original research proposal:

> The assumption of the present system is that the choices are made rationally, on the basis of full information and a proper appreciation of the implications of a particular choice. For example, the prescribed forms of words used in putting the choice of court to the defendant are an attempt to provide the minimum necessary information upon the choice and its implications. There is however room for considerable doubt whether defendants are fully aware of the range of decisions which they have to make before the decisions are thrust upon them, and whether they appreciate what the decisions entail. It may be that the safeguards of our rules of criminal procedure, superficially impressive, afford little real protection to the defendant.

Once again, it seemed worth investigating whether this was so.

Having thus concentrated upon the idea of choices made by the defendant, we considered systematically what these choices were.

There were, we concluded, five substantial decisions to be investigated:

(i) Plea—the crucial decision to plead guilty or not guilty;

(ii) Venue—the defendant's choice of court, as between the magistrates' court and a higher court, open to him in many but not all indictable offences and in some summary offences;

(iii) Representation—the decision whether or not to have a legal representative;

(iv) Bail or custody—the decision whether to apply for bail (or to oppose a request for a remand in custody) or not;

(v) Appeal—the decision, if convicted, whether to appeal against conviction, or sentence, or both.

The Home Office generously agreed to finance a research project to investigate the defendant's view of these five decisions. The project was officially entitled 'Decision-making by Defendants in Criminal Cases'; it will be seen that from the outset it was concerned with the tension between defendants' legal rights and the needs of courts for smooth administration.

Modifying the research: 'appreciation'

The term 'decision-making' appeared in the original title of our research, but does not appear in the title of this book. This represents a significant shift in our thinking which it is important to explain.

The original focus was somewhat psychologistic: we would approach the defendant's decisions after the manner of decision-making research in psychology. The most obvious criminological parallel, much in our minds at the outset, was sentencing research—and, like the two most recent major sentencing research workers (Hogarth, 1971; Hood, 1972), we thought in terms of applying batteries of psychological tests to our subjects.

This intention we quite soon abandoned, for two main reasons. First, at a simple practical level our pilot interviews in defendants' homes suggested that it would be difficult to switch attention from the case and its details—about which most defendants seemed willing to talk freely—to an instrument obviously designed to probe the subject's own personality, at a time when he was often still naturally defensive and wounded after the recent court experience. Second, we consulted the Director of the Sheffield University MRC Unit for Research in Social and Applied Psychology, and received the discouraging reply that there were no simple standard tests available which were likely to test all the kinds of personal attribute that seemed hypothetically likely to be associated with our defendants' decisions. Thus we could either (i) use a whole battery of different available tests; (ii) select one simple test (such as Eysenck's EPI) in the hope that the few attributes it measured would be relevant to our research; (iii) create our own psychological instruments as in Hogarth's sentencing research; or (iv) abandon formal tests altogether, and treat the research as descriptive and exploratory. Since alternatives (i) and (iii) were for different reasons impracticable, and (ii) seemed an extremely crude procedure, we chose the fourth option, and were fortified in that choice by the knowledge that this would also have been the choice of the MRC Unit.

As the pilot work proceeded, the wisdom of this choice was reinforced. It became clear that in many cases defendants simply did not 'take decisions' in any formal sense. Events at the scene of the crime, or in the police station, or in subsequent legal processes, often seemed to the defendant himself to render meaningless the formally available decision to opt for (e.g.) a guilty or not guilty plea. Events had taken such a course that there was no real option. In such cases, the analogy with formal sentencing decisions by judges or magistrates breaks down almost completely.

Furthermore, early interviews emphasised the magnitude of the problem if true explanation of defendants' decisions was to be attempted. Inevitably, to create an adequate explanation we would need to have a good deal of information about the defendant's past life, including his previous dealings with legal and other authorities, his personal and family history, and so on. Thus one man might approach the court in a very meek and submissive, even self-punitive way, while another might be full of bombast and extremely right-assertive; but to understand and explain these attitudes fully one would need to explore very deeply and widely into defendants' past experiences and beliefs. One of us had experience in another context of the complexity of classifying offenders' criminal and social histories (Bottoms and McClintock, 1973, part I), and it was obvious that in the limited space of the interviews we were able to conduct, no such exploration was likely to be possible, even if defendants had allowed us to attempt it.

For all these reasons we shifted the focus of the research from 'explaining decisions' to a more general description of the criminal justice system by defendants, centring around the five key areas of plea, venue, representation, bail and appeal.

This shift was much in line with a shift in criminological thinking taking place at about the same time. For in recent years there has been a marked increase of interest in what may be described as 'subjectivist' approaches in criminology, first with Matza's (1969) 'naturalism', and then more fully with the growth of the phenomenological school (see Phillipson, 1971; Phillipson and Roche, 1974). Matza (1969, pp. 24-5) describes 'appreciation' as entailing

> a commitment ... to render [the phenomenon] with fidelity and without violating its integrity. ... The view of the phenomena yielded by this perspective is *interior*, in contrast to the external view yielded by a more objective perspective. The...phenomenon is seen from the inside. Consequently, many of the categories having their origin in evaluations made from the outside become difficult to maintain since they achieve little prominence in the interpretations and definitions of [the] subjects.

We have already seen an example of this: what appears externally as a 'decision' to be 'made', may not appear in such a way at all to the defendant. Thus the appreciative stance could shed light on the topic in a way not otherwise available (for an illustration of this in relation to the American public defender system, see Sudnow, 1965).

We were influenced by Matza's concept of appreciation in the final stages of the development of our research interview schedules. Our shift of focus from psychological explanation to description had facilitated a marriage with 'appreciation', and we thus deliberately decided to phrase as many questions as possible in an open-ended way, and to allow the subject to talk freely, to maximise the appreciative aspect of the study. At the same time we did not abandon our original focus upon five specific 'decisions', so that we have adopted an appreciative stance only to a limited extent. Furthermore, as we have made clear above, our view of explanation in social science is very different from that of the phenomenologist, and we should not be taken to have written a phenomenological book.

In short, during the course of our pilot work we shifted our framework of study from psychologistic explanation to appreciative description, while adhering to a focus upon the five decisions of plea, venue, representation, bail and appeal. But to our original interests in administration and in a civil rights perspective had been added the important goal of more fully understanding and appreciating the defendant's point of view for its own sake, i.e. to understand its interior logic rather than categorise it with the labels of an external system.

'Appreciation' and 'consumer research'

In passing one should note the close connection between the appreciative stance and so-called 'consumer research'. In Britain at least, the two have developed rather separately. The appreciative/phenomenological school of sociology has developed largely for theoretical reasons, but also often in close harmony with a concern for the apparently powerless and oppressed in our society (for an example of research with these mixed concerns, see Cohen and Taylor's (1972) account of prisoners in the maximum security wing at Durham Prison). Developing at the same time, but independently, has been a strong movement among social workers and social administrators to consider the consumer's view of official administrative agencies and of social casework as provided by professional social workers: here perhaps the seminal work has been that of John Mayer and Noel Timms (1970). (For other work see references at pp. 174-5 of Mayer and Timms; also Timms, 1973; Goldberg, 1970.) Despite different theoretical approaches and policy concerns, these two traditions obviously have some common features; it is a sad comment on the institutional separation between sociology and social work in Britain that they have remained as separate as they are.

Our own research was not much influenced, in any direct sense, by the 'consumer research'/'client speaks' group. Nevertheless, in one way it is obviously part of that tradition, since it provides for the first time an overall consumer's eye-view of the English criminal justice system. This is a neglected approach to an important social institution. Interestingly, the nearest direct parallel to our own research (the American study by Casper, 1972), was written explicitly from a consumer research perspective (p.3).[2]

Modifying the research: the court sample

The shift from psychologistic explanation to appreciative description was the most important alteration made to the original research proposal; but one other modification is worth brief notice.

Originally we intended simply an interview study of defendants concentrated on the five selected defendants' decisions. In theory this could have been done without any court observation on our part (simply selecting defendants to be interviewed from lists supplied to us by the court authorities), but from the outset we decided against this. We wanted to have our own observation of the court proceedings, partly as a check against the defendant's perhaps imperfect comprehension of the legal and procedural events; and partly so that we would have our own notation of any special events in court which our defendants might not have thought necessary to tell us about, and which our specific questions might miss. In practice we later found that the presence of a research observer in court was helpful in another way; especially when the interviewer herself had been present in court, but also in other cases, 'the fact of having been in court was a major influence on the relationship established between interviewer and offender. In a curious way it formed a link between the two individuals' (Martin and Webster, 1971, p. 20).

Having decided to monitor the court proceedings of the interviewed defendants, we were in practice committed to observing, at least initially, all cases coming within certain offence categories, since there was no way of knowing in advance which way defendants would make certain decisions (e.g. plea and venue) and these were to be key factors in the stratification of our sample, as we explain more fully below. We could still have decided to make no detailed notes on cases falling outside the interview sample, or to destroy or ignore what notes we had made on these cases. But we decided instead to record it all. The extra investment in terms of time and effort was relatively slight, and there seemed to be important secondary advantages in full recording. There is no previous research in England which has recorded details on a complete sample of indictable cases over a certain time span, monitoring in detail items such as we were to be concerned with. What research there has been has been concentrated on specific aspects of the system, such as bail (Bottomley, 1970; King, 1971; Zander, 1971), appeal (Zander, 1972a) and so on: yet there seemed to be important advantages in viewing the system as a whole, and considering these various matters as interrelated parts. This conclusion was reinforced as we continued with the research. As we did so, it struck us as the more remarkable that government committees had also not really considered the criminal justice system as a whole. Once again, there have been various recent inquiries into specific aspects of the system, such as the Widgery Committee on criminal legal aid (Home Office, 1966), the Home Office (1974) working party on bail, and the Streatfeild (1961) and Beeching (1969) inquiries into the higher criminal courts, but there was no overall consideration of the whole system. The Beeching Report, with its special statistical survey (see Rose, 1971), came nearest, but this too had not adequately considered the genesis of higher court caseloads through decisions made in the lower courts.

Thus we provide details in this book of a complete population of cases falling within a specified offence parameter during the research period. This (although it is not strictly a sample) we refer to throughout as the 'court sample'; it naturally includes within it all the cases we eventually interviewed (the 'interview sample').

The total number of defendants' cases observed in the court sample was 1,696; 1,367 defendants were male and 329 female. Of these cases, 24 are excluded for most purposes for the reasons set out at the foot of Table 1.3.

Methodology: general considerations

These then, are the broad features of our research—a defendant's eye-view of the criminal justice system, attempting an appreciative description of the defendant's perspective, but also having very much in mind the relevance of defendants' decisions to the system as a whole, and their crucial place in the tension between lawyers' civil rights rhetoric and the needs of court administrators for a smoothly running system. As a secondary aim, we tried to monitor a complete set of cases in one area, to provide a fuller account than before of the inter-related working of our system.

How should such a research project be carried out?

For practical reasons, we decided from the outset to monitor only one local court system, as any other decision would have been outside the realm of practicality. Our research, therefore, is limited to cases originating in the Sheffield magistrates' court (even if going on to a higher court)—or in other words, to prosecutions relating to alleged offences committed within the city of Sheffield. Only the adult court system was considered, so that (with very rare exceptions)[3] our samples contain only persons aged 17 and over.

We were anxious to avoid overwhelming our sample with minor cases. On Home Office advice (discussed more fully below) we also totally excluded motoring offences. We therefore chose to study all indictable prosecutions, and all non-indictable (other than motoring) prosecutions in which the defendant had a choice of venue between the magistrates' court and the higher court (in practice those where the maximum penalty on conviction is imprisonment for more than 3 months). Readers who find this terminology confusing will find a full explanation in chapter 2, where we discuss court business in detail.

Within this geographical and offence framework, we monitored (as already explained) all cases in our court sample (a few cases in the higher courts were transferred to Doncaster, Leeds or York, but we obtained details from local observers so far as possible). In order to obtain a sufficient number of 'not guilty' pleas to interview, the minimum period for which we could carry out the research would be six months, so the court sample includes all relevant offences originating in the Sheffield magistrates' court from 1 November 1971 to 30 April 1972. Owing to a research complication which could not be avoided, this period included a changeover in the administrative system of the higher courts, since on 1 January 1972 the old Quarter Sessions and Assizes were abolished, and the Crown Court was instituted (in implementation of the Courts Act 1971).[4] In fact this complication does not much affect our results, but readers should be aware that we sometimes refer, using modern terminology, to the 'Crown Court' where strictly we should add 'or, before 1972, Assizes and Quarter Sessions'. Elsewhere we refer generically to 'higher courts' to denote all three.

A sample of the court population then had to be interviewed. We stratified the sample according to the various decisions taken by the defendant: we explain this fully in the next section.

Interviews were carried out, so far as the practicalities of the fieldwork situation permitted, one to two weeks after the final disposal of the case by the courts of first instance (i.e. one to two weeks after either acquittal or sentence, as the case may be). This was usually within the time limit for possible appeal, but apart from this the case was no longer sub judice. We originally intended two separate research samples, one of defendants interviewed prior to court appearance about the extent of their knowledge of the various decisions they had to make, and a second of defendants interviewed after the trial to ascertain the way in which decisions had been taken. It was then intended to match these two samples (inevitably only in a crude fashion) in order to relate information data from the pre-court sample to decision data on the post-court sample. It was however put to us by the Home Office not only that the sub judice nature of the case at the pre-court stage presented difficulties for government-sponsored research, but also that, if we were to ask persons interviewed after the court hearing about the state of their information prior to the court appearance, the resulting inevitable inaccuracy would be no greater than that engendered by the matching process, and would avoid what appeared to be very considerable practical problems in obtaining valid interviews in the rushed atmosphere on the morning of a court appearance. We accepted these views, and the research is consequently restricted to post-court interviews only.

Interviews in social science research are of many kinds. Ours could best be described as a 'semi-structured interview'. A fully structured interview would have allowed few open-ended questions, and would have given the interviewers little or no authority to change the order of the questions, or not to ask questions already answered by the defendant in a narrative response to an earlier question. Such an interview was not what we sought: it would have denied the 'appreciative' aim of the research, and it would have imposed too much rigidity upon interviews which often had to be conducted in far from ideal conditions (see further below). On the other hand, an 'unstructured' interview, with the interviewer having only an 'interview guide' or 'checklist' of things to be asked, with complete freedom to handle these as she chose, was also impracticable, despite its many attractions. Such a 'guide' would have maximised the appreciative aspect of the research, and would also have been advantageous given the 'very wide variety of circumstances we had to cope with', and for 'reasons of approach, contact, rapport, co-operation' (the reasons given by Martin and Webster (1971) for their use of this method in a study of the social consequences of conviction which, like our research, observed court cases and subsequently interviewed both those in custody and those in freedom). Yet we could not adopt it, for we had some highly technical material to handle. It was simply impracticable to assume that interviewers could, without a relatively structured interview schedule, consistently come back with the answers to some of the questions we wanted answering, such as:

> 'Now, I noticed that you did not have a lawyer when you first appeared in court, but you did have one later on. Can you tell me why you did not have one at the beginning?'

'You were told that you could apply for bail to a judge in chambers. Did you make an application?' Yes/No
'*If yes,* what happened?'
'*If no*, did you know how to go about applying to a judge in chambers? Yes/No
If yes, why didn't you apply?'

Thus a structured recording schedule was required, and used. But within this, we gave our interviewers considerable freedom to vary the order of questions or to rephrase questions in the light of what defendants had already said—and as already indicated, as many questions as possible were left open-ended so that the respondent could tell his own story in his own words.

Recording of interviews was done in longhand in the defendant's own presence. Tape-recorders were avoided as being too threatening to (mostly) recently convicted defendants. Notes were usually made in brief and amplified immediately after the interview: but some defendants took great interest in ensuring that the full account was written down in their presence (and they were allowed to see the schedule if they wished).

A complication of the research was that we had to interview defendants who had taken many different routes through the courts. It would have been extremely clumsy to have attempted to construct completely different schedules for every possible route; rather, we worked out different possibilities within each of the five major decision areas, and then took the appropriate recording schedule for each defendant depending on his actual decisions. The full list of 'scheduled routes' was as follows:

I Plea
- (a) Guilty plea.
- (b) Not guilty plea.

II Venue
- (a) Defendant elects summary trial and is tried and sentenced by magistrates.
- (b) Defendant elects summary trial but after conviction is sent to higher court for sentence.
- (c) Defendant elects jury trial at higher court.
- (d) Defendant not given choice, magistrates order higher court trial.
- (e) No choice of venue, higher court trial legally mandatory (no schedule,

		defendant not interviewed re venue).
III	Representation	(a) Unrepresented.
		(b) Legally represented at all court appearances.
		(c) Not represented at first, represented at later appearance.
IV A	Police bail	(a) Defendant appears for first court appearance from police custody.
		(b) Defendant appears for first court appearance from police bail.
IV B	Court bail[5]	(a) One court appearance only, no question of court bail/custody (no schedule, defendant not interviewed).
		(b) On court bail throughout, no police opposition.
		(c) On court bail throughout, despite police opposition.
		(d) In custody at all times after first appearance, application(s) made for bail.
		(e) In custody at all times after first appearance, no application made for bail.
		(f) On bail at one stage after first appearance, in custody later.
		(g) In custody at one stage after first appearance, on bail later.
V	Appeal	(a) Acquitted, no appeal possible (no schedule, defendant not interviewed re appeal).
		(b) Convicted person planning to appeal.
		(c) Convicted person not planning to appeal.
		(d) Convicted person unsure (at time of interview) whether to appeal or not.

Thus for example, suppose that Mr C fell to be interviewed. The interviewer would study the court observation forms, and note that he had pleaded guilty; chosen summary trial and been finally dealt with by the magistrates; had been unrepresented at first but represented later; and had been in custody at first appearance and subsequently (although he had applied for bail). She would therefore take with her an individual interview schedule for Mr C consisting of forms I(a), II(a), III(c), IV A(a) and IV B(d); she would also take forms V(b), (c) and (d) and complete the appropriate one according to C's intention about appeal as expressed in the interview.

It remains to indicate a series of reasons for excluding particular types of defendants from the interview sample.

As already stated, motoring offences were excluded from the court and interview samples, even if (as in the case of dangerous driving) they would otherwise have qualified. In fact initially we had intended to include such offences, on the grounds that the social class background at least of 'moving' motoring offenders (see Steer and Carr-Hill, 1967) was very different from that of the usual indictable defendant, and their pattern of defence (including, perhaps, calling in a legal representative from a motoring organisation) might also be different.[6] We were dissuaded by the Home Office from including such cases, on the grounds that the matters we were interested in were already being covered in T.C. Willett's then ongoing interview study of motorist defendants. In fact this research, when published (Willett, 1973, chapter 5), was rather less extensive and intensive on the question of court processes than we had been led to believe; nevertheless, where appropriate we refer to Willett's results for comparative purposes.

The court sample consisted of indictable cases plus non-indictables with a choice of venue. The interview sample however excluded from its ambit four groups who fell within the court sample, namely:

(i) Females As this was an exploratory study, it was decided to study one sex only, to avoid over-complications of analysis. Furthermore, on practical grounds it was appropriate to exclude females, since some of the rarer court choices (e.g. defendant opting for higher court trial) would have required a study taking much longer than six months to ensure an adequate statistical representation of females.

(ii) Non-Sheffield cases Cases come before the Sheffield court if the alleged offence was committed in Sheffield, regardless of where the defendant lives. However, to have attempted to interview defendants from all over the South Yorkshire and Derbyshire region (or even beyond) would have placed too great a strain on our limited fieldwork resources. We therefore confined our attention to defendants residing within the administrative boundaries of the city of Sheffield.[7]

(iii) Sex offences Most of the interviews took place in defendants' homes. Our two principal interviewers were young women in their early 20s. At their express request, we excluded the small number of sex offences from the interview sample in order to avoid embarrassment to them and to the defendant.

(iv) Other cases A very few defendants spoke no English at all, a fact which naturally became obvious in court. We made no attempt to interview such defendants, though where a defendant had limited English we always did attempt an interview. Similarly, there were a few cases where the defendant had already been interviewed, or refused to be interviewed, earlier in the research or during the pilot period: obviously, we did not seek another interview. Finally, there was one case of murder during our six months' observation, and we made no attempt to interview him because of the known special Home Office rules surrounding defendants on murder charges and life-sentence prisoners.

Methodology: drawing the interview sample

When we started our research, there was very little guidance available from published sources as to the number of cases we might expect to find pleading guilty or not guilty, choosing lower or higher court trial, or being represented or unrepresented. We therefore carried out a preliminary documentary study of Sheffield court records for a three-month period (1 April to 30 June 1970), the results of which for male defendants are summarised in Table 1.1.

Table 1.1 Analysis of Sheffield court records, 1 April to 30 June 1970

	Male defendants	No.
1	Elected summary trial, pleaded guilty, represented	104
2	Elected summary trial, pleaded guilty, unrepresented	452
3	Elected summary trial, pleaded not guilty	35
4	Defendant chose jury trial, pleaded guilty	56
5	Defendant chose jury trial, pleaded not guilty	20
6	Other higher court cases, pleaded guilty	108
7	Other higher court cases, pleaded not guilty	24
	Total	799

It was clear from Table 1.1 that we must stratify our sample with different sampling fractions for the various strata. Otherwise, if we had taken say every fourth case throughout a six-month period, we would have finished up with over half our interviews being of the second category (elect summary trial, plead guilty, unrepresented), whereas we would have had only 10 cases to interview in the 'defendant chose jury trial, pleaded not guilty' category. This was clearly unsatisfactory. To obtain adequate representation of each stratum, but not too many cases in each, different sampling fractions were decided as in Table 1.2.[8] This table is also very important in introducing to the reader a terminology of abbreviations for the sub-samples which we use throughout the book.

Table 1.2 Abbreviations and sampling fractions of sub-samples

Category	Abbreviation	Sampling fraction
1 Elected summary trial, pleaded guilty, represented	SGR	1 in 2
2 Elected summary trial, pleaded guilty, unrepresented	SGU	1 in 8
3 Elected summary trial, pleaded not guilty	SN	all
4 Defendant chose jury trial, pleaded guilty	DG	all
5 Defendant chose jury trial, pleaded not guilty	DN	all
6 Other higher court cases, pleaded guilty	HG	1 in 4
7 Other higher court cases, pleaded not guilty	HN	all

The abbreviation terminology is simple to handle: it will be seen that there is a consistent division by plea (G or N) in all groups, and a three-way split by venue (S = summary trial; D = higher court trial by defendant's option; H = higher court trial other than by defendant's option). Among the higher court cases, there is no division by legal representation (R and U) because in practice all are represented; such a division is however very important among the SGs. We did not introduce an official SNR/SNU distinction (though we could have done), mainly because there were only a handful of SNUs, which are separately considered where appropriate. Finally, readers might like to note that where we give case examples in this book, the first digit of the case number refers to the seven sub-sample categories as set out in Table 1.2, e.g. case 1049 is an SGR, case 5013 is a DN, and so on.

Two of the three distinguishing features (plea, venue, representation) require some further explanation. Some cases are not represented at one court appearance, but represented at another. These we have grouped in as 'represented', though where necessary we make the distinction between 'partial' and 'full' representation. 'SGUs' however, are unrepresented at any stage. Second, the plea distinction as between guilty and not guilty, apparently simple, can get very complex where the defendant pleads guilty to some charges, but not guilty to one or more others. In practice we solved this by calling all cases where there was any plea of not guilty an 'N', except where there were 'alternative charges' on the charge sheet (e.g. theft or receiving of the same goods), the defendant pleaded guilty to one but not the other, and the prosecution accepted this before the beginning of the final trial. Hence any substantive not guilty defence, and any more technical defence not accepted by the prosecution, is coded as 'not guilty'.

A complicating feature of the research was that the business of the courts turned out not to have been accurately predicted by the preliminary documentary study. In theory, we should of course in a six-month period have got twice the total number of cases as that found over three months, i.e. $2 \times 799 = 1{,}598$ males. In fact we got only 1,344, a shortfall of 15 per cent. Rather more seriously, the distribution of cases as between the various sub-sample groups was somewhat different, as Table 1.3 shows: in particular, there was a marked decline in the proportion of DGs (from 7 to less than 2 per cent) and a rise in the SGRs (from 13 to 17 per cent).

The overall shortfall seems to reflect seasonal trends, since the annual totals appearing before Sheffield benches in 1970-2 did not decline. No explanation is readily apparent for the change in distribution of type of business: a close examination of court records for several years would be necessary before one could begin to unravel the possible factors involved.[9]

These changes meant that our final interview sample was smaller, and differently distributed among the sub-sample groups, than was originally intended. This did not become apparent for some time, and by the time it had appeared it was impossible (for practical reasons) to adjust the research design by e.g. taking extra cases or altering a sampling fraction. Fortunately, however, we were left with

Table 1.3 Distribution between sub-sample groups of cases involving male defendants (i) in the preliminary documentary study, April-June 1970; (ii) in the final court study, November 1971-April 1972

Sub-sample group	1970	1971-2
SGU	56·6	54·9
SGR	13·0	17·3
SN	4·4	3·7
DG	7·0	1·5
DN	2·5	3·0
HG	13·5	16·1
HN	3·0	3·4
Total (%)	100·0	100·0
No.	799*	1,344*

*These figures exclude a few defendants who were not categorised because their cases were dropped due to the mental illness, death or disappearance of the defendant; or because the court sent the case to the juvenile court for sentence.

reasonable sub-sample sizes for all groups except one (the DGs, only 17 interviews completed); also fortunately, our interviewers were very successful in obtaining response, and satisfactory success rates of interviews sought were obtained in all sub-sample categories, as Table 1.4 shows. The final overall success rate was 85 per cent of interviews attempted. This conceals an important difference between interviews sought in custody and those sought of men not sent to a prison, borstal or detention centre: 99 per cent of the former, but only 78 per cent of the latter, were successful. (This largely explains the high response of the HG sub-category, since 39 of the 46 cases in that group were given custodial sentences.) However, even when one looks at non-custodial interviews, the success rate falls below 70 per cent only for one sub-sample group (the HNs), which can be considered a highly satisfactory overall result.

The 293 successfully completed interviews form the basic material for most of this research report. The representativeness of the respondents is considered in the final section of this chapter.

Methodology: field experience

Field researchers tend to become fascinated by, and nostalgic about, the details of their fieldwork procedure. We shall try to avoid this

Table 1.4 Availability for interview sample and response rate among possible interviewees

Sub-sample group	Total male cases (court sample)	Available for sample*	Sample intended†	Sample possible‡	Successful interviews	% success §	% success, non-custodial interviews
SGU	738	614	77	77	69	90	87
SGR	233	196	98	98	78	80	70
SN	50	42	42	42	33	79	77
DG	20	20	20	19	17	89	85
DN	40	33	33	30	25	83	76
HG	217	178	46	46	46	100	100
HN	46	36	36	32	25	78	61
Total (unweighted)	1,344	—	—	343	293	85	78

*Excludes non-Sheffield cases and those charged with sex offences and murder.

† Available for sample' multiplied by appropriate sampling fraction (see Table 1.2).

‡ Excludes those selected for interview but having no English or already interviewed.

§ Successful interviews' expressed as percentage of 'sample possible'.

danger, but there are some aspects of our fieldwork programme which require brief mention.

A severe practical problem throughout the research was the difficulty of providing observers for cases, particularly at times when one might have say three courtrooms with Crown Court business and one magistrates' court to cover. We made extensive use of law students for court observation, and also towards the end employed an additional full-time observer to supplement our two full-time interviewers—who were sorely needed to catch up on interviews rather than spend time on court observation. By one expedient or another, we managed to cover most of the cases, though sometimes we had to rely on an excellent liaison with the court probation officer to obtain details of cases that had suddenly been put on in extra courtrooms.

Our occasional observers, such as students, had little problem with the question of relationships with others in the courtroom—they simply went, recorded, and left. Our three regular observers were in a different position. They were well known to various court personnel, and aware that they were. Because of this, they were acutely conscious of possible cues they were feeding to defendants about themselves, and so far as possible they dissociated themselves from all those in authority (especially prosecution, police and clerk) and from the press (which was known to cause distress to some defendants—see Appendix). The fact that our three main observers were all females in their 20s, and usually fairly casually dressed, may have assisted in this regard. It was hoped that this dissociation might help with defendants' subsequent response both in the obtaining and in the quality of interviews.

How far this is so is difficult to judge. Numerically, there is little evidence for it: Martin and Webster's (1971) interview team were 'openly on good terms with people in authority' (p. 18) and they were all males in their late 30s, yet ironically their response rates for first interviews were almost identical to ours (100 per cent in custody and 77 per cent of the non-custodial cases: p. 292). Whether we got better quality results than theirs is anyone's guess, as the two projects were researching different matters.

The approach to the subject was obviously an important matter. Martin and Webster used three approaches: if a custodial sentence was given, they simply went to the prison; if probation, an introduction through the probation officer; in other non-custodial cases, a verbal approach on the steps of the courthouse (pp. 18-19). We adopted the first of these procedures, but not the last two (and the last category in our case included acquitted defendants also). We found it impracticable to attempt courthouse introductions and go on observing the next case; we therefore developed a standard practice of sending a letter signed by the senior interviewer a day or two before we proposed to interview. Inevitably we lost a few cases of men who vanished from the address given on the court sheet, but on the whole the letter was a successful device.[10] We discussed possible approaches to probationers with the probation service: they said they wished probationers to be treated like any other defendant, and as this was also our preference, letters were sent to them in the normal way.

Getting interviews, and getting good quality interviews, was inevitably the hardest part of the research, methodologically speaking. All interviews in freedom (65 per cent of interviews sought, and 60 per cent of interviews obtained) were conducted by our two principal interviewers, Isobel Todd and Elizabeth Elston; they also carried out most of the custodial interviews, though the two principal authors did some.

Interviews in freedom were almost always conducted in the defendant's home (or temporary abode), but a few defendants chose to call in at the university of their own volition to be interviewed. The interviews varied widely with the age, social status and previous penal experience of the defendants. A recurring problem was that of the presence of third parties such as wives and parents: this could not be avoided, but attempts were made to direct the questioning to the defendant wherever possible. In fact this proved particularly difficult in the case of young (17-22-year-old) defendants interviewed in their parents' presence. A further problem was that of the interviewer's presentation of herself and of the purpose of the research: there were various difficulties in being initially regarded as a social worker; as the defendant's girlfriend (or occasionally, by a suspicious wife, as his mistress); or (by student defendants, of whom there were quite a few) as a fellow-student with whom the subject should be discussed in a light-hearted way. Various techniques were developed by our interviewers for dealing with these situations.

Interviews in custody were mostly conducted in Leeds Prison, where the Governor kindly made available appropriate facilities in the Observation and Classification Unit. Transfers out of Leeds were often very fast, however, and we also chased interviewees through the prison system to places such as Manchester, Preston, Thorp Arch and Ranby Camp. Detention centre inmates were seen at North Sea Camp, Sheffield's 'local' senior centre (but actually 75 miles away!). In all custodial interviews, there were few if any technical problems such as presence of third parties or interruptions; but the pervading difficulty, which outweighed these advantages, was that of possible identification with the official prison system, especially at a time when prisoners were receiving a number of induction interviews with a view to security classification and allocation, and particularly as we could send no letter in advance of our visit but had to explain ourselves from scratch to a prisoner fetched to see us by a prison officer. These difficulties were overcome so far as possible by detailed and patient explanation, and it may have helped that we were clearly concerned with the defendant's legal case rather than his personal circumstances, as well as being explicitly concerned with *his* point of view of that case.

There remains the question of the veracity of our interviews. Apart from observation of the court proceedings, there is no independent check on the truth of defendants' replies to our questions. We do not doubt that some defendants may have glossed the relevant events to present a more favourable picture of themselves; for this reason we nowhere assume, for example, that a convicted defendant's protestation of innocence is necessarily true. But the primary focus of our inquiry is on the criminal justice system, not on the defendants' prior conduct; there is no reason to suppose that defendants have any vested interest in lying on such matters as their reasons for choosing a solicitor, or higher rather than magistrates' court trial. Certainly our interviewers were quite satisfied that in all but a tiny handful of cases, our men were giving us their sincere opinions, and doing their best to cope honestly with a fairly complex interview.

In some cases it was clear from our court observation that a defendant's replies were based on a misunderstanding of what had happened in court, or a prejudiced view; but such replies, if sincerely given, are very much part of the defendants' perspective. They have an importance in their own right both for research purposes and in making assessments of the criminal justice system. To give one example: some defendants form a poor opinion of the work of their barristers. It may be that the assessment is mistaken, that 'objective' standards of professional competence, taking into account work done by the barrister which was invisible to the client, would give a more favourable assessment. But if many defendants form such mistaken views, that fact is important; it raises questions, for example, as to the wisdom of the barristers' traditional policy of maintaining a certain aloofness from their clients.

In short, defendants' sincerely held perspectives constitute very important but neglected data on the criminal justice system—and we are in no doubt that the great majority of our defendants were sincere. For these reasons, we frequently in later chapters give verbatim quotations from defendants, and it is a cardinal principle that we do not interfere with such quotations.

Characteristics of the sample

We have discussed the evolving aims and scope of our research project, and given an account of the methods used. It remains to consider briefly the main characteristics of the defendant populations sampled, examining at the same time the extent to which the interview sample was representative of the court sample as a whole.

In some respects of course the interview sample was wholly unrepresentative, because certain classes of defendants were deliberately excluded—notably, as already explained, all female defendants. In the court sample, 19 per cent of defendants were women; it is clear from the annual *Criminal Statistics* that, at least for indictable offences, the proportion of Sheffield defendants who are women is rather above the national average. One element in this is the high incidence in Sheffield of prosecutions for shoplifting and meter-theft. The presence in our sample of a large group of women charged with these offences shows itself in the significantly higher proportion of women in the SGU group (55 per cent of men were SGUs as against 66 per cent of women); and correspondingly in the significantly lower proportion of women in the HGs (16 per cent of men, 4 per cent of women).

The age distribution, ignoring a small number of cases in which the defendant's age was unclear, is set out in Table 1.5. There were significantly more men in the under-21 age group, and significantly more women in the over-50s. Careful tests were made for differences in the age distribution between the men in the interview and court samples, and between the interview sample and those men in the court sample with whom interviews were unsuccessfully sought (i.e. excluding sex offenders, those living outside Sheffield, etc.). Tests were made for each sub-sample group (SGU, SGR, etc.); but no significant differences were found at any stage.[11]

Table 1.5 Age distribution in court and interview samples (%)

Age	Males		Females
	Court sample	Interview sample	
Less than 21	26	24	17
21-29	39	37	34
30-39	18	20	21
40-49	10	10	10
50-59	6	7	13
60+	1	2	5
Total	100	100	100

The only point on which the interview sample was at all unrepresentative of the men in the court sample as a whole emerged on analysis of the principal offence with which defendants were charged. The distribution of offences is set out in Table 1.6: sex offenders, who were excluded from the interview sample, are wholly omitted from this table. The difference in the distribution as regards those charged with burglary is almost significant, and when the analysis by groups was carried out, there were significantly more of such defendants in the interview sample for the larger groups, i.e. SGU, SGR and HG ($p < 0{\cdot}05$). In two of these groups (SGR and HG) this slight over-representation of burglars is due to the higher success rate in obtaining custodial interviews, as burglars were more likely to be sent to prison than others.

Table 1.6 Principal offences alleged against male defendants in court and interview samples (%)

Offence type	Court sample	Interview sample
Aggressive	13	16
Burglary	18	23
Shoplifting	10	6
Meter-thefts	8	5
Other thefts and frauds	33	36
Taking car without consent	7	6
Handling stolen goods	4	4
Criminal damage/arson	4	1
Drugs offences	3	3
Total	100	100

We applied for, but were not granted, access to the criminal records of those in our samples, and had to rely on court observation. This is not entirely satisfactory: information is sometimes made available to the bench in written form and so is not heard by the observer; and some previous convictions will be omitted from statements of antecedents when they are some years old and unrelated to the subject-matter of the current charge. Table 1.7 sets out the information available to us in respect of the men in the court sample; it covers only 1,236 men as no information was available for the remaining 108. (See also Table 4.4, and note 4 to chapter 4.)

It is immediately obvious that the SGR group is in this respect much more like the typical higher court group than the other groups of defendants tried summarily.

We used previous custody as a test of the representativeness of the interview sample. Twenty-two per cent of the men interviewed had served a custodial sentence as against 19 per cent of men in the court sample. This difference is not significant, nor were any significant differences revealed on more detailed analysis within groups. None

Table 1.7 Previous record, by sample group (males)

	SGU	SGR	SN	DG	DN	HG	HN	All
Previous convictions								
and custody	8	30	9	37	27	34	22	18
but no custody	35	23	20	5	21	31	5	30
unclear re custody	16	24	24	21	27	17	35	18
No previous convictions	42	23	47	37	24	19	38	34
Total	100	100	100	100	100	100	100	100

of the women in the court sample had served a custodial sentence.

We were anxious from the outset to obtain information as to the socio-economic grouping of our defendants; questions as to the use of a solicitor, for example, seemed likely to be affected by class attitudes. In practice it was very difficult to get the data we needed, and the social class results were not as important as we had expected.

Court observers noted the stated occupation and income of defendants, but in many cases this information was not given or was unhelpful for research purposes, as where a defendant was merely described as having lost his job at the time of his arrest. We therefore decided instead to obtain for the court sample details of the rateable value of the house occupied by each defendant, also taking into account whether the house was council-owned or not. The information so obtained was limited to defendants with an address in the city of Sheffield, 85 per cent of the court sample; only such men were eligible for the interview sample.[12] A summary is contained in Table 1.8; there were no significant differences between court and interview samples on a detailed analysis by groups.

For defendants in the interview sample only we were able to obtain, through the kindness of the police, details as to the last known occupation of all defendants who were unemployed or for whom information was not otherwise available. We were thus able to classify defendants in the interview sample according to the Registrar-General's scheme of classification.[13] We examined many factors in the court process in relation to social class data, using both the court sample (rateable value) and the interview sample (Registrar-General's classification). Very few statistically significant interactions were found; the major exception, examined more fully

Table 1.8 Rateable values of defendants' houses (male defendants resident in Sheffield) (%)

Rateable value	Court sample	Interview sample
Less than £100	37	39
£100-£149	33	33
£150 +	20	21
Others (hotels, NFA, etc.)	10	7
Total	100	100

in chapter 5, was that using both types of data the guilty sample groups were more likely to be of lower social class, as well as younger, than the not guilty pleaders.[14]

The most important conclusion to emerge from this brief survey of the main characteristics of defendants is that on the available tests the interview sample does not differ significantly from the population of defendants from which it was drawn; moreover, the interview sample is for the most part very similar to the non-respondents, and to those whom we did not seek to interview because they were sex offenders or lived outside Sheffield. We can therefore confidently treat our interview sample as reasonably representative of male indictable offenders generally.

2 Court business: legal and administrative considerations

As discussed in chapter 1, both researchers and official committees have shown a remarkable lack of consideration for the overall structure and business of the English criminal courts. Particular aspects have received close attention from time to time, but seemingly no one has stopped to think about the system as a whole. From an administrative point of view, however, this is the only way in which it can meaningfully be considered, since changes in one part of the system often have important effects in other areas (for a similar point in relation to the English prison system, see Sparks, 1971). In this chapter we look in an administrative context at the overall structure of criminal court business in Sheffield at the time of our research; particularly for non-legal readers, we also set out some of the legal considerations relating to the distribution of business.

The basic pattern of the English criminal courts is deceptively simple. With numerically insignificant exceptions, all criminal cases involving adults begin in the magistrates' court covering the area in which the alleged offence is said to have been committed. There are two possible modes of procedure. The first, known as 'summary trial', is a trial in the magistrates' court, i.e. the issue of guilt or innocence is dealt with by the magistrates. If guilt is established (as it is in the majority of cases by a simple plea of guilty from the defendant), then the magistrates consider the question of the appropriate sentence, although (as we shall see) the case is sometimes sent up to the Crown Court at this stage. The second mode of procedure is entirely different: it is used when (for various reasons which we shall discuss) it has been decided that the trial is to be in the Crown Court. In this case the prosecution must satisfy the magistrates (who are now technically acting as 'examining justices') that there is sufficient evidence to put the accused to trial by jury. If the decision is that there is such evidence, then he is committed to the Crown Court; otherwise he is discharged. These latter proceedings are known as 'committal proceedings' and since 1967 have in the overwhelming majority of cases been of a very formal nature.

We discuss in detail below the criteria for deciding which of these two modes of procedure is to operate. First, though, let us consider how a typical 100 cases eligible for our sample (i.e. excluding cases which must be tried summarily) flow through the system. Table 2.1 gives details of the national and the Sheffield picture.[1] Both show the well-known difference in the pattern of cases involving male and female defendants: the latter, partly because of the kinds of offences they are charged with, are much more likely to be dealt with by summary trial.

Table 2.1 Distribution of criminal cases (other than those triable only summarily) in magistrates' courts

	Males		Females		Total	
	E.*	S.*	E.	S.	E.	S.
Dealt with by examining justices						
Committed for trial	18	23	8	10	16	21
Discharged	0·3	0	0·2	0	0·3	0
Dealt with by summary trial						
Convicted and sentenced	71	69	84	87	73	72
Convicted; committed for sentence	4	5	1	0·5	3	4
Charge withdrawn or dismissed	6	1	6	1·5	6	1
Other cases						
Incomplete, etc.	2	2	2	1	2	2
Total	100	100	100	100	100	100

Sources: (England and Wales) *Criminal Statistics 1972,* tables I(b), (c); (Sheffield) data from court sample.

*E. = England and Wales; S. = Sheffield.

Of more interest to our research are two contrasts between the Sheffield and the national data. The first is that the acquittal rate, or more strictly that of charges withdrawn or dismissed, is much lower in Sheffield. This may be the result of a lower proportion of not guilty pleas in Sheffield summary trials, a matter which is examined in chapter 5.

Of greater importance to the flow of business is the fact that a larger proportion of Sheffield male defendants are committed for trial than the national figures lead one to expect: 23 per cent as opposed to 18 per cent. This merits close examination, but analysis is made difficult by the number of factors involved. As will be seen, however, we believe that the particular factors operating in Sheffield can be identified.

Choice of procedure

Three distinct factors control the distribution of business as between the two modes of procedure. One is the nature of the offence, which wholly determines the matter in a large number of cases; additionally, there remains room for the exercise of choice by both the defendant and the magistrates. As one commentator has well observed, 'the policy issues involved in the choice of mode of trial are confused by the extraordinarily and unnecessarily complicated legal framework within which the decision must be made' (Thomas, 1972b, p. 477).

There are at least five types of offence for this purpose (more detailed classification is possible, but will not be pursued here). The five categories are:

(i) *offences which can only be tried on indictment in the Crown Court* Here there is no room for discretion once the charge has been laid, and accordingly no problem for the courts as to mode of trial. Murder is the obvious example of an offence in this category; in practice, burglary in a dwelling house and certain types of wounding are the most frequently encountered cases.

(ii) *offences which can only be tried summarily* This category includes such things as drunkenness and most motoring offences. As we have seen, it is excluded from both our research samples.

(iii) *indictable offences triable summarily* This is by far the largest category in our study, including as it does most thefts and related offences. It is governed by s.19 of the Magistrates' Courts Act 1952. This provides that the magistrates must begin as examining justices, but may at any time change to summary trial provided that the defendant consents: there is thus a choice first for the magistrates, and then if that choice is for summary trial, for the defendant. Before the magistrates can choose summary trial, they must be satisfied

> having regard to any representations made in the presence of the accused by the prosecutor or made by the accused, and to the nature of the case, that the punishment that the court has power to inflict [on summary trial] . . . would be adequate and that the circumstances do not make the offence one of serious character and do not for other reasons require trial on indictment (s.19(2)).

In practice, in the majority of cases the procedure is more formal than the wording of the Act would lead one to expect. Frequently in the Sheffield courts one sees the prosecutor rising to say 'Request summary trial, your Worships', and obtaining the automatic response 'Agree to summary trial'. Only in types of cases where the prosecutor knows that the bench is likely to consider seriously the possibility of Crown Court trial will he outline the facts (according to the prosecution view) so that the magistrates can decide whether to allow summary trial or act (at least for the time being) as examining justices. Thus we can generalise and say that the prosecution almost always takes the initiative in seeking summary trial, but the agreement of the magistrates, and the consent of the defendant, is essential in every case before summary trial can actually occur for offences falling within this category. We discuss below the detailed operation of this practice.

(iv) 'hybrid' offences This group (which mainly contains some of the more serious motoring offences, but also some offences in our sample, e.g. some drugs offences) may be dealt with under either mode. Section 18 of the 1952 Act contains an elaborate set of provisions as to how the choice is made. In practice the prosecution makes the choice, but if it wants summary trial it must obtain the court's agreement at the outset of the hearing (s.18(1)), and the court can revert to committal proceedings at a later stage (s.18(5)), or transform what began as committal proceedings into a summary trial after hearing representations from either prosecution or defence (s.18(3)).

(v) non-indictable offences in which the defendant can elect for trial on indictment in the Crown Court In a number of non-indictable offences (both hybrid and summary), principally those punishable on summary conviction with imprisonment for more than 3 months, the defendant is entitled to elect trial by jury (1952 Act, s.25). The choice is his alone; neither the prosecution nor the magistrates can overrule him.

It will be seen that in categories (i) and (ii), the procedure to be followed is governed solely by the nature of the offence charged. The procedural implications of this may well affect the original prosecution decision as to which charge should be brought: for example, a man who grabs a woman's arm and wrenches a handbag out of her hand could probably be convicted of robbery (which can only be tried at the Crown Court), but the circumstances may be such that the prosecution want summary trial, in which case they can charge theft instead of robbery. Matters such as this are part of the wide discretion vested in the prosecuting authorities (including the police). They operate at the charging stage, out of court, and could not be examined in this research, although they would constitute an important research topic in their own right.

Much more visible are the factors operating when a case falls into categories (iii), (iv) or (v). The prosecution may apply for summary trial in the first two of these categories: as Lord Parker, CJ, remarked, with notable frankness, in R. v. Coe ([1969]1 All E.R. 65): 'No doubt it is convenient in the interests of expedition, and *possibly in order to obtain a plea of guilty* [italics added], for the prosecution to invite the justices to deal with indictable offences summarily.' The 'expedition' point is the one most usually stressed: see, for example, Lord Parker himself in R. v. King's Lynn Justices, ex parte Carter ([1969] 1 Q.B. 488). But as we shall see in a later chapter, some defendants believe that they are more likely to be acquitted by the Crown Court than by magistrates, before whom, they think, a 'not guilty' plea has little chance of success. Hence, if the prosecution obtains agreement to summary trial in such cases, the chances of a not guilty plea are much reduced.[2]

Of course the defendant himself has an important influence on the nature of the proceedings. He can insist on trial in the Crown Court whenever the case is in categories (iii) or (v), and can make representations to the same effect in a category (iv) case. We examine this defendant's choice of venue in detail in chapter 4.

There remains the discretion vested in the magistrates. In cases falling within categories (iii) and (iv), the magistrates must give their consent before the case can proceed to summary trial. The magistrates may feel that the case must go for trial in the Crown Court, and s.19(2) of the Magistrates' Courts Act 1952, already set out, indicates the criteria as they apply in category (iii) cases. Similar considerations would seem relevant in category (iv), but the statute is silent on the point.

There now exists a considerable body of case law on the magistrates' discretion in this matter. In a number of cases decided in or about 1950, Lord Goddard, CJ, stressed that 'serious cases ought to be dealt with by the superior courts' (R. v. Middlesex Quarter Sessions, ex parte D.P.P. (1950), 34 Cr. App. Rep. 112; R. v. South Greenhoe Justices, ex parte D.P.P., [1950] 2 All E.R. 42, sub nom R. v. Norfolk Justices (1950), 34 Cr. App. Rep. 120). In a case involving unlawful wounding, in which the victim nearly died, Lord Goddard described the magistrates' decision to proceed summarily as 'a most extraordinary state of affairs'. He went on:

Justices should remember that they have to deal with matters of

> this sort judicially, and they are not bound to assent to dealing with a case summarily because the prosecution want to get the matter dealt with there and then, without the necessity of going to the assizes (R. v. Bodmin Justices, ex parte McEwen, [1947] K.B. 221).

It follows that the magistrates should make some inquiry into the facts before deciding to agree to summary trial. As Lord Parker, CJ, made clear in R. v. King's Lynn Justices, ex parte Carter ([1969] 1 Q.B. 488) they are not doing their duty if they act in any other way.

In practice there are many cases in which the charge itself contains all the relevant details. A charge of stealing a small sum from a gas meter is almost self-explanatory. But a charge of stealing from a named person may not indicate the important fact that the victim was the employer of the defendant, and 'specimen charges' may not indicate the scale—in value or time—of a series of crimes. The magistrates have to rely in practice upon the prosecution to go into these details whenever there is any chance that summary trial might be thought inappropriate; as the prosecution is often anxious to secure summary trial (for the reasons summarised in the quotation from R. v. Coe, above) there is an almost classic conflict of duty and interest. When the magistrates make a decision which attracts criticism, it is usually the prosecution who are really at fault in failing to alert the bench to the full facts. That the appeal courts realise this is illustrated by R. v. Pitson ((1972), 56 Cr. App. Rep. 391) where the prosecution were roundly criticised by Lawton, LJ, for having requested summary trial in a case involving theft of goods worth £7,000 from National Carriers Ltd by some of their employees over some two years. In R. v. Coe ([1969] 1 All E.R. 65) the prosecution sought and obtained summary trial of 6 offences of burglary (with property worth £3,500 being stolen) and 11 offences of taking a car without consent; the prosecution knew that the defendant would ask for 18 other offences to be taken into consideration. Lord Parker, CJ, said that it was difficult to understand the prosecution's action, but also criticised the justices for failing in their duty to make a proper inquiry.

Court practice

Table 2.2 sets out data from the Sheffield court sample as to the selection of trial in the higher court. We were able to distinguish between cases in which that decision was dictated by the nature of the offence, or was made by the defendant or the magistrates. (The published national figures are not broken down in this way, so we cannot draw any conclusions as to the pattern of magistrates', or indeed defendants', decisions over the whole country.) It was something of a surprise to discover that, taking all offences together, cases in which the magistrates exercised a discretion in favour of Crown Court trial were more numerous than were cases in either of the other two categories. If this were true in a substantial number of other areas as well as Sheffield, it might suggest that one way of cutting back the business of the Crown Court (and hence of reducing delays in being dealt with by that court) would be for magistrates to be more ready to try serious indictable offences summarily.[3] This of course would require a reversal of the caselaw already discussed.

Table 2.2 Choice of mode of trial, by offence type (males)

Offence class	Sheffield Offence	Sheffield Defendant	Sheffield Magistrates	Sheffield Total	England & Wales, total
Aggressive	19	6	35	60	36
Sex	32	7	4	43	39
Burglary	19	4	19	41	39
Handling	3	2	22	27	24
Other thefts/frauds	1	6	7	14	11
Taking car without consent	—	5	8	13	10
Arson/damage	2	2	6	10	7
Shoplifting	—	4	2	6	4
Meter-thefts	—	—	—	0	3
All offences	7	4	13	24	18

Source (England and Wales data): *Criminal Statistics 1972,* tables I(b),(c).

This table indicates the percentage of cases involving male defendants in each offence type which are dealt with by trial in the higher court. The Sheffield figures indicate whether this form of trial was dictated by the nature of the offence, chosen by the defendant, or chosen by the magistrates.

Differences in the offence/defendant/magistrates distribution as between different offence types, as shown in Table 2.2, are largely accounted for by detailed legislative provision. Thus, only handling emanating from offences abroad is compulsorily dealt with in the

Crown Court, so there are very few such cases; conversely, rape charges are relatively common, and this largely accounts for the high 'offence only' proportion among the sexual offences.

The fourth and fifth columns of the table show that for almost all offence groups the proportion of cases going for trial in the Crown Court is higher in Sheffield than one would expect from the national figures. The greatest difference is in the aggressive group with 60 per cent of all cases going to the higher courts in Sheffield, as against 36 per cent nationally. It seems clear that only a marked difference in the magistrates' exercise of discretion can explain the different pattern in this particular offence group. Two illustrative cases are taken from the court sample:

> Case 6231 B (aged 27) a self-employed newsagent and motor mechanic with no previous convictions, visited the home of his wife, from whom he was separated, to give his daughter a birthday present. He got into an argument with his wife and hit her about the head with his fists. He was charged with assault occasioning actual bodily harm. The magistrates committed him for trial in the Crown Court. No penalty was imposed by the Crown Court, which bound him over to keep the peace and ordered the payment by B of £25 towards prosecution costs.

> Case 6247 R (aged 19) returned home drunk. He hit his wife on her face and body, later kicked her and turned her out. Before R's first court appearance he and his wife were reconciled. He had one previous conviction for assault. He was committed for trial, and was ultimately placed on probation for 3 years.

There is little doubt that many courts would have dealt with these cases summarily. Why should the Sheffield pattern be different?

It is possible to give a very specific answer. In 1968, a man called Everest came before the Sheffield magistrates charged with having cut a woman's face with a glass. The bench agreed to summary trial, fined him £10 and bound him over to keep the peace. Sixteen days later, Everest threw acid into the same woman's face, doing damage to both eyes and causing 'appalling injuries'. He was sent to prison for 8 years, the sentence being upheld on appeal. The appeal court, with the advantage of hindsight, deplored the fact that the earlier assault had been dealt with summarily. Had it not been, the later assault might never have happened (R. v. Everest, [1968] Crim. L.R. 688; *The Times,* 8 October 1968).

This decision, and the somewhat harsh criticism made of the magistrates, made a great impact on the Sheffield bench. It is regularly referred to in training sessions and discussions. It seems quite clear that the recollection of the Everest case, and the painful thought of possible further disapproval from the Court of Appeal, is a major influence on the practice of the local court in cases involving aggressive offences. One of the disadvantages of the former system of Assizes and Quarter Sessions was that liaison between the magistrates and the higher courts on matters of policy was very difficult: there was no judge of the higher courts regularly available to whom the chairman of the bench or the clerk to the justices could go with current problems. The Crown Court's administrative structure has removed this difficulty, and the sort of problem which caused such disquiet after the Everest decision could now be discussed with the presiding judge for the circuit in a more relaxed and constructive way.

We have seen from Table 2.2 that Sheffield also has a slightly higher proportion of Crown Court property cases than is the case nationally. It seems plausible to suggest that the post-Everest policy in aggressive offences may well have an indirect influence on the way in which the magistrates' discretion is exercised in these other cases. Examination of individual files suggests that the bench is normally likely to order Crown Court trial in cases involving high-value thefts (over about £400),[4] or where there was some special feature (e.g. persistent theft from employer, theft of special-quality metal in small quantities, a clerk in the magistrates' court office engaged in petty deception and destruction of records). On the other hand some relatively serious property cases are granted summary trial: we give examples below, in discussing committal for sentence.

Two special types of case deserve comment. The first is exemplified by the following incident:

> Case 6026 O (aged 50) a labourer with no previous convictions, got involved with another man in a rather petty offence of burgling a store and stealing scrap metal valued at £1. His codefendant had to go to the Crown Court because of other offences alleged, and it was conceded on all sides that under normal circumstances O would have been allowed summary trial. But the magistrates refused such trial on the grounds that codefendants in the same case should be tried together. At the Crown Court, he pleaded guilty and was given a conditional discharge.

A number of other similar cases were observed, and it seems that this principle may be observed more strictly in Sheffield than elsewhere.

The second special type of case is again best introduced with an example:

> Case 6340 J (aged 18) was charged with two offences of obtaining goods (worth a total of £40) by deception. The prosecution indicated that he had used worthless cheques and had admitted other offences. On this information the bench ruled that the case must go to the higher court.
>
> J was later charged with burglary and theft of £640, and asked for 17 other offences to be taken into consideration, but this was, of course, not revealed to the magistrates at the time of their decision as to mode of trial.

We identified a number of other, very similar, cases during the research period. The observer is forced to suspect that some other information is available to the bench which is not revealed in court, but we are assured that this is not the case. Informal negotiations sometimes take place between the defence and the prosecution: in one case a middle-class defendant told us that his solicitor tried to ensure summary trial in this way. The clerk can sometimes be involved, but not the magistrates.

Finally, we would not wish to be thought to be asserting that the prosecution's view is always decisive for the magistrates' decisions. Two contrasting cases give the lie to this view, though they were the exception rather than the rule:

> Case 6014 M, a foreman in a firm, and a highly respected man in many walks of life, was charged with three cases of corruptly obtaining money. These were specimen charges relating to 1958, 1969 and 1971 respectively of a long history of petty exploitation of workers at the firm, from which he had netted approximately £1,000 in all. The prosecution requested summary trial, the magistrates refused. At the Crown Court, the judge commended the lower bench and remarked that he was 'very pleased that the magistrates saw fit to send this case to this court'.

> Case 1037 O, a 21-year-old labourer, was charged with 4 offences of petty theft (total value £16) from his blind and crippled landlady whose husband was at that time in prison.

> The prosecuting solicitor outlined the facts to the bench, and requested trial at the Crown Court on the grounds that 'such a mean crime should maybe go for trial'. The magistrates, however, agreed to summary trial, which the defendant also elected when the choice was put to him.

Committal for sentence

A closely related matter is that of committal for sentence to the Crown Court. Section 29 of the Magistrates' Courts Act 1952, as amended, provides that when an adult is convicted by the magistrates after summary trial of an indictable offence

> then, if on obtaining information about his character and antecedents the court is of opinion that they are such that greater punishment should be inflicted for the offence than the court has power to inflict, the court may . . . commit him in custody or on bail to the Crown Court for sentence.

There has been much discussion of the phrase 'character and antecedents'. On the face of it, it certainly includes details of previous convictions, and of offences which the defendant admits and asks to be taken into consideration. It has been less clear to what extent the magistrates can rely on the nature of the offence of which he was convicted. It was said in R. v. Vallett ((1950) 34 Cr. App. Rep. 251; see Thomas, 1972b, at pp. 481ff) that 'character' referred to more than previous convictions, and 'antecedents' 'is as wide as can possibly be conceived'.

The matter was fully considered in R. v. King's Lynn Justices, ex parte Carter ([1969] 1 Q.B. 488), a case already referred to. Lord Parker, CJ, discussed the proper practice and related it to the question of the decision as to mode of trial:

> As I see it, speaking for myself, the expression 'character and antecedents' being as wide as it possibly can be, justices are entitled to take into consideration in deciding whether or not to commit, not merely previous convictions, not merely offences which are asked to be taken into consideration, but matters revealed in the course of the case connected with the offence charged which reflect in any way on the prisoner's character. Of course, in the ordinary way where justices do their duty under s.19(2) of the Act, the circumstances of the offence which reflect on character and antecedents will already have emerged,

> and if, notwithstanding that, the justices decide to deal with the case summarily, they cannot take those matters into consideration again when they are considering committal under s.29; there must be something more than has been revealed at the stage when they decided to deal with the case summarily. On the other hand where, as in the present case, they have either been persuaded to deal with the case summarily, or have embarked on the summary trial without making any proper enquiry, or without conducting their enquiry as examining magistrates far enough to understand the nature of the case, then, as it seems to me, they are fully entitled to take into consideration those matters relating to the offence which had been revealed at the trial and which do reflect on the character and antecedents.

Lord Parker later admitted that this statement could be taken as a charter for magistrates to deal with cases summarily; but he stressed that they would only have power to commit for sentence if new facts were revealed after the decision to proceed to summary trial. He was speaking in a case, R. v. Tower Bridge Magistrate, ex parte Osman ([1971] 2 All E.R. 1018) in which the charges themselves indicated thefts from a railway goods depot over a considerable period; the stipendiary magistrate himself knew that a number of cases had arisen in the past of thefts from the same depot. In those circumstances, he had no fresh information on which to base a decision to commit for sentence. In contrast is R. v. Lymm Justices, ex parte Brown ([1973] 1 All E.R. 716). Brown pleaded guilty at a summary trial to thefts at an airport. At the sentencing stage it became known to the bench that he was employed as a policeman by the Airport Authority, and had used his post to steal. This additional information justified the magistrates in committing for sentence.

Court practice

Table 2.1 shows that the proportion of cases tried summarily and leading to a committal to the higher court for sentence is slightly higher in Sheffield than the national average. This is despite the high rate of committal for trial.

Of the 64 cases in the Sheffield court sample, every one involved a defendant with previous convictions. At least 34 had previously served a custodial sentence; there were 13 cases in which this point was not made clear in court. Twenty-two cases involved defendants who asked for other offences to be taken into consideration. There is no evidence, therefore, to suggest that the Sheffield court is departing from the criteria laid down in s.29 of the 1952 Act, as interpreted in the King's Lynn Justices case.

On the other hand, some of those 64 cases cause surprise on the grounds that they might be thought more suitable for trial in the Crown Court. We have seen that the local bench is very ready to refuse summary trial, especially in the case of offences against the person; the following illustrative cases, all involving property offences, show the other side of the picture:

> Case 1297 H (aged 19) was charged with burglary of a store; theft of money; permitting premises to be used for smoking cannabis; stealing prescription forms; forgery of prescriptions; and attempting to obtain drugs and money using a forged instrument. Summary trial was agreed to, but he was sent to the Crown Court for sentence.

The odd feature of this case is that H was serving a prison sentence at the time of his trial. There would seem to have been no particular reason why trial on indictment would cause difficulty. He was eventually given 3 years' probation to follow his prison term.

> Case 1032 B (aged 29), a scrap metal dealer. He was charged with 2 offences of handling stolen goods and 2 of obtaining money by deception. These were clearly 'specimen' charges; he asked for 36 offences to be taken into consideration, and had a record of similar offences going back some 6 years—but no custodial sentence. He was sent to the higher court for sentence, and received concurrent sentences totalling 9 months' imprisonment.

> Case 1301 E (aged 45) was charged with 3 offences of burglary, of a shop, an office and a café, and with thefts in connection with two of those burglaries. He asked for 7 burglaries and 10 attempted burglaries to be taken into consideration; he ultimately received sentences totalling 18 months, despite a good record in recent years.

A feature common to the three cases just considered is that the value of the property concerned was low; in each case it was below the £400 level which the local bench seems to have adopted as indicating Crown Court trial. Of course the value factor is only one of many which are to be taken into account.

In view of the practice of the Sheffield bench in committing for trial a high proportion of cases of aggressive crimes, it is not surprising that there are few such cases among those committed to the higher court for sentence. The pattern of the 64 cases is shown in Table 2.3.

Table 2.3 Pattern of cases committed to higher court for sentence

Type of offence	No.
Burglary	27
Taking vehicle without consent	6
Shoplifting	2
Other thefts/frauds	25
Assault occasioning actual bodily harm	3
Drugs offences	1
Total	64

The time factor

To many defendants, a pressing question is, 'How soon will it all be over?' To a few, delays in dealing with a case, with the attendant need for several appearances, lead to loss of earnings which creates hardship. Others, uninterested in and dissociating themselves from the whole court process, simply wish to be rid of the whole irritating irrelevance of the case. To a larger number, however—including some with considerable criminal experience—the court appearance, the attendant publicity, and most of all the uncertainty as to the outcome are matters creating a (sometimes very marked) state of anxiety, which can only be alleviated by the termination of the case. Additionally, for those in custody and hoping for a non-custodial sentence, there are special reasons for wishing a speedy conclusion.

Not surprisingly, the considerable delays which have been caused by the post-war increase in criminal proceedings have attracted the attention of writers and of government. This attention has been directed principally to delays in the business of the higher courts. The Streatfeild Committee (1961) and the Beeching Commission (1969) were concerned primarily with the business of the higher courts, and the full range of magistrates' court work was not covered by Gibson (1960).[5] It may be that there is no real problem at the lower court level in London, with its system of stipendiary magistrates. For example, Zander (1969, at p.639) reports that of 136 cases in which a not guilty plea was made in metropolitan magistrates' courts, 109 were brought to a conclusion within his one-week study period. As we shall see, the pattern is very different in Sheffield.

In the pages which follow, we have some harsh comments to make about the position in the Sheffield courts. It is fair to preface them with two points. The first relates to the local situation, with a large number of very busy courts meeting in a building which was chronically overcrowded (see Preface). Even if staff and magistrates were available, courtrooms would not exist in sufficient numbers to ease the flow of business. This congestion is undoubtedly a factor in the delays we describe and the construction of a new courthouse, now taking place, will ease the situation.

A more general point is as to 'justified delay'. From the point of view of the defendant, unless he himself is anxious to secure an adjournment, all waiting time is bad. We have followed the Streatfeild Committee which recognised that the preparation of the case, the logistics of mounting a trial, or a court hearing of any sort, all require time. This waiting time is of benefit to the defendant, though he may not be disposed to see it in this light, as contributing to the proper administration of justice. Our criticisms are directed not at this type of delay, but at the very considerable periods of time over and above a generous allowance of time for preparation, which some defendants have to endure.

Summary trials

Table 2.4 sets out the length of time it took for Sheffield magistrates' courts to deal with cases which were tried summarily. The period is that from first appearance in court to the date of final disposition, including where appropriate committal for sentence. The table shows that cases in which the defendant is represented take longer to dispose of than those in which he is unrepresented; that there are significantly greater delays in unrepresented cases involving female defendants than those involving males; and, most important, that cases in which there is a plea of not guilty take much longer than those in which the defendant pleads guilty.

The first of these points, the greater delays in cases where there is legal representation, might be attributed to the activities of the defence lawyers in seeking adjournments. It is certainly the case that unrepresented defendants very seldom ask for an adjournment. The lower part of Table 2.5 sets out the position as regards the male

Table 2.4 Summary trials: percentage periods in magistrates' court

Period (days)	Guilty pleas				Not guilty pleas	
	Unrepresented		Represented			
	M	F	M	F	M	F
Immediate	88	69	43	57	2	5
6 or less	1	0	3	7	0	0
7-13	1	2	18	2	0	0
14-20	2	12	14	7	0	0
21-34	6	15	12	14	6	23
35-55	1	1	5	9	34	23
56-83	0·5	0·5	3	5	42	36
84-99	0	0	1	0	10	9
100 +	0	0·5	0·5	0	6	5
Total	100	100	100	100	100	100
No.	764	215	207	58	50	22

'Represented' includes all cases in which there was legal representation at one or more appearances. Twenty-six cases included in the first column are in our sub-sample category SGR because they were represented on committal for sentence, but were unrepresented at all appearances before the magistrates.

defendants who plead guilty: there is only 1 adjournment at the request of the defendant in every 100 unrepresented cases, but 20 adjournments at the request of the defence in every 100 cases in which there is representation.[6] But the same table shows that adjournments at the request of the prosecution are also very much more frequent in cases in which the defendant is represented. Such cases tend to be the more serious, and both sides need to prepare themselves before the trial can proceed. Table 2.5 reflects what actually happens in court; there may be cases in which it is more convenient for the prosecuting solicitor or police officer to make the formal application for an adjournment, having agreed to do so in discussion with the defendant or his solicitor.

The significantly greater delays experienced by unrepresented female defendants than by their male counterparts may be surprising at first sight. The explanation lies in the nature of the adjournment, with a much greater use of (post-conviction) adjournments for social inquiry reports where women are concerned. Taking all summary trial cases, there were 28 such adjournments in each 100 cases

Table 2.5 Adjournments in cases tried summarily (adjournments of particular types as a percentage of cases)

	Males		Females	
Plea:	G	NG	G	NG
Prosecution sought adjournment	15	58	3	36
Defence sought adjournment	5	78	3	68
Adjournment for reports	8	6	30	4·5
Non-appearance of defendant	1	2	3	4·5

	Male defendants pleading guilty	
	Unrepresented	Represented
Prosecution sought adjournment	4	48·5
Defence sought adjournment	1	20
Adjournment for reports	9	6
Non-appearance of defendant	1	1

involving women, but only 8 in cases with male defendants. A number of factors are operating here. The greater use of reports for women is probably just one more example of the tendency of penal agents to view the female offender in more 'pathological' terms than the male—a subject on which much could be written, though this is not the place for it. There is also a slight tendency to use reports more often in unrepresented cases, whatever the sex of the defendant: reports were called for in 15 per cent of the unrepresented cases we observed as against 11 per cent of represented cases. One reason which prompts magistrates to adjourn for reports is that they feel that they do not know enough about the case. This is more likely when the defendant is unrepresented and inarticulate than when he has a solicitor to present a plea in mitigation.

The difference in waiting period between men and women who plead not guilty is not statistically significant. One possible reason for this, suggested by Table 2.5, is that when there is a not guilty plea it is possible to prepare a social inquiry report in advance of the trial and an adjournment for reports is unnecessary; accordingly, the special delaying factors affecting women offenders are inoperative. In fact, this is unlikely to be the full explanation, for defendants pleading not guilty will sometimes object to the preparation of pre-trial reports, and such reports are rare in Sheffield.

Over and above all these points is a much more important one; for by far the most striking feature of Table 2.4 is the discrepancy between guilty pleas and not guilty pleas. Over 90 per cent of guilty pleas are disposed of within 34 days, or about a month. But of those who chose to plead not guilty, only 8 per cent of men and 28 per cent of women had been dealt with in the same period.

What this discrepancy means in practice is that a defendant who indicates that he wishes to plead not guilty normally has his case adjourned at once to an afternoon court some 6 or 8 weeks later. At one point during our observations, the period reached 3 months.[7] Not surprisingly, a number of those who had experienced such a delay commented adversely upon it during our interviews, though we had not asked a specific question about it: in the words of one of them, 'it lasted ages—from December to March. I never expected it to drag on so long'.

The really important factor, however, is the possible effect of the delay on the defendant's choice of plea. In one or two cases during our observations, the announcement of the adjournment produced an immediate and public change of plea, the new guilty plea being accepted by the court. No case of this nature fell within the interview sample, but we did find a number of cases where the defendant had partly or wholly determined his plea because of the known delay factor in 'not guilty pleas'. One such case, no. 1049, was quoted at the beginning of chapter 1; other examples were:

> Case 1070 T, a 31-year-old lorry driver, was charged with theft of a tumbledown van (value £20). The van was derelict and T, who had a van of the same model, had used many important parts from his own van to make good the derelict van, and had then driven it away. He claimed he thought the van was abandoned, but that after the police had informed the true owner, he had actually bought the van off him for £20. T was legally represented, and his solicitor told him that he could plead not guilty and would probably get away with it. The solicitor also said, however, that this would mean a delay of 2 to 3 months in the case; and on the morning of the court appearance he added that 'today's is a lenient bench'. T decided to plead guilty in order to 'get it over with'.

> Case 1040 B, a 'young, friendly, extravert Irishman', to quote our interviewer, was charged with burgling a shop with intent to steal. He said in interview that he was drunk at the time and, while he had certainly smashed the shop window, he

hadn't taken anything and didn't intend to. He had talked to a CID officer, who had said 'if you plead guilty, it will be finished; if not, you'll be on remand in Leeds'. B decided to plead guilty.

Case 1034 S, aged 21, lived with his parents in a large detached house in one of the most affluent areas of Sheffield. He had never been in court before, but was charged with possessing cannabis. A policeman had seen another youth handing S an envelope in a lane and arrested them both; S, who had not opened the envelope when arrested, said he had no idea that the stuff inside was cannabis. If true, this constituted a rare legal defence to a charge of possessing drugs. But S had pleaded guilty, he said, for two reasons: (i) because his mother thought it best as 'she worries a lot and with not guilty pleas it drags on and on'; (ii) because the police had threatened to charge him with supplying, so that it was 'perhaps best to plead guilty to the lesser charge'.

These last two cases, of course, indicate the additional importance of charging procedures and of pre-trial custody in relation to plea, and they emphasise—what we must constantly reiterate—the often close relationship between the different aspects of the criminal justice process and the defendant's responses to them. We shall return to the specific question of custody again in chapter 8; here it can just be noted that all the eventual 'SN' cases (i.e. those actually pleading not guilty before the magistrates) finished up on bail, apparently largely because of the long waiting periods known by the magistrates to be routinely involved in this category of case.

In connection with this topic we note one set of facts which is highly suggestive, though inconclusive. We have already referred to a study of magistrates' court cases by Zander (1969) in which the delay experienced by those pleading not guilty seems to have been minimal. He found that 19·8 per cent of his defendants pleaded not guilty; in Sheffield, where the penalty in terms of delay was much heavier, only 6 per cent chose to plead not guilty. It is very tempting to jump to the obvious conclusion, but we must exercise caution before doing so. Despite the above cases, there were in fact relatively few who gave delay as a direct reason for pleading guilty in our interview sample (see chapter 5), largely because this plea is often constrained by other factors. Even so, we cannot rule out the possibility that those who saw any hope of defence in their cases might be much more disposed to plead not guilty in the circumstances pertaining in the court Zander studied; the total effect on the pattern of pleas is impossible to calculate.

But one thing we can and must say. The sort of pressure operating at the time of our research upon defendants in summary trials who wished (or may have wished) to exercise their undoubted right to plead not guilty, is quite unacceptable by any standards of justice. It is greatly to be hoped that improvements in court accommodation will go some considerable way towards the elimination of this problem.

Committal proceedings

Part of Gibson's study (1960, pp. 18ff) was concerned with delay at the magistrates' court level in cases to be tried in a higher court. Her sample was of 781 cases dealt with by 100 different courts in 1958; her table 17 indicated delay between first appearance and committal for trial, and distinguished between those committed in custody and on bail. Our Table 2.6 sets out similar information derived from the Sheffield court sample. In fact a comparison of the two sets of findings is very difficult: quite apart from the considerable extension of the magistrates' jurisdiction since 1958, which will have changed the types of case involved, Gibson's figures are expressed in categories of '1-2 weeks', '2-3 weeks', etc., and it is not clear how a 14-day delay would be treated. The fact remains that delays in Sheffield in 1971-2 were apparently greater than the national level in 1958.

On the Sheffield figures, 14 per cent of those committed in custody had waited for 28 days or more before the committal proceedings; of those committed on bail, 25 per cent had such a wait. The equivalent proportions in Gibson's study were 3 and 12 per cent.

Gibson's study was carried out at a time when 'full' committal proceedings were required in each case, i.e. each prosecution witness had to give evidence orally, this had to be written down, and the magistrate(s) then had to decide whether there was sufficient evidence to commit for trial. The system was amended by s.1 of the 1967 Criminal Justice Act to allow formal proceedings whereby the bench could commit for trial on the basis of the unexamined written statements, provided that the accused were legally represented: 'in effect this means committal for trial by consent provided the accused is so advised by his lawyer' (Jackson, 1972, p. 197). During our period of observation in the Sheffield court, only 1 case (out of 356) was dealt with by 'full' committal proceedings, the remainder being given the shortened 'section one' procedure: hence Napley (1966b, at p. 556) was correct in predicting that a reform along the lines of the 1967 Act would mean the effective demise of committal proceedings in their traditional form.[8] The effect of this change on our comparison with Gibson's figures is difficult to assess. The new procedure was designed to save time in actual court proceedings, not to reduce waiting periods; the shorter form of hearing could have reduced delays by obviating the need for advance booking of time in a special court, but on the other hand the necessity to prepare written evidence in advance could have lengthened the delay.

Finally, in our data we distinguished (as Gibson was unable to do) between cases tried on indictment because the defendant so opted, and other cases. From columns 3 and 4 in Table 2.6 it will be seen that where the defendant makes the choice, he is likely to experience greater delays; this despite the lower proportion of such defendants who are remanded in custody. A partial explanation may be that work on the papers for committal proceedings may begin late when the defendant's decision comes as a surprise; but it is still remarkable that 33 per cent of defendants opting for jury trial wait for 28 days or more, as against only 18 per cent of other defendants.

Delays in the higher courts

Here again comparison with earlier studies is difficult. Both Gibson (1960) and Rose (1971) studied the question of delays in the higher courts closely, but the changeover to the Crown Court at the end of 1971 makes comparisons of limited value. In addition there are difficulties in defining the period of delay.[9]

Gibson found an average delay between committal and trial, in the case of persons committed for trial to a court in their own area, of 37 days (Gibson, 1960, table 1). Persons on bail waited an average of 40 days, as against 31 for those in custody. Delays were significantly less in 'breaking and entering' cases, but the transfer of many such cases to the magistrates' jurisdiction in 1962 makes that fact of little value for present purposes.

The Streatfeild Committee reporting in 1961 was much concerned at the high proportion (22 per cent) of defendants who experienced a delay of more than 8 weeks between committal and trial: their

Table 2.6 Waiting time before committal for trial (% distribution)

Time (days)	In custody	On bail	Defendant's choice	No choice
Immediate	3	6	1	6
6 or less	5	4	3	5
7-13	51	23	19	37
14-20	18	23	42	18
21-27	9	18	3	16
28-34	8	15	15	8
35-55	3	3	7	6
56-83	3	4	5	2
84-99	0	2	3	1
100 +	0	1	3	1
Total	100	100	100	100

proposals were designed to ensure that 8 weeks was, so far as possible, a maximum. Yet Rose found that the pattern in 1967 was much the same: 22 per cent of defendants committed for trial waited 60 days or more between committal and sentence (Rose, 1971; table 24).

It is necessary to distinguish various groups of defendants. Rose found that 14 per cent of those in custody at the time of their appearance before the higher courts waited more than 60 days, but 26 per cent of those on bail. The rate was 12·5 per cent for those committed for trial and pleading guilty, but 34 per cent for not guilty pleas; only 3 per cent of those committed for sentence endured such a delay.

The Sheffield figures are set out in Table 2.7, and present a dismal picture. Except for committals for sentence, all figures show that the proportion of those waiting more than 8 weeks was at least twice as large as in the corresponding survey by Rose. It is difficult to select one particular set of figures for especial comment, for all indicate intolerable delays with the Streatfeild target disappearing without trace.

In mitigation it must be said that the early months of our research period coincided with the last months of the system of Assizes and Quarter Sessions which was seen by the Beeching Commission as the cause of much delay. Forty-three per cent of cases which began in the magistrates' court in November or December 1971 were subject

Table 2.7 Waiting periods in higher courts (% distribution)

Period (days)	Committed for trial		Committed for sentence only	Committed for trial	
	G plea	NG plea		Bail	Custody
Less than 14	4	0	15	2	4
14-20	7	4	19	3	10
21-27	9	3	25	7	8
28-34	10	6	15	8	11
35-41	16	8	12	12	16
42-55	15	12	10	15	14
56-69	19	16	2	20	15
70-97	11	22	2	13	17
98-125	4	15	0	8	5
126-153	3	7	0	7	0
154-182	2	4	0	4	1
182 +	0·5	5	0	3	0
Over 56	39·5	69	4	55	38
No.	245	103	59	214	134

Note: 13 cases are excluded from this table (and from Table 2.8) because the date of final disposal of the case was not recorded and not readily ascertainable.

to delays of over 8 weeks. The rate rose to 55 per cent during the following two months, perhaps a transitional period before the Crown Court got into full working order. During the final two months the rate settled back to 42 per cent, much the same as in the first period. It would be unwise to base firm conclusions on such figures, but they seem to indicate that the new system of courts was not able to make any dramatic impact on a very bad pattern which it inherited. The Lord Chancellor's Department's *Statistics on Judicial Administration* for 1972 (Table 3.4) indicate a similar picture in England and Wales as a whole: 43 per cent of cases waited more than 8 weeks (calculated to the start of the trial in the Crown Court).

Overall waiting periods

From the point of view of the defendant the waiting period which matters is the whole period, that is in court terms from first appearance before the magistrates to the final disposal of the case. It is of importance to the court administrators to know whether the delay is in the magistrates' court or the Crown Court, but this is of no great interest to the defendant. Table 2.8 sets out the melancholy figures of this overall delay in cases eventually reaching the higher courts.

Table 2.8 Overall waiting period, higher court cases (% distribution)

Period (weeks)	Committals for trial		Committal for sentence only	Committals for trial	
	G plea	NG plea		Bail	Custody
Less than 3	2	0	14	0·5	4
3<4	3	3	26	2	5
4<6	13	6	36	7	17
6<8	19	7	19	13	19
8<10	22	12	2	20	16
10<14	22	30	2	25	23
14<18	9	13	0	10	11
18<22	3	10	2	6	4
22<26	4	12	—	9	1
26<30	2	3	—	4	1
30 weeks < 8 months	0	1	—	0·5	—
8 months +	0·5	5	—	3	—
Total	100	100	100	100	100

If we allow 8 weeks, the Streatfeild target, for the waiting period in the higher courts and a generous 6 weeks for other waiting time, we get 14 weeks as an upper limit for acceptable delay. Yet we find 18·5 per cent of guilty plea cases, 44 per cent of not guilty cases, and even 2 per cent of committals for sentence going beyond that limit in Sheffield; taking the first two of these groups together, 32·5 per cent of those committed for trial on bail, and 17 per cent of those in custody were made to wait for at least 14 weeks.

We can only repeat that we consider such delays quite unacceptable.

By way of comment we may quote from the Streatfeild Committee's report (1961, paras 15-19) the grounds on which that body described as indefensible lesser delays than we found:

> First, all the benefits which flow from justice being done will be more potent if it is done quickly. Where a crime has caused concern and anxiety, whether nationally or locally, it is in the public interest that there should be no avoidable delay in determining the guilt or innocence of the accused person and, if he is found guilty, in fixing the penalty . . .
>
> Secondly, if there is a long delay, there is a risk that the evidence may be stale and that in consequence justice may not be done . . ..
>
> Thirdly, some witnesses, especially the victims of assaults, view with apprehension the prospect of describing an unpleasant incident in formal evidence for the second time . . ..
>
> Fourthly—and this consideration is no less important than the other three—the interval is an anxious period for the accused himself. If he is one of [those] who plead not guilty, he wants the matter determined as soon as possible; and if he is eventually acquitted . . . the criminal charges publicly made against him have gone unrebutted during the waiting period. Even if the accused intends all the time to plead guilty, he should know his fate, in terms of a sentence, within a reasonable period.

3 Approaching the court: the defendant's perspective

To the court administrator, to the judge or magistrate, to the professional lawyer, the court is a familiar place. Familiar rituals are re-enacted daily, often many times a day. These men know with almost unfailing precision what will happen next—a prosecutor's speech, or the introduction of evidence, or whatever. They share also a common stock of experience which, despite their different roles in the courtroom drama, pulls them together, and enables them to communicate with each other in ways which are incomprehensible to an uninformed outsider.

There is nothing sinister about this. No overt collusion to manipulate justice exists; what does exist are the shared understandings of habitués. These understandings may become so routine and commonplace that the habitué forgets that the outsider finds them strange, and often alienative. Some time ago, for example, one of us spent some time with a group of experienced but disbelieving magistrates, explaining not only that this sort of verbal shorthand exists, but, specifically, that the defendant may be alienated by the routine and wholly innocent pieces of verbal shorthand at the beginning of a summary trial. It is true that his rights are in no way being eroded in these exchanges, but the point is that only the habitué can be sure of that. The defendant, unsure as to what exactly is going on, can be excused if he is suspicious that exchanges which he does not understand might in some way be affecting his interests adversely.

For the defendant is usually not an habitué. First-time defendants in particular expressed to us their sense of confusion and exclusion in the court process:

> 'I felt awful: I was in a daze most of the time.'

> 'The police statement of the facts [after defendant's guilty plea] gave completely the wrong impression. But I wasn't given a proper chance to explain—I was so amazed at what the police said that I couldn't say anything.'

'When I was in the dock I felt very nervous—I tried hard to be subservient, and not to smile nervously.'

'I've never been in court before, and I found it all very interesting—but considering what I was up for [a minor shop-lifting charge], I felt so scared.'

'It was all unexpected—I've never been through it before—it was very nerve-racking.'

The second and third of these quotations are perhaps of special interest. In the second case, the defendant had, formally speaking, been given his chance to explain the incident to the court: but to him, he hadn't had a proper chance, because of his astonishment and confusion in the court situation. The third defendant, a skilled technician, expressed his uncertainty of role in the dock, a feeling of a need to be subservient rather than assertive in the courtroom situation.

Such feelings and reactions are not confined either to the first-time defendant or to the less educated groups within society:

Case 1045 B, aged 32, had a number of previous convictions, and had not long been released from a sentence of 2 years' imprisonment. He obviously knew all about courts and the legal system—for example, he had deliberately not applied for legal aid for his first court appearance because 'to begin with in the magistrates' they are just kicking you backwards and forwards'; later he had got a lawyer, but commented that your chances were better if you paid for one yourself, rather than getting one on legal aid. Despite this and other comments on the legal system, he said that he still disliked the trial: 'it all seems so very confusing.'

Case 2070 S, aged 18 was a student at a local institution of higher education; he had 1 previous conviction. One day he and a friend found an unattached roadsign by the road, and took it. They did not think this was theft, and when interviewed by the police said they had stolen nothing: the police said it was theft, and that ignorance of the law was no excuse, so S pleaded guilty, as 'once I knew it was theft there was no case for a not guilty plea'. (Actually, the police view that S's actions clearly amounted to theft was legally doubtful.) He did not obtain a lawyer because 'I did not think it was worth it—there were no mitigating circumstances'. In court the police said S had initially 'denied theft': this, said the defendant, gave a misleading impression, but he had not felt able to say anything in court, so his version of the incident went unheard by the magistrates.

Other respondents isolated other factors which help to produce confusion and lack of articulation in the typical defendant. One factor was the agony of uncertainty, the need to have the matter settled one way or the other: one defendant of the 'passive inadequate deviant' type (see West, 1963) had been given 4 years' imprisonment for a series of relatively minor burglaries, but refused to re-open the issue on an appeal, because 'while you are waiting, you don't know what you'll get'. To the defendant in this state of worry and uncertainty, the possibility of effective personal intervention in the court scene is remote. Second, some defendants perceive themselves to be placed in a subordinate and confusing position even before they reach the dock—before the case they have had to surrender to their bail, and for administrative convenience all defendants are then grouped together in a special part of the court, waiting until their case is called. One defendant, a technical representative, strongly disliked being thus 'herded around like a gang of labourers'; another saw it as simply the first stage in a cumulative process of humiliation: 'It is unfair from the moment you go into court—the police say "sit there" and so on—it's a very small-minded attitude.'

Nor was the contrast between their own position and that of the court staff and lawyers lost on defendants. As one first-offender eloquently put it: 'To them, it's everyday life. It's just like a hospital: to relations, sickness is a worry, but to staff it's an everyday thing.'

The defendant in court, then, is typically confused, worried and relatively inarticulate, and the court processes themselves often do little to alleviate this position. For a fuller statement of this picture of the defendant in court, the work by Pat Carlen (1974) should be consulted.

But this perspective on the defendant, accurate enough in itself, is not the whole truth. In approaching the court, the defendant has (as we have seen) a number of specific choices open to him, in particular as to plea, legal representation and venue. By making certain of these choices, or by consulting friends or relatives, or by adopting an ideology which rejects the court as irrelevant, or by accepting for himself a deliberately humble, passive role in the court, the defendant may reduce the impact upon himself of the worry and humiliation of being 'the man in the dock'.

In reviewing our interview data, we were struck by the variety of styles of defendants' approach to the court. To make adequate sense of these varying approaches, it seemed to us that we must create a classification, or typology, of defendants from the point of view of the way they had faced up to the confrontation with societal-legal authority in the form of the court.

There are many and various classifications for different purposes in the criminological literature (for a review, see Bottoms, 1973). Only one, however, was of the type we felt was needed to characterise our defendants. This is the classification by Cohen and Taylor (1972, chapter 7) of types of response to long-term imprisonment—a classification which was deliberately 'appreciative' (in the sense outlined in chapter 1) without confining itself entirely to the subject's own statements about himself; which allowed a prisoner's overt ideological position full recognition; and which was explicitly a 'characterisation of relationships with authority'. Despite this degree of accord, their classification could not be adopted by us, since (i) the confrontation with authority in the court setting is very different from that in the prison setting, and (ii) their sample was confined to 'Category A' prisoners (requiring conditions of maximum security) who had committed certain grave crimes wholly different from the run-of-the-mill episodes of most of our sample.

We created, then, our own typology of defendants' approaches to the court. The rest of this chapter is devoted to an explication of the various categories of this typology, from which the rich variety of approaches to court should be plain.

Strategists

The first group is of various kinds of 'strategists'. A strategic approach to the problematic situation of being charged as a defendant is an approach which tends to stress elements of rational planning, to maximise the benefit and payoff to the defendant (or perhaps more accurately, to minimise the potential damage or punishment). Just as the good military general thinks strategically, just as the football manager creates strategic defensive and offensive patterns, so the strategic defendant is able (or is enabled by others) to think ahead to the next stages in the court process, to plan an overall strategy which seems to him most likely to create advantages such as acquittal or a lighter sentence. Such a strategy may be mistaken (the strategy may in fact increase the sentence), but this does not alter the strategic quality of the thinking and planning behind the approach, and it is this which is crucial.

The first and most numerous type of strategist in our sample was the 'recidivist strategist'. This kind of strategist had learned his strategic thinking through previous personal experience in the criminal courts, and was able to anticipate various eventualities as a result. We give an example of one of the most sophisticated recidivist strategists in the sample (in this and other case examples in this chapter, we have indicated the main ways in which the five major decisions of plea, venue, representation, bail and appeal were approached by the interviewee).[1]

> Case 4022 E had 7 previous convictions, including 4 prison sentences; he was currently charged with a variety of sophisticated property offences, plus some motoring and drugs charges.
>
> Plea Originally told police that he had bought the property; but then codefendant told them the truth (that the goods were stolen samples to obtain orders). After the police had seen codefendant, it was pointless to plead not guilty, so 'I made a statement of guilt to get it all sorted out and dealt with quicker' (but in the event they were held 3 months on remand).
>
> Venue Elected Crown Court trial. He was intending to plead guilty at the Crown Court, but still chose that court because he thought he would be sent there for sentence under s.29 of the Magistrates' Courts Act (he knew the section number!) if he pleaded guilty at the magistrates', and (i) he thought there was a greater chance of bail being granted if he opted for Crown Court trial than if going under s.29; (ii) even if remanded in custody he would be an 'unconvicted remand' and therefore have greater privileges in the prison than as a convicted remand, which he would be if committed for sentence.
>
> Legal representation Decided 'straight away' to have a lawyer; a lawyer can express the case a lot better, he knows the technicalities involved and can put it across better so as to 'make it sound feasible'. Also the bench will take more notice of a lawyer than of the defendant.
>
> Custody Police custody before first appearance. 'I asked for the phone, for writing material, and to see a lawyer—but they never allow it.' Applied for bail at all court appearances, also applied to judge in chambers unsuccessfully. The difficulty was,

he had committed this offence while on bail for another charge (see further below, chapter 8).

Appeal Will appeal if solicitor considers that sentence (3½ years) is excessive. He had tried to discuss it with an appeals officer in Leeds Prison, 'but they can't advise on something they know nothing about'. [Prison legal aid officers are instructed to give advice about available facilities, but not to discuss individual cases with prisoners.] He would rely entirely on the solicitor's opinion.

We identified also three other main types of strategist. The first two of these, the 'entrepreneur strategist' and the 'middle-class strategist', might seem superficially similar, but in fact they are very different types. The distinctive feature of the entrepreneur strategist is that he treats the court proceedings and their preliminaries very much as he would approach a business deal: all entrepreneur strategists were of social class II or III, being in business as scrap metal dealers, haulage contractors, etc. A brief example will suffice:

Case 3004 S was a metal dealer living in comfortable surroundings. He was charged with handling stolen metal: he agreed the thief had offered him the goods but said he instantly refused them. He was convinced of his innocence, but worried because of a previous conviction some time before on a similar charge. He therefore wrote extensive notes on all his interviews with the police immediately they were finished, and got his secretary to type up the notes for him. He secured a lawyer (privately paid for) at once; he thought there was no question of custody as he knew many policemen socially. He chose the magistrates' court for his trial ('I knew I was not guilty, so why go further?') and was acquitted.

The middle-class strategist, of all the various kinds of strategists, is the one most likely to be ignorant of court proceedings, yet because (i) his social training and cultural expectation is to think in the long term, in a strategic way, and (ii) he almost immediately obtains legal services to help him in his predicament, he can truly be called a strategist. A difficult problem of allocation is created by the few company director defendants, who in a sense are both middle-class and entrepreneurial strategists; this has to be resolved in the individual case, but in our sample usually resulted in placement in the middle-class category. Some middle-class strategists are, however, not businessmen at all:

Case 3038 B was a university student, and was charged with (i) being drunk and disorderly, (ii) criminal damage to a car aerial. Kept in the cells overnight, he appeared next morning and pleaded guilty to the first charge but not guilty to the second, 'because I thought I could get off, and I didn't want a record'. His case was duly adjourned: as soon as he got home, he realised he should have a solicitor. He consulted (through his father) an ex-senior magistrate, who in turn wrote to a senior solicitor asking him to defend B: on this solicitor's advice, B withdrew his guilty plea and denied the drunk and disorderly charge. Meanwhile B had also consulted one of his lecturers about the incident, and he had advised a civil suit against the complainant in the case, since this man had allegedly broken B's nose in the incident. B was eventually found guilty on both charges and fined; he did not consider an appeal would be worth it because 'I might be found guilty again and it would be more expense'.

The fourth kind of strategist is very different—he is the 'alternative-society strategist'. That is, he is ideologically committed to a different set of values than those enshrined in our existing legal system; his strategy is to cope with his predicament as a defendant by rejecting the legitimacy of the court, while at the same time giving it sufficient external cognisance and subservience so as not to increase the penalties likely to be inflicted upon him. Most of the few alternative-society strategists in our sample were charged with drug offences; one such case gives a very clear example of the type:

Case 1009 R, a 21-year-old unemployed clerk, on a suspended sentence for cannabis possession, was charged again with that offence. In interview he admitted he had been 'pushing' cannabis in Sheffield for some time, but in fact denied that particular activity in connection with the current charge. He said he saw drugs and drug-use as 'part of a larger revolt against society'; he disliked magistrates, whom he saw as sitting in judgment not just on the facts of the case but on defendants' life-styles, and said, 'we are out to smash their kind of society'.
Plea He had hoped to get away with a not guilty plea and acquittal; he couldn't, because a codefendant had 'shopped' him. Once this had happened he felt he had little choice but to plead guilty, because he thought magistrates were very severe in

sentencing people who had pleaded not guilty without adequate reason.

Venue Chose magistrates' court to get a lesser sentence; also to get it over with, 'waiting is bad'.

Representation He 'needed someone to speak' for him. His codefendant had wanted to 'tell the court straight' about their views on drugs; that would have been a tactical mistake. In fact the lawyer put their point of view in a simplified and modified way, which was helpful. Mr C (solicitor) was chosen because 'he has a good reputation in drugs cases'.

Custody No appeal to judge in chambers, but 'would have done if remand had been for longer'.

Appeal Uncertain about appeal, said it would depend on 'personal reasons' to do with his girlfriend.

Finally, there was a handful of defendants whose approach seemed most correctly described as 'strategic', but who did not fall readily into any of the above four specific sub-categories. These were described as 'other strategists'.

Respectable first-timers

The second major type of approach is in some ways the antithesis of the first; and especially of the recidivist strategist. It is adopted by the man who is respectably established in society, at least in his middle 20s, and who suddenly has to face a court appearance for the first time. There are two variants of the approach. The first we called the 'remorseful one-time loser': the man who recognises his guilt, is very remorseful about the offence, and typically anxious to make amends, to apologise to the court, and to pay his fine or to serve his sentence without fuss. The second approach is one of outraged innocence, which we have described as the approach of the 'mistakenly indicted citizen': the man with no criminal record who is charged with an offence which he strongly denies.

Of course, not all first-offenders (or first-time defendants) would fit these descriptions. The young dependent 17-year-old, living with his parents, usually does not, for he is not sufficiently respectably established to qualify. Nor does the first-offender who has been on the fringe of a criminal sub-culture for some time, as one or two in our sample were; and some first-offenders fit better into some other category, such as 'middle-class strategist'. Furthermore, in one or two cases we extended the respectable first-timer category to include those with an isolated previous conviction, usually many years ago as a juvenile, where their reaction was otherwise typical of the respectable first-timer.

The following is an example of the remorseful one-time loser:

> Case 2057 M was a door-to-door salesman; he kept some money given him for goods by customers, bet it on greyhounds, and lost it. When he realised he could not pay the money to his firm, he went to the police and confessed. His reactions to the various court decisions show his anguish at his whole situation, facing his first conviction, and also his determination to face up to his guilt.
> Plea 'I was guilty, it was a stupid thing to do. It would be stupid to deny it.'
> Venue Magistrates' court—'to get it over—I had been through so much already'.
> Representation Unrepresented. The police told him about legal aid, but 'I was guilty so there was no point in a lawyer. The police had all the facts in my statement'.
> Appeal 'I was guilty, I must pay the consequences. There is no question of an appeal'.

By contrast, the following case exemplifies the 'mistakenly indicted citizen'.

> Case 3039 S was a 52-year-old storekeeper in a factory, with no previous convictions, except one as a juvenile for riding a bicycle without lights. He was charged with theft of margarine, value 16p, from a shop—he denied this very strongly, and told a complex story about shopping bags and the checkout point.
> Plea He refused to plead guilty, although he said the police tried to make him do so, and had told him he would only get a 'lecture' if he did. He could not plead guilty, he said, because he had not done it.
> Venue He didn't know about venue choice until he got to court; then his solicitor said 'be tried here'.
> Representation Decided on a lawyer as soon as police tried to make him admit it: 'I needed help.'
> Appeal Solicitor advised against it, although S was found guilty and fined £5. S was also influenced by his supervisor at the factory telling him to drop the case, and saying the firm believed him and would not sack him.

In these two cases, there is also a contrast of pleas. However, although many 'mistakenly indicted citizens' do plead not guilty, as many as half in our sample did not. For one reason or another, although strongly believing themselves innocent, they had decided or been persuaded to plead guilty. An example is case 1049, already given at the beginning of chapter 1; the general group of self-styled 'innocents pleading guilty' is discussed further in chapter 5, where reasons for such behaviour are examined more fully.

Right-assertive defendants

A further reaction, characteristic of only a small number of defendants, is that of the strong assertion of rights. To an extent, some of the 'mistakenly indicted citizens' are right-assertive (see case 3039's reaction concerning the question of plea), but the right-assertive defendant is usually more forceful, and of course he need not be a first-time defendant. Almost by definition, virtually all right-assertive defendants plead not guilty; the following is an example:

> Case 7003 E was charged alternatively with burglary in a dwelling house and handling stolen goods. He strongly denied his guilt of burglary, and in interview at one point denied guilt of handling too, but also said 'I suppose I did know the goods were stolen eventually'. He had 7 previous convictions.
> Plea Barrister strongly advised a guilty plea to the handling charge; E resisted this and pleaded not guilty to both charges (he subsequently regretted this and thought his sentence might have been less had he followed his barrister's advice: he was in fact convicted on the burglary charge).
> (Venue Not relevant: no venue choice, case had to go to Crown Court.)
> Representation 'I wanted a lawyer from the start, to protect my interests.' But he claimed that the police wouldn't let him contact a solicitor until after the first court appearance; he said, 'you should be able to have one in the police station when you are interviewed'.
> Custody In custody throughout, but he made strenuous efforts to resist this result. He said he had written ten letters to different people about bail, and had asked his solicitor five times to apply to the judge in chambers for bail, but he had said it was a waste of the taxpayers' money.

Appeal At time of interview, uncertain about appealing: he said 'my solicitor says there's no chance, but if my fiancée thinks I have a chance I will have a go'. He did subsequently make application for leave to appeal—see chapter 7.

While not all defendants in the right-assertive category are quite as assertive as this in every department of their case, they all show similar qualities of persistence and of a strong civil rights approach.

Ordinary respondents

The fourth major approach in our defendants' typology is that of the 'ordinary respondent'. Such a man shows no evidence of strategic thinking in his approach to the court, he is not right-assertive, he does not have the special features of the 'respectable first-timer', and his approach is not markedly passive (see below). Rather, the approach is that of the straightforward, matter-of-fact man, taking decisions as they come in a commonsense manner.

As we shall see in more detail later, the 'ordinary respondent' approach is particularly strong among not guilty pleaders, and among the SGU group. We give one example briefly from each category:

Case 5034 E was charged with malicious wounding, in a domestic incident involving a fight with his brother-in-law. He had a previous conviction for common assault eight years previously. He said he had acted this time in self-defence, that it was a miscarriage of justice that he had ever been charged, but that he was 'worried sick' about it. He pleaded not guilty, and chose Crown Court trial, 'because I just thought a jury would be fairer'. He was legally represented because 'I felt it needed it—it was a more serious case than last time'. E was acquitted.

Case 2002 J, aged 21, had several previous convictions, the last one five months previously when he had been given a 3 months suspended prison sentence. He was charged with burglary and theft from a shop.
Plea 'I denied it at first, but it was obvious they knew, so I had no case and told them it was me.'
Venue 'I was sure to get a prison sentence, so decided to get it over, avoid a remand in custody and start the sentence.' (The

defendant did not know the rules too well: remands in custody in fact count as part of the prison sentence.)
Representation Unrepresented: 'there was no point, I was pleading guilty and it was a straightforward case.'
Appeal 'I'm satisfied with the sentence' (six months' imprisonment); 'I only got three months on top of the suspended sentence, and that's light.'

Passive respondents

A further response to the confrontation with societal authority in the courtroom is the approach of passivity. In this approach, or rather in the several variants of the approach, the defendant's characteristic stand is that of acceptance of and submission to the court processes.[2]

The first variant of the type is that of the dissociative defendant. This is a concept culled from the work of Downes (1965, pp. 237f) on adolescent delinquent groups. Such boys typically 'dissociate' from school (and later from official work norms); they reject official values subscribed to by the dominant society, but this rejection 'is not one of structured protest, defiance and rebellion . . . but of . . . inertia, boredom and passivity'. In an analogous way, some of our defendants passively dissociated themselves from courtroom processes, and reacted with inertia and boredom to the whole tedious official ritual of 'dealing with' their behaviour in the court. Typically, too, such defendants were bored by our interview, and could see little purpose in going over all this ground again in detail; their interview reaction was therefore very often monosyllabic and relatively unhelpful to us:

Case 2052 C, aged 32, was charged with intercepting a neighbour's Giro order and obtaining £6 after forging a signature. He had previous convictions, the last one eight years before.
Plea Pleaded guilty 'to get it cleared up, no point in delaying it'.
Venue Magistrates' court 'to get it cleared up there and then'.
Representation No lawyer: 'knew I would be found guilty; lawyer would be waste of money.'
Appeal 'Didn't know I could. I wouldn't anyway; the fine was what I expected.'

The second variant of passivity is a very different one; we referred to it as the 'moralistic-passive' approach. The few defendants in this category applied strongly to themselves a conventional moralistic attitude typical of more censorious judges or magistrates; there was a strong tendency for them to accept and endorse the court world-view, and/or to display a self-punitive attitude. The following is an example:

> Case 1022 S was charged with aiding and abetting an attempt to obtain a watch at a Sheffield department store. X proffered a cheque with a false signature at the store; S had given him the cheque.
> Plea He heard the police were looking for him, so went to them and made a complete confession. 'I find it difficult to tell lies—I wanted to get it over and take my punishment, because I knew I had done it.'
> Venue Magistrates' court, 'to get it over and done with'.
> Representation Not represented at magistrates' court: 'I didn't think about applying for legal aid.' Was then committed to Quarter Sessions for sentence: 'I was told I was to have a barrister—it was decided for me.'
> Custody Didn't apply for bail: 'X asked and he was refused, so I didn't bother.'
> Appeal 'No point: I was given probation, which is what I wanted. I finished my last probation in June and I still feel the need to talk to someone about personal matters.'

The third variant of the passive approach is that of the 'immature-passive' defendant. These men were all very young (without exception, in the age group 17-23) and their approach to the court displayed a passivity based on youthfulness and inexperience. The following is an example (it is in fact the same case referred to in chapter 2, note 4, concerning theft of stamps):

> Case 1005 T, aged 17 and with no previous court appearance, was charged with burgling the attic of an unoccupied house and stealing stamps; he was jointly charged with his older half-brother. He was described by our interviewer as 'having little to say, very shy and immature, and knows little about court proceedings'.
> Plea 'We knew we had done it and we were told it was wrong. We didn't think we had stolen anything [thought stamps belonged to no one and of no value] but we were told it was wrong, so we pleaded guilty.' Now wishes they had pleaded not guilty: 'we might have got off.'

Venue Magistrates' court 'to get it over with'. Now regrets decision.
Representation Brother got a solicitor (brother lived apart from T), and by mistake the solicitor spoke for both boys at the first appearance; but not at the second as T had not applied for legal aid. T seemed rather bewildered by all this.
Appeal No appeal: 'we found the stamps and they call it stealing, so we have to agree with them, and admit we deserve to be punished for it.'

The final variant of the passive defendant we describe simply as 'other passive'. This type of defendant does not display the special kind of passivity of the dissociative man, nor is he necessarily moralistic like the second variant, nor does his passivity seem to be simply the result of youthful inexperience like the third sub-type. In the following case, for example, although the defendant was aged only 22, he was classified as 'other passive' rather than 'immature passive' because his passivity seemed to be more deep-seated than is typically the case with the immature passives:

Case 6009 With others, G took part in a bank raid, wearing a stocking mask and carrying a pistol and an axe. He had 2 previous convictions and was currently on probation.
Plea Pleaded guilty because, he said, the police beat him up and forced him to tell the truth and admit guilt.
(Venue Not relevant; compulsory Crown Court trial.)
Representation 'They gave me legal aid: everyone has a lawyer.'
Custody No application for bail: 'I thought I might as well start serving my sentence immediately and get the time knocked off at the end.'
Appeal Received 9 years' imprisonment, and urged by other prisoners to appeal, especially as his codefendant was appealing. But he wasn't going to: he said 'it's too much bother; anyway I've nothing to lose by being in prison'. Our interviewer described him as 'very apathetic', and noted that his cellmate (whom she also interviewed) described him as 'completely unable to cope with society outside'; it seemed he was very much an accomplice rather than a planner in the robbery.

Other-dominated respondents

Many defendants seek advice from many different quarters about various aspects of their court appearances: in later chapters we examine in some detail the pattern of advice concerning each type of decision. Here, however, we must note a special kind of defendant who forms a small but interesting part of our sample: the defendant whose approach to decisions is dominated by the advice of others.

Some friends and colleagues with whom we discussed our research from time to time queried whether it was worth asking the legally represented defendant about decisions and choices made: surely all such decisions will be made for him by the lawyer? This is a serious misconception. Many lawyers do not wish to take decisions for their clients, but would rather spell out the options available and leave the final decision to the client; even where this is not so, the client's behaviour and choices at a stage before the lawyer reaches the case (e.g. during interrogation in the police station) often severely limit the range of action open to the lawyer. So, while 44 per cent of our interview sample were legally represented, only 8 per cent were in the 'other-dominated respondent' category; and of defendants in that category one-third were unrepresented, for dominant advice may be received from many other sources than the lawyer, e.g. relatives, probation officers, policemen.

The following two cases illustrate this category of defendant: in the first case it is the police advice which is decisive, in the second case it is that of the defendant's solicitor:

> Case 2028 E had previous convictions for dishonesty, and had only just been released from prison. He was charged with theft of lead sheeting.
> Plea 'Police said "if you plead guilty it will be easier; if you deny it, we will lock you up, and you're only just out of prison; if you plead guilty you will only get a fine". I had wanted to deny it, but I decided to go along with them. My brother had advised a not guilty plea and I wish I had followed his advice' (because after pleading guilty E received a 3-months prison sentence).
> Venue 'Chose magistrates' court, because police said I'd only get a fine, and the Crown Court would mean a long wait.'
> Representation Not represented—police had said he would only get a fine, so he saw no point in a lawyer. His brother had advised him to get one, and he regretted not having done so.
> Bail After admission to police; 'they said they would lock me up otherwise.'

Appeal No appeal; short sentence, by the time appeal came through he would be out of prison anyway.

Case 5025 J, aged 17, was charged with assault on a policeman, occasioning actual bodily harm to him. It was alleged that after a Christmas Eve party, J was behaving in a disorderly manner, a policeman had come up to him to quieten him, and J had kicked him in the groin. J disputed this and had another version of the incident.
Plea Seriously considered guilty plea, and only finally decided on not guilty plea at third court appearance. Solicitor advised him that the prosecution evidence was poor: 'I pleaded not guilty completely on the advice of the solicitor.'
Venue At first intended magistrates' court and a guilty plea: 'Solicitor advised me to plead not guilty and go to the Crown Court.'
Representation 'A serious case—I wouldn't have liked to have gone on without a solicitor.'
Appeal Convicted and sent to detention centre for 3 months but no appeal planned: 'It would have to go to London, and I'm only here for a short time.'

It will be seen that not all the decisions taken in these cases are taken on others' advice: both men decided against an appeal on their own initiative. Yet the dominant theme of their main decision pattern is undoubtedly the influence of third parties.

Other types of defendants' response

The seventh main type of defendants' response is a somewhat heterogeneous one which we described as 'dominated by external circumstances'. There are two variants of this. The first, found overwhelmingly in the SGU category, was of a case being dominated by the triviality of the offence. Defendants in this group would, if charged with more serious offences, have taken a wholly different approach to the case, a fact they usually made clear to us (they might, for example, have normally taken a recidivist strategist or a right-assertive approach, but felt that the offence circumstances simply did not warrant taking the case so seriously). It was for this reason that they were almost all in the SGU group; they did not consider it worth getting a lawyer or being tried in a higher court for such a trivial offence. The single exception to this rule was a recidivist charged with a 40p theft, who took the precaution of getting a lawyer, but otherwise made no effort to fight the case—by way of denial, etc.—in the way he normally would. The offences charged against members of this group were all thefts of very low value, and in two-fifths of the cases the man was charged with theft from the gas or electricity meter in his own home.

In some other cases also, a decision pattern was wholly or largely determined by external circumstances surrounding the case. These circumstances were very heterogeneous, and depended very much upon the individual case: in a few cases, for example, it was the defendant's lack of command of the English language which dominated all aspects of the case; in one case a man about to go to prison for non-payment of motoring fines deliberately went to the police to confess his guilt of theft from his meter, so as to obtain a prison sentence concurrent with that he was about to serve; in one or two cases codefendants' decisions almost forced the defendant into a decision pattern of a like kind; some cases were made very different from the usual simply because the defendant perceived himself to be in a very special risk situation because he was in breach of a suspended prison sentence order; and so on. Because of the heterogeneity of the category, little purpose is served in providing an illustrative case.

Finally, there were a few defendants who did not really fit into any of the above seven major types and variants within them. Men with long histories of mental illness, for example, sometimes produced idiosyncratic decision styles; and there were one or two other special cases. This is the inevitable 'miscellaneous' category to which almost all typologists are driven in the attempt to classify all their cases.

Operationalising the defendants' typology

When the criteria for allocation into the categories of a typology are relatively 'soft' and imprecise—as in the instant case—there are always difficulties in operationalising the typology. 'Polar' or 'ideal-typical' cases can relatively easily be identified and classed; but there are inevitably marginal cases which present problems. For our typology, for example, there were some cases which showed elements of strategic thinking but no fully consistent strategy—were they to be 'strategists' or 'ordinary respondents'? Again, a lawyer might have strongly influenced a couple of decisions taken by a defendant who otherwise showed marked passivity—was the case to be 'other passive' or 'other-dominated'?

No hard and fast rules could be laid down, but we endeavoured to classify each case into the most appropriate category, bearing in mind all the circumstances of the case. The overall result for our whole sample (reweighted according to sampling fraction as appropriate) is shown in Table 3.1. The largest major category is of passive respondents, who make up one in three of the sample; of these about a third are dissociative, and the rest other kinds of passive. One in five cases are 'ordinary respondents', and another fifth are dominated either by others' advice (8 per cent) or by external circumstances (12 per cent). That leaves one in six defendants as a 'strategist' of one kind or another; one in twelve as a 'respectable first-timer'; and a handful remaining as right-assertive (1 per cent) or miscellaneous (4 per cent).

For the purpose of statistical cross-tabulation with other factors, the full classification in Table 3.1 is too elaborate; we have simplified it for operational use by taking simply the major type (I-VIII) in all instances except among strategists (where we have preserved a distinction between recidivist strategists and the rest) and among passive respondents (where we have distinguished between the dissociative and the rest).

Using this simplified version of the typology, we can relate it to the various sub-sample categories based on decisions as to plea, venue and representation. This is shown in Table 3.2. Comparing categories within the lower court (S) and higher court (D and H) groups, we find that:

(i) SGRs have significantly more strategists than SGUs, but correspondingly less in the group of ordinary respondents, dissociatives and other passive respondents;

(ii) SGRs have significantly more passive respondents than SNs, but significantly fewer respectable first-timers;

(iii) DGs have significantly more strategists and significantly less ordinary respondents and (almost significant) respectable first-timers than DNs;

(iv) HGs have significantly more passive respondents, and significantly less right-assertive defendants, than HNs.

If we compare different venue types within the group of defendants pleading guilty or not guilty, we find that:

(i) the three not guilty groups (SN, DN, HN) do not differ significantly. When taken together, however, they have significantly

Table 3.1 Proportionate distribution of interviewees in defendants' typology

	%	Total %
I Strategists		
(a) Recidivist strategists	8·9	
(b) Entrepreneur strategists	2·5	
(c) Middle-class strategists	1·9	
(d) Alternative-society strategists	1·2	
(e) Other strategists	0·6	
Total class I		15·1
II Respectable first-timers		
(a) Remorseful one-time losers	5·1	
(b) Mistakenly indicted citizens	2·8	
Total class II		7·9
III Right-assertive defendants		1·3
IV Ordinary respondents		19·7
V Passive respondents		
(a) Dissociative	12·6	
(b) Moralistic passive	2.2	
(c) Immature passive	7·3	
(d) Other passive	10·0	
Total class V		32·1
VI Other-dominated respondents		7·6
VII External circumstances dominate response		
(a) Response dominated by triviality of offence	5·8	
(b) Response dominated by other circumstance	6·5	
Total class VII		12·3
VIII Miscellaneous		4·0
Grand total		100·0

more right-assertive and ordinary respondents than do (SGR + HG).

(ii) SGRs do not differ significantly from HGs for any type, but

Table 3.2 Defendants' typology, by sub-sample categories (%)

	SGU	SGR	SN	DG	DN	HG	HN
Recidivist strategists	3	15	12	23	12	17	20
Other strategists	4	8	9	35	4	7	16
Respectable first-timers	7	5	18	—	16	9	16
Right-assertive	—	1	9	—	20	—	12
Ordinary respondents	25	10	24	—	28	13	20
Dissociative	16	10	—	—	—	11	4
Other passive	22	17	3	6	—	24	4
Other-dominated	3	17	15	24	16	11	—
External circumstances	16	13	6	6	4	4	8
Miscellaneous	4	4	3	6	—	4	—
Total	100	100	100	100	100	100	100
No.	69	78	33	17	25	46	25

both groups have significantly less strategists and significantly more passives than do the DGs.

It will be seen, therefore, that there are many important differences in defendants' approach to the courts when we compare them on the basis of administrative routes through the criminal justice system. To summarise, we can say that the SGU group is, not surprisingly, the least strategic and the most passive; it also has more ordinary respondents than any other guilty plea group, but not than the not guilty pleas. Right-assertive defendants are found almost exclusively among not guilty pleas. Passive respondents are found much more among HGs than any other higher court group, while the small DG group is confined almost exclusively to strategists and to other-dominated defendants (as we shall show later, legal advice plays a very special role among this group). 'Respectable first-timers' are found proportionately more frequently among the not guilty groups than the guilty groups.

We also examined the defendants' typology in relation to two major items of data on the individual characteristics of defendants, i.e. age and social class. The results are shown in Table 3.3. The first part of the table shows that the sub-group with significantly the highest social class position is the 'other strategists' group: this of course is accounted for by the presence of entrepreneur strategists and middle-class strategists within the group. Rather surprisingly, the lowest social class position is held by the 'external circumstances' group; also passive (including dissociative) and 'recidivist-strategist' defendants tend to be of lower social class than respectable first-timers, right-assertives and ordinary respondents, though these differences are not statistically significant.

Table 3.3 Defendants' typology, by individual characteristics

	Social class (%)				Age (%)				
	I,II	III	IV,V	Total	<21	21-29	30-39	40+	Total
Recidivist strategists	3	43	54	100	8	36	27	29	100
Other strategists	41	43	16	100	21	48	18	13	100
Respectable first-timers	3	63	34	100	—	22	18	60	100
Right-assertive	—	62	38	100	15	62	—	23	100
Ordinary respondents	7	53	40	100	27	44	23	6	100
Dissociative	—	43	57	100	26	53	21	—	100
Other passive	—	42	58	100	44	22	18	16	100
Other-dominated	6	49	45	100	48	25	20	7	100
External circumstances	7	19	74	100	8	41	19	32	100
Miscellaneous	—	39	61	100	—	30	28	42	100
All offenders	5	44	51	100	24	37	20	19	100

The respectable first-timers are markedly the oldest group, with three-fifths aged 40 or more; recidivist strategists also tend to be older than average. The youngest two groups are the 'other passives' (strongly weighted, of course, by the inclusion of the 'immature-passive' group), and also the 'other-dominated respondents', who in the youngest age group tend to rely especially upon the advice of parents.

These data tend to confirm the meaningfulness of the defendants' typology. Ideally, of course, one would want a full explanation of the reasons for the adoption of a particular style in the approach to the court process: this we are unable to provide, given the descriptive and exploratory nature of the research (see chapter 1). But now that we have explained the various categories of our typology, we may appropriately mention one other similarity between our typology and that of Cohen and Taylor (1972). Their book views the prisoner's response to long-term imprisonment as a problem of survival. In a real sense too, our typology is about survival: the defendant (and his self-concept) is seen struggling to survive with minimum damage in a situation usually perceived as offering a not inconsiderable threat—to liberty, to financial resources, or to reputation. We have seen that in the courtroom the defendant is typically confused, apprehensive and relatively inarticulate. But the various decisions available to the defendant—decisions which may be taken away from the court setting, although formally pronounced there—give the defendant some chance of exercising choice and imposing order in a difficult and perplexing situation. There are many different ways of ordering these choices, and our typology has sought to capture some of the main styles of approach. How far these different styles are differentially successful in resolving the 'survival' problems of different defendants is a highly complex matter which was not within the scope of our research.

But we have used the defendants' typology in later chapters, to throw some light on the differential incidence of reasons for various decisions among the various groups of the typology. We turn now to our substantive investigation of the defendants' approach to these five main types of decision—the issues of venue, plea, representation, appeal and bail.

4 Venue

When lawyers talk of 'venue' they usually mean where a case is to be tried: which town, or county, is the proper venue. We use the term in a second sense: in which court, or under which mode of procedure, is the trial to take place. In particular we are concerned with the choice between summary trial and trial on indictment, between trial in the magistrates' or the Crown Court.

We have already seen (chapter 2) that the nature of the offence and the wishes of the prosecution and of the magistrates are relevant to this question of venue. This chapter is concerned with the defendant's views. In very many cases the defendant can control the decision; he must consent to the summary trial of an indictable offence even if the prosecution and the magistrates agree that summary trial is appropriate; he can claim trial by jury for many offences which would otherwise be tried summarily.

If all considerations are eliminated other than the need for cases to be disposed of quickly and economically, it is highly desirable that as many cases as possible are disposed of summarily. A defendant who goes to the higher court for trial may save a little time for the justices and their staff, but on balance his decision greatly increases the amount of work to be put into the case. Papers have to be prepared by the prosecution for use at committal proceedings. A number of adjournments may take place pending these proceedings, especially where the defendant is in custody and can only be remanded for 8 days at a time. This involves extra court appearances, and the bringing of a prisoner remanded in custody from Leeds Prison to Sheffield on each occasion. The work load of the Crown Court is increased, and the defendant has to be represented by counsel who must be given a brief with adequate instructions by the defendant's solicitor. From the point of view of economy and smooth administration, it is a good thing that only a very small proportion of defendants opt for trial by jury.

On the other hand, it is perfectly possible to argue that, as in many other legal contexts, the demands of adequate justice are opposed to those of economy and administration. On this view, everyone pleading not guilty is entitled to a judgment by his peers, the twelve good men and true of the English jury, the bulwark of liberty; while even those pleading guilty have every right to expect the fuller and more leisurely consideration of sentence which the Crown Court gives, aided as it is in almost every case by a defence lawyer[1] and a social inquiry report from a probation officer. On this view, trial by the magistrates is a form of second-class proceedings.

Despite the interest of these conflicting considerations, choice of venue has received very little attention in the recent upsurge of interest in English criminal proceedings. Bail, legal representation, plea, appeal—each has its literature, both academic and governmental. Venue, in the sense of the defendant's venue choice, has not; hence the importance of the James Committee, set up in July 1973 jointly by the Home Secretary and the Lord Chancellor to consider all aspects of distribution of business as between magistrates' courts and the Crown Court.[2]

Table 4.1 shows the overall pattern of defendants' venue decisions in our court sample.

Table 4.1 Pattern of defendants' venue decisions

	Male		Female	
Defendant elected summary trial (S)	1,021	(76%)	295	(90%)
Defendant elected higher court trial (D)	60	(4%)	14	(4%)
Case to higher court; no election by defendant (H)	263	(20%)	19	(6%)
Total	1,344	(100%)	328	(100%)

Where the defendant had a choice, he opted for summary trial in 95 per cent of the cases. The remaining 5 per cent of cases make a considerable impact on the business of the higher court, for they represent 21 per cent of higher court cases (18 per cent of male, 42 per cent of female cases).

It is this 5 per cent of cases, the 'D' group, which is of special interest. But the overall figure masks considerable variation by offence type, as Table 4.2 shows. The main feature is that assaults and sexual offences far more often resulted in the choice of higher court trial. In a sense, this is rather surprising in view of the high proportion of such cases already siphoned off by the bench for higher court trial without putting the option to the defendant (see chapter 2). The explanation seems to lie in the special issues arising in contested cases for such offences, especially problems of (i) identity, and (ii) the involvement of the complainant, leading to defences of consent and self-defence; no doubt it is felt by legal representatives that such matters are best handled at the higher court.[3] Another feature of the table is the low proportion of those charged with handling who opted for Crown Court trial; the explanation here seems to be that in Sheffield the more serious handling cases are almost all handling of scrap metal, and these tend to be refused summary trial by the magistrates (see Table 2.2).

Table 4.2 Proportions of defendants charged with different offences who chose higher court trial ('choice of venue' cases only)

Offence	%
Assaults and woundings	14
Sexual offences	11
Thefts (not shops or meters)	9
Burglaries	6
Frauds	6
Taking car without consent	6
Shoplifting	5
Handling	2
Criminal damage	2
Meter-thefts	0
Drugs offences	0
All offences	5

Before turning to the main research results on venue, we must notice three rather special features about the relatively small 'D' group, each of which in some way affects the interpretation of some of the figures.

(i) Our final sample contained (as we showed in chapter 1) fewer 'DG' cases than we had expected, only a half of the prediction based on the examination of earlier court records. This makes it rather more difficult than it might have been to draw firm conclusions from our data.

(ii) The distinction between the DN and DG groups is to some extent artificial. At the time of making their choice of venue, only 5 of the 17 interviewed DGs had intended to plead guilty; the other 12 were late change-of-pleas. We examine plea-changes in chapter 5; for the moment, it is crucial to bear in mind that in our sample the

'D' choice is, at the time it is made, overwhelmingly a choice for full jury trial. This does not mean there are no differences between the DNs and the change-of-plea DGs; indeed, we have already seen that the former group contains more 'ordinary respondents' and 'respectable first-timers', and fewer 'strategists', than the latter (see chapter 3).

(iii) There was one particular case causing special problems. Four university students appeared as codefendants; one was a law student, and this led the group to act as 'middle-class strategists', consulting a Professor of Law, getting legal representation, etc., despite a relatively trivial charge arising out of a celebratory party. They eventually (after a plea change) pleaded guilty in the Crown Court, and thus constitute 4 of the 17 defendants in the DG category. This special quartet tends to distort the data for that category; that this category tended to be younger than some others, and had significantly more single men, is largely due to the presence of this group of students, which took its decisions as one body but does of course count as 4 separate defendants.

Knowledge of the system

The assumption behind the present practice of asking the defendant to decide venue is that his choice is an informed and intelligent one. This assumes in turn that defendants have some knowledge of the courts, and also some advance knowledge that a choice of venue has to be made by them. Defendants in our interview sample were questioned on these matters, and some information about the extent of knowledge of the courts among the population as a whole is available in a study prepared for the Home Office by the Office of Population Censuses and Surveys (Durant et al., 1972).

The OPCS survey found that 47 per cent of informants had attended a court of law at some time, 14 per cent as defendants; although the question asked ('Have you ever been inside a court yourself?') was in the context of an interview about the criminal courts, some of the answers related to civil cases, with 6 per cent of respondents indicating that they had been to court as a plaintiff, to bring a case against someone (Durant et al., 1972, table 3, p.12). When the results were analysed by sex, there was a sharp difference: 63 per cent of men, but only 32 per cent of women had been in court; of the men 26 per cent had been as a defendant as against only 2 per cent of the women (Durant et al., 1972, table 4, p.14). As our interview sample was exclusively male, the higher figures are the relevant ones for purposes of comparison. An outline comparison is given in Table 4.3.

Table 4.3 Proportions of males attending magistrates' and higher court

	OPCS males	Sheffield sample (%)	
		Tried summarily	Tried in higher court
Had attended a magistrates' court	50	76	82
Had attended a higher court	20	32	44

The difference between the Sheffield sample and the OPCS data is entirely expected. Those Sheffield defendants who had previous experience of the criminal courts had gained it mostly as defendants, but, as we have seen, only 26 per cent of male respondents to the OPCS survey had (or admitted to having) been defendants in the past. (The OPCS survey does not indicate the experience as defendant separately for the different types of court.)

Table 4.4 gives the results of interviews with defendants.[4] Of those who in the current case had elected summary trial, 21 per cent had never been in a magistrates' court in any capacity, and 69 per cent had never been in a higher court. It is noteworthy that SGRs had greater experience, especially of the higher courts, than the other groups. The SNs are more likely to have been litigants in civil cases than the other groups, perhaps a reflection of the higher socio-economic status of defendants pleading not guilty (see chapter 5).

The lower half of Table 4.4 shows the data for those who were tried for the current offence in the higher court. It will be remembered that only the Ds had themselves chosen trial in that court, the Hs being sent for trial there because the law so required or the bench so determined. So far as experience of the magistrates' courts is concerned, these groups of defendants are very similar to those whose current case was tried summarily, except that the higher court groups seem to have had more juvenile court experience. Differences begin to emerge when we examine the extent of experience of the higher courts: DGs, HGs (and SGRs) present one pattern, all with 47 per cent having had experience as a defendant in the higher

Table 4.4 Court experience of interview sample (%)*

I Defendants tried summarily				
Experience of magistrates' courts	SGU	SGR	SN	All
In previous criminal cases	70	77	71	71
In civil cases	1	0	6	
In juvenile court case	5	4	0	8
As spectator	3	1	0	
Total	79	82	77	79
No experience	21	18	23	21
Experience of higher courts				
In previous criminal cases	25	47	31	30
In civil cases	0	0	3	1
As spectator	0	4	0	
Total	25	51	34	31
No experience	75	49	66	69

II Defendants tried at higher court					
Experience of magistrates' courts	DG	DN	HG	HN	All
In previous criminal cases	65	68	77	64	73
In juvenile cases	0	8	10	5	8
As spectator	6	0	0	5	1
Total	71	76	87	74	82
No experience	29	24	13	26	18
Experience of higher courts					
In previous criminal cases	47	32	47	36	43
As witness	0	0	0	5	1
Total	47	32	47	41	44
No experience	53	68	53	59	56

*In most categories a small number gave answers to the question as to whether there was experience of court which cannot be classified satisfactorily.

courts, while DNs, HNs (and SNs) have a 'score' of between 30 and 36 per cent.

Overall the main finding is that for only one group of defendants, those in our SGR category, can it be said that a majority made their choice of venue on the basis of some first-hand experience of both types of court. This does not necessarily mean that our defendants were ill-informed about the court system; we examine the state of their knowledge below. We must look first at the other requirement we have suggested for an informed and intelligent choice: advance warning that the defendant has a choice of venue.

This choice of venue is always made in open court, and the procedure is regulated by s.19 of the Magistrates' Courts Act 1952 so far as the most common case, involving an indictable offence triable summarily, is concerned. This section (as amended) provides, in part:

> (3) . . . [T]he court . . . shall tell [the defendant] that he may, if he consents, be tried summarily instead of being tried by a jury and, if the court thinks it desirable for his information, shall explain what is meant by being tried summarily.
> (4) The court shall also explain to him that if he consents to be tried summarily and is convicted by the court he may be committed to the Crown Court [for sentence] . . . if the court, on obtaining information of his character and antecedents, is of opinion that they are such that greater punishment should be inflicted than the court has power to inflict.
> (5) After informing the accused as provided by the last two preceding sub-sections, the court shall ask him whether he wishes to be tried by a jury or consents to be tried summarily . . . .

This procedure will be gone through perhaps as often as a dozen times in a morning's sitting; anyone spending any time in a magistrates' court becomes quite familiar with it. We have seen that the great majority of all defendants have spent time in a magistrates' court before their current case, and they may well have sat through several other cases on the day they had to make the choice as to venue. So it might be expected that few defendants would be unaware of the choice before them.

On the other hand, it may be that this bit of court procedure makes little impact on the observer. It forms part of a larger set-piece at the beginning of each case in which the prosecuting solicitor or officer and the chairman also have speaking parts; it is delivered at some speed by a clerk who has done it a thousand times before; it may simply not 'register'. Certainly there are occasions on which the defendant who is being addressed has to be woken from his trance-like state, and the question repeated. It has something of the quality of a television washing-powder commercial: slick, rapid, familiar—and yet the viewer may pay so little attention that he could not tell you the name of the product at all. As one defendant put it:

> 'I found this very confusing—so quick that I didn't really know what was going on. I didn't really choose—I thought, go to prison or Assize or something—I just said 'tried here' to get it done there and then.'

And several other interviewed defendants also (though less articulately) indicated this sense of bewilderment at the whole venue set-piece.

It will be recalled that we were not able to ask defendants any questions before their appearance in court; we had to ask them to recollect the state of their knowledge as at that time, which perhaps involved looking back over several weeks and a number of subsequent court appearances. Those who did in fact choose summary trial were given this question:

> 'Now, you know that your case was dealt with by three magistrates. Before you went into court, did you know that you were going to be asked if you wanted to be tried by a different court?'

If the answer was 'yes', then they were asked how they knew. Table 4.5 summarises the answers.

Table 4.5 Advance knowledge of venue decision, defendants tried summarily (%)

	SGU	SGR	SN	All
Not known beforehand	24	13	25	21
Only from watching earlier cases	7	0	6	6
Advance knowledge				
own previous criminal cases	56	62	31	56
general knowledge	2	0	28	6
police advice	4	1	9	4
solicitor's advice	0	20	0	4
Other answers	6	4	0	5
Total	100	100	100	100

The main result is that 27 per cent of defendants who consented to summary trial report that they were unaware as they entered court for the start of the day's sitting that they had a choice of venue. The proportion was 31 per cent for those pleading not guilty, for whom trial by jury might be an important matter. This raises a serious question as to the need for some formal notice of this right to be given in advance of the court hearing.

There are some interesting variations between the sub-sample groups. The SGRs are much the best informed; their past experience and the help of their solicitors explains that. The SNs were the only group to treat this to any extent as a matter of general knowledge. This is intriguing, for they had just, in the immediately preceding question in the interview, admitted to as great an experience of the criminal courts, as defendants, as that possessed by the SGUs; and the majority of SNs were represented even at their first court appearance. Neither fact shows itself in the answers given to this particular question, and it could be that the SNs' response is again an indication of higher social class composition. However, even if the SN group was an unusually well-informed one, it seems doubtful if this matter of choice of venue really is general knowledge in the sense that 'every schoolboy knows' it; though unfortunately this was not one of the points investigated in the OPCS survey.

Although represented defendants were better informed than unrepresented defendants about the existence of venue choice, there was a surprising number of represented cases where the solicitor had not told the defendant about the decision he faced, and thus left him unprepared for it. While almost all such cases will seem to the solicitor to be obvious common sense choices in favour of summary trial, to give the defendant no warning at all about the choice seems irresponsible at best, and not unnaturally some defendants complained about it. This reinforces the case for some more official prior notice to be given to the defendant.

The questions asked of those tried in the higher courts as to advance notice of choice of venue were rather carefully devised to avoid undue complexity. The defendants were in one of three groups: those who opted for trial by jury (corresponding to sub-sample groups DG and DN); those whose cases were sent to the higher court because the bench refused to try the case summarily (making up part of sub-sample groups HG and HN); and those whose cases went to the higher court because the offence could only be tried there (the remainder of groups HG and HN).

Only the first group had actually made a choice of venue. Their answers to the question as to advance knowledge corresponding to the one already quoted are given in Table 4.6.

Only 7 per cent were unaware of the choice of venue as they

Table 4.6 Defendants' advance knowledge about choice of venue (defendants choosing higher court trial)

	%
No advance knowledge	5
Only from watching earlier cases	2
Advance knowledge	
own previous criminal cases	43
solicitor's advice	48
friend's advice	2
Total	100

entered the court, a much lower proportion than was found among those electing summary trial.

It is possible to examine separately those defendants (wherever ultimately tried) who had advance knowledge, gained before entering the courtroom, and those who had not. Seven per cent of those with such knowledge chose trial in the higher court, as against only 1·5 per cent of those without such knowledge. It is also possible to make a further, if rather speculative, calculation of the effect of ensuring that all defendants did have advance knowledge, by notice or otherwise. If we assume that such a notice would be read, and that all defendants would make an election in the proportions found for those who have advance knowledge under the existing arrangements, we find that the business of the Sheffield Crown Court derived from the local magistrates' court would rise by some 32 cases a year, an increase of about 5 per cent. In practice this would probably be an overestimate, as the assumptions we make would not be fully justified.

Of defendants who did not themselves have a choice of venue, these general issues were discussed only with those in the second group, those who were sent for trial in the higher court by decision of the magistrates. These defendants would have been given a choice of venue had the magistrates not pre-empted the matter; those in the third group could in no circumstances have been asked to choose.

This second group was asked if they knew in advance that the bench had the option of sending the case for trial in the higher court. In all 63 per cent of defendants had advance knowledge, 61 per cent of those pleading guilty and 77 per cent of those pleading not guilty. Those pleading not guilty were better informed because they were more likely to receive legal advice, and also (and this point applies in other contexts) because they were more likely to be on bail, and so more likely to spend time waiting for their case to come on in court, able to observe other cases, rather than in the cells. Of those who knew that the magistrates had the option, 56 per cent expected to be sent for trial in the higher court, 7 per cent were uncertain, and the remaining 37 per cent had not expected their committal for trial.

Defendants in this group, had they themselves been able to choose (and 26 per cent had expected to), would have elected trial in the higher court in 25 per cent of cases; as we have already seen only 5 per cent of all defendants with the choice made that decision.

Perceived differences between courts

Before we examine the reasons given by those of our defendants who were able to make a choice of venue, it is important to see how in general terms they perceived the differences between the magistrates' and the higher courts. The OPCS survey (Durant et al., 1972) contains some useful background information about the views of the population at large. It is an interesting commentary on the English attitude to the law that one of the test questions adopted in that survey was about the practice of wearing wigs!

The OPCS survey found that 14 per cent of respondents did not appear to realise that there were different types of criminal court; they replied that offenders convicted of drunkenness would be sentenced at the same type of court as those convicted of robbery with violence. It having been made clear that there are in fact lower courts called magistrates' courts, and higher courts, 14 per cent thought that magistrates wore wigs (they do not, or rather not the obvious off-white ones beloved of lawyers) and 14 per cent thought that magistrates' courts had a jury (as they do not) (Durant et al., 1972, p.17). The rate of wrong answers was as high as 10 per cent for those who had actually attended a magistrates' court (ibid., p.19). The survey also asked respondents whether the higher courts had a jury, and if so whether always or only sometimes. The correct answer was given by only 32 per cent, if one accepts the view that the correct answer is 'sometimes'. This answer was chosen because there is no jury on a committal for sentence (ibid., p.21); of course there is also no jury on a plea of guilty, an equally pedantic point. The present authors would have given the wrong answer to that question, and are vain enough to conclude that the question was badly drafted!

We shall see below that sentencing considerations enter into decisions as to venue. The OPCS study contains some information relevant to this. Of all respondents 67 per cent thought that most judges would give similar sentences for similar offences, but only 40 per cent thought that magistrates showed the same consistency, a rate which fell to 33 per cent among those respondents who had actually appeared before the magistrates as a defendant (ibid., pp.42-3). Although questions were not designed with the point in mind there is other evidence in the OPCS data that judges were regarded as 'better' sentencers than magistrates (e.g. the respondents who replied to the question whether it was right that the magistrate or judge is the person who decides the sentence by saying that it was right for the judge but not the magistrate; those who volunteered at another point that a judge or someone superior to a magistrate should pass sentence: ibid., pp.44-6).

Most of the questions in the OPCS survey concentrate on the magistrates' courts and the magistrates themselves, but one question sought views on the jury. Seventy per cent of respondents thought that juries made the right decision about the guilt or innocence of the accused 'always' or 'nearly always'.

In our Sheffield study we contented ourselves with asking those electing summary trial the very open question, 'What difference do you think there is between the magistrates' court and Quarter Sessions/the Crown Court?' Some replies were factual statements about the composition of the court, but others were more revealing about perceptions and attitudes. The replies are summarised in Table 4.7.

We have already seen that the SN respondents emphasised their 'general knowledge'; here, they tended more often to give the 'factual' answer about the composition of the two courts, i.e. that the higher court has judge and jury. The SGUs were the only ones to comment on the greater expense of the Crown Court. The most interesting response comes from the SGR group: those in this category tended to have a high opinion of the 'fairness' of the Crown Court, but stressed the lower sentencing powers of the magistrates and—as we shall see later—made their venue choice largely on these grounds.

This raises a more general issue of some importance. From the more qualitative data of our interview schedules, including some

Table 4.7 Perceived differences between courts (defendants electing summary trial)

% answering*	Sub-sample group SGU	SGR	SN	All
Higher court has judge and jury	28	34	45	30
Different sentencing powers	16	27	13	18
Magistrates more lenient	15	27	6	17
Higher court deals with more serious cases	18	5	10	15
Higher court more expensive	12	0	0	9
Higher court wants to know more about case or defendant	6	7	6	6
Higher court more formidable, more fuss	6	0	6	5
Higher court gives a fairer trial	3	14	6	5
Others	10	4	13	8
Don't know	16	12	13	14
Not much or no difference	3	2	3	3

*The columns do not total 100 as some respondents gave more than one answer.

final general questions about those parts of the whole proceedings considered to be especially good or especially unfair, there can be no doubt but that defendants in general have a higher opinion of the Crown Court than the magistrates. Of course, some Crown Court defendants thought the judge, or his direction to the jury, unfair; and on the other hand a few praised the 'fairness', 'patience' or 'sympathetic' nature of the magistrates, or eulogised the 'quick and simple' nature of the lower court proceedings. But a more common response, especially among recidivists with a knowledge of the system, was to contrast the magistrates unfavourably with the higher court: as one defendant put it, summing up so common a view that we dubbed it 'the recidivists' refrain', 'At Sessions you have a chance, at the magistrates' you have no chance'.

The reasons for this unfavourable view of the magistrates were many and various, but really centred round three points: that magistrates were too pro-police; that the proceedings were not full and careful enough; and that the magistrates were amateurs without training who could not be expected to do a decent job. Some defendants' remarks illustrate these three themes:

Case 5023 'Magistrates are useless in most towns: they work with the police.'

Case 1001 (A 'recidivist strategist' who opted for lower court trial for sentence reasons) 'Crown Court is more fair—the police have less influence, and cases are less cut and dried.'

Case 6020 'I've never been in Crown Court before' (he was charged with burglary in a dwelling house, which normally has to go to the Crown Court). 'It seems much fairer in the Crown Court, they listen to what you say.'

Case 1080 'In the Crown Court all the people are trained professionals, they don't rely on the clerk like the magistrates do. Magistrates' is more like a conveyor belt.'

Case 1067 'Magistrates' courts should be abolished. They are manned by shopkeepers who have no idea, they have to consult the clerk: it's not their job. Crown Court is much better, it's run by the judge, he knows what's what and listens to everything.'

Case 1058 'Magistrates are mostly business people, stealing to them is commerce and money but to the judge in the Crown Court it's just crime. Crown Court is more fair—they're professionals, not amateurs, like having a doctor instead of a medical student.'

Other examples could be given, but these sufficiently indicate the three themes we have outlined. Of particular interest to us, and worthy of further examination in a later research project, was our defendants' approach to professionalism among court staff: there was an overwhelming tendency to accept the professional's evaluation of himself as a more 'objective' and 'expert' person. Meanwhile it should be noted that all the illustrative cases above, except the first and the third, chose trial in the magistrates' court. Clearly, then, such choice is not in itself a vote of confidence in the magistrates; equally clearly, there is a substantial body of opinion among our defendants endorsing the view that lower court proceedings are second-rate justice.

Reasons for venue choice: summary cases

Having considered knowledge of the system and perceived differences between courts, we are at last in a position to look at the reasons given by our defendants for their choice of venue.

The reasons given by those who elected summary trial are given in Table 4.8. The dominant reason is clearly the wish to 'get it over with', which in all was mentioned in 60 per cent of cases where summary trial was chosen. This certainly includes fear of delays if the case goes to the higher court, but may also include a wish to avoid more court appearances as such; probably the overwhelming motivation is simply to get the case settled and put a stop to the anxiety it has brought.

Table 4.8 Reasons for electing summary trial

% answering*	Sub-sample groups SGU	SGR	SN	All
Get it over with, avoid delay	65	51	34	60
Get a lighter sentence	18	44	19	23
Offence too trivial for higher court	12	15	12	13
Solicitor's advice	0	19	30	5
To avoid remand in custody	4	4	3	4
No point in going to higher court	4	0	3	3
Better chance of acquittal	1	5	3	2
Police advice	1	8	0	2
Magistrates' court less frightening	0	4	3	2
Other reasons	6	1	19	8
Don't know	0	0	3	1

*The columns do not total 100 as some respondents gave more than one reason.

We were able to examine the delay factor a little more closely. Respondents were asked how long they thought they would have had to wait if they had opted for trial in the higher court. The answers are summarised in Table 4.9.

Those who claimed to know the actual date were referring to the old Quarter Sessions, the sittings of which were advertised on quite enormous posters which could hardly escape the attention of anyone entering the courthouse. Those who gave an estimate of the likely delay were for the most part a little optimistic. Very few cases would complete the committal proceedings stage and reach trial in the higher courts in less than a month, yet a quarter of those giving an estimate of the delay chose such a period. On the other hand, some of the SNs in particular had overestimated the length they would have to wait for Crown Court trial, and had not realised the delays attached to not guilty pleas in the magistrates' court (see chapter 2).

Table 4.9 Knowledge about delay for trial in higher court (respondents choosing summary trial)

	%
Knew actual date of sitting	2
Didn't know at all	41
Estimated up to	
1 month	14
1 < 2	13
2 < 6	26
more	4
Total	100

A few of them said explicitly that they now wished they had opted for jury trial, as the delay involved would be little if any greater.

Returning to Table 4.8, the second major reason for summary trial was the 'sentencing' reason, based partly on the knowledge that magistrates have a limited 'ceiling' of sentencing powers, and partly apparently on the view that magistrates were more likely to be lenient anyway.[5] What is particularly notable about this reason is that it is far more often given by the recidivistic SGRs than by the other two groups; and many of those (like case 1001 above) who chose summary trial despite an unfavourable evaluation of the magistrates did so for this reason, though some did so also for the 'delay' reason.

A final point about table 4.8 concerns solicitors' advice. Not unexpectedly, this featured prominently in the reasons given by SNs, but it was less important to the SGRs with their greater experience of the court system, and for whom a choice of the Crown Court would usually have been a choice of sentencing tribunal only.[6]

We compared the incidence of the two main reasons for electing summary trial in the various categories of the defendants' typology developed in chapter 3. Table 4.10 gives the results. Some of these, such as the high proportion of 'other' reasons among those respondents dominated by others' advice or by external circumstances, are not surprising and in a sense simply confirm the reliability of the typology. The highest proportions of those wishing to 'get it over with' are found, also not surprisingly, among the respectable first-timers, the dissociatives and the other passive respondents; the high placing of 'other strategists' on this reason was more unexpected. The outstanding result of the table is undoubtedly the very high proportion (89 per cent) of recidivist strategists who gave 'lesser sentence' as their main reason; this was significantly in excess of the proportion for any other group. From the recidivist's point of view, if he is pleading guilty, it makes obvious sense to opt for summary trial: there is always the chance that the magistrates will be in a lenient mood and will not send him to the Crown Court for sentence, so that he gets two bites at the sentencing cherry instead of one, even though the Crown Court is usually considered by such defendants to offer a fuller and fairer hearing.

Table 4.10 Reasons for electing summary trial, by defendants' typology

	% answering*		
	Get it over	Lighter sentence	Other
Recidivist strategists	9	89	3
Other strategists	72	31	10
Respectable first-timers	78	17	9
Right-assertive	(60)	(20)	(20)
Ordinary respondents	70	19	29
Dissociative	77	23	8
Other passive	74	6	26
Other-dominated respondents	34	36	74
External circumstances	58	20	76
Miscellaneous	32	39	29

*The rows do not necessarily total 100 as some respondents gave more than one reason.

Some further information about the importance of sentencing factors was obtained by asking summarily convicted defendants (other than those committed to the higher court for sentence) whether they thought their sentence would have been any different if they had been tried in the higher courts. It is clear from Table 4.11 that the overall expectation is that a heavier penalty would have been imposed by the higher court. This view was particularly strongly held among the SGUs, a group which did not rely strongly on sentencing factors as a reason for electing summary trial. The explanation may well be that the answers summarised in Table 4.11 indicate the respondents' reaction to the sentence they actually received. If they receive a light sentence from the magistrates, as many SGUs did, they are more likely to express the fear that another court would have imposed a heavier penalty. The SGRs, normally so well informed, are strongly 'don't know' on this point; the SNs, for whom the verdict was the important thing, are more inclined to say that the higher court sentence would be no different.

Table 4.11 Expected court sentencing patterns (convicted defendants tried and sentenced by the magistrates)

% thinking that a higher court sentence would be	Sub-sample group SGU	SGR	SN	All
Heavier	71	49	55	65
No different	6	4	23	6
Lighter	6	9	9	6
Don't know	15	35	14	20
Other answers	2	3	0	2
Total	100	100	100	100

If they had been tried in the higher courts, 96 per cent of those pleading not guilty would have tendered the same plea, but only 79 per cent of those pleading guilty. Some defendants therefore would see their chances of acquittal as better in the higher courts, and 17 of the 23 interviewed defendants who were convicted by the magistrates after a not guilty plea felt that a jury would have acquitted.

Finally, one uncommon but still important misconception by some of our defendants must be recorded. There were a few cases of not guilty pleas where the defendant had been advised by his solicitor to go to the higher court, and had not realised that it was possible to plead not guilty before the magistrates. Conversely, there were a few guilty plea cases who said they thought they had to elect summary trial just because they were pleading guilty. It is easy to understand how such misconceptions occur, even if they only occur rarely. Once more it suggests that if venue choice is to be treated seriously as a part of English criminal procedure, rather more effort should be expended in explaining to defendants what it is all about.

Reasons for venue choice: higher court election

The defendants who opted for trial in the higher courts were also asked to give their reasons: they are set out in Table 4.12. In interpreting the table it must be remembered that all but five of these defendants were intending not guilty pleas at the time of making the venue choice, and most were legally represented at that time. Hence it comes as no surprise that the dominant reasons given were 'fairer trial', 'better chance of acquittal' and 'lawyer's advice'. It is clear once more from these figures that the higher court is seen by our respondents as offering a fairer trial, and that with this group in particular any legislative change to reduce the opportunities to claim trial by jury would be unpopular.[7]

Table 4.12 Reasons for opting for trial in the higher courts

% answering*	Sub-sample groups DG	DN	All
Fairer trial	41	56	50
Solicitor's advice	23	32	29
Better chance of acquittal	17	12	14
Lighter sentence	12	4	7
Wanted to fight case	6	0	2
Would have ended in higher court anyway	0	12	7
Friends advised	0	4	2
Others	35	20	26

*The columns do not total 100 as some respondents gave more than one reason.

We looked more closely at the question of legal advice. It is clear from table 4.8 (the SN column) and 4.12 (which deals with defendants most of whom were, at the time of venue choice, planning to plead not guilty) that about 30 per cent of such defendants stated that legal advice was an important factor in their venue decision. But this overall figure conceals an interesting difference. As we shall see more fully in chapter 6, there are in Sheffield three solicitors who (in one case, with a partner also) dominate the criminal court business to the extent that together they carry 60 per cent of the total workload.[8] We analysed the number of cases handled by each of these three which, at the time the venue choice was made, were intended for higher or lower court trial, guilty or not guilty plea (i.e. we have used our SGR, SN, DG and DN categories, but reallocated 'DG change-of-pleas' into 'DNs' for the purpose of this table only).

Table 4.13 shows the results. Since almost all 'D' cases are intended not guilty pleas at this stage, the crucial comparison is that between the SN and the DN columns. It is obvious from this that solicitor C differs very much from his two colleagues.[9] Fourteen of his 15 intending not guilty pleas are channelled to the Crown Court, while the other two solicitors are much more evenly balanced between lower court and higher court trial; and it is also clear from material in the interviews how strongly solicitor C pushed his intended not guilty pleas towards jury trial, believing in a much higher acquittal chance there. Indeed, 12 of the 14 cases mentioned the solicitor's advice as the major determining reason for the choice;[10] typical comments were:

> 'Mr C said the best chance was before a jury.'
>
> 'At first I intended magistrates' trial and a guilty plea. Mr C persuaded me to try a not guilty plea and go to the Crown Court.'
>
> 'Mr C's advice: he said not a good chance for not guilty plea before the magistrates.'

Table 4.13 Distribution of business of three leading solicitors (measured at time venue choice was made)*

	SGR	SN	DG	DN
Solicitor A	36	5	1	6
Solicitor B	22	11	1	8
Solicitor C	18	1	0	14

*Actual numbers are given, not percentages; but the SGR group has been doubled because of the one-in-two sample taken for this group.

We examined also the cases of the other two solicitors. Legal advice was much less dominant in the reasons expressed (both by the DNs and the SNs) in the interviews, suggesting that neither of these solicitors has a hard-and-fast rule on the venue question; indeed, even in those cases where legal advice was mentioned, we were unable to discern any obvious features of discrimination between lower court and higher court cases, suggesting that each case is looked at on its merits by these two solicitors, judging the quality of the evidence, how difficult the defendant would find the greater drama of a Crown Court trial, etc. That they should differ so markedly from their colleague C in their perception of the venue question raises fascinating issues about legal perceptions and legal strategies which we were unable to pursue in this research.[11]

As with those electing summary trial, we explored with the D defendants (and with the Hs also) the question whether they thought the sentence would have been any different if they had been tried at the magistrates' court. The answers are set out in Table 4.14. The question was of course unrealistic for those whose trial had to be in the higher court, the Hs, and yet 13 per cent of that group replied that the magistrates would have given a heavier sentence.

Table 4.14 Expected court sentencing patterns (defendants tried in higher courts)

% thinking that magistrates' court sentence would be	Sub-sample groups Ds	Hs*
Heavier	31	13
No different	3	16
Lighter	41	58
Don't know	21	9
Other answers	3	4
Total	100	100

*The question was only asked in respect of those Hs where the magistrates had refused summary trial, and hence the column does not include those compulsorily sent to the higher court because of the offence charged.

Overall the view was that magistrates would impose lighter sentences, but defendants who had actually been sentenced in the higher court were less clearly of that opinion than those who had opted for summary trial (and whose answers to the converse question are in Table 4.11).

We also asked defendants who had chosen the higher court how much delay they expected as a result of their decision. Their answers are summarised in Table 4.15.

If these are compared with the answers given to the corresponding question by those who decided against claiming trial in the higher court (set out in Table 4.9), it is seen that defendants actually incurring the delay were more pessimistic as to its length than those who avoided it. Of those estimating the likely delay, 17 per cent of those choosing the higher courts thought it would amount to a month or less as against 25 per cent of those tried summarily. The more realistic answers in this group may reflect more extensive legal

Table 4.15 Expectations of delay for trial in higher court (respondents choosing higher court trial)

	%
Didn't know at all	33
Estimated up to	
1 month	12
1 < 2	24
2 < 6	29
more	2
Total	100

advice. Although waiting periods were often longer than expected, only 2 defendants, both of whom pleaded guilty in the Crown Court, would have opted for trial in the magistrates' court had they realised the true extent of the delay.

Finally, we must consider the 'true' DGs, that is, those who chose higher court trial in the full knowledge at the time of making the venue choice that when they reached the higher court they would plead guilty. Legal commentators often assume that this group does not exist, but it manifestly does, even if in small numbers. As we have said, there were only 5 interviewed cases of this type in our final sample,[12] so any kind of statistical analysis is obviously impossible. We shall confine ourselves to setting out brief details of the cases: one of them (no. 4022) has already been fully described as an example of the 'recidivist strategist' in chapter 3, the other four were as follows:

> Case 4003 H, aged 33, was described in court as having 'spent all his life in hospitals and institutions', or, when outside such places, 'travelling as a vagrant'. He was charged with attempting to obtain a pecuniary advantage by deception—to wit, offering a taxi driver toy money instead of real money for an 86p fare. He was unrepresented at the beginning of the case, and at that stage elected Crown Court trial. He said in interview he had done so because he didn't want to go back to the reception centre where he had been living, and also didn't want to have to pay the taxi fare—he thought it best to spend 'a few days in prison' before he eventually got fined (though actually the Crown Court gave him probation).

Case 4007 T, aged 44, had been a patient at a local mental hospital since 1955. He threw a brick through the window of a local tobacconist's shop and was charged with burglary with intent to steal, and criminal damage, to both of which he eventually pleaded guilty. He told our interviewer that he did it because he wanted a change of air—he was tired of his ward and didn't like the other patients or the nurses there, and 'something came over me: I was very angry'. He elected Crown Court trial at his first appearance, when he was unrepresented: the case was stood down so that a probation officer could see him partly about his stated desire to go to Leeds Prison on remand rather than back to the hospital, and partly (according to our court observer) to try to make him change his mind about the Crown Court decision. But he maintained his decision, and said in interview he had done so because 'at the magistrates' they don't look into the case—they say "Oh, common thief" and don't want to understand why I did it. At Sessions they want to know'.

Case 4021 L, a 23-year-old labourer with 5 previous convictions, was charged with taking a car without consent, and with assaulting a policeman. He chose Crown Court trial at a time when he was unrepresented. He said that he never had any intention of pleading not guilty as he was 'obviously guilty'. At the start, in the police station, he had thought of asking for summary trial, but as soon as the police added the assault charge he was determined to go to the Crown Court. His reason, he said, was that 'there they go into the case in far more detail. If anyone was going to listen, it would be the Crown Court. Magistrates never listen, they just sentence you purely on your record; and they're so quick they don't know anything about the cases'. At the Crown Court he received a suspended sentence; he was lyrical about the fairness the court had displayed and was very pleased with himself for having made the right decision as to venue.

Case 4027 L, a 25-year-old machinist, was charged with two counts of theft from a fellow-lodger in a rooming-house. He was on a suspended sentence, and seeing a probation officer on a voluntary basis 'four to five times a week', because he needed help. When he was first charged, he was held overnight in custody, during which time the probation officer came to see him. The probation officer suggested getting a lawyer, and contacted a solicitor on L's behalf (L said 'I'd have thought that was probably a waste of time'). The solicitor came to see L in the morning, advised him there were no grounds for a not guilty plea (L had thought there might be, as the complainant owed L money), but said the magistrates were sure to 'jump on' L in view of the suspended sentence. 'So let's fight it to the Crown Court', he said, and L took his advice. The strategy paid off—the Crown Court did not implement the suspended sentence, and indeed simply imposed another one concurrent with the first.

Obviously these five cases are very different. Cases 4022 and 4021 are both 'recidivist strategists', though taking the venue decision on different grounds. Cases 4003 and 4007 are both importantly affected by their special personal histories. Case 4027 is an interesting example of a passive man taking a strategic route through the courts because of the intervention on his behalf of a probation officer and solicitor. This is also the only case of the five where the decision was effectively taken by the lawyer rather than by the defendant; in a sense this may be thought surprising, as there are other grounds for thinking that in the general run of cases the Crown Court may be more lenient than the magistrates (see note 5 to this chapter). Perhaps the answer is that lawyers fear reprisals on their clients in the form of heavier penalties if Crown Court judges think the strategy is being regularly employed—and there are some good grounds for this, as we shall show in a moment.

Venue choice: discussion with others

Respondents, whatever their venue choice, were asked with whom they had discussed the decision as to venue. The questions asked were on a pattern which recurred in the interview as each decision taken by the defendant was examined: hence they sometimes partially overlap with other material, in this case for example with our earlier discussion of the three solicitors.

Each of the tables in this particular series (i.e. Tables 4.16, 5.10, 5.13, 6.8, 7.3) shows a distinction between two groups of potential advisers, an 'unofficial' group, family and friends mainly, who had no official connection with the criminal justice system, and an 'official' group, lawyers, policemen, probation officers, who were 'insiders' in relation to the system. The groups are not necessarily in watertight compartments, as even lawyers have friends, but the division is a useful one. In the tables we use the cryptic 'others in trouble' as a shorthand term for the cumbersome but more accurate 'people who had been in trouble with the law other than codefendants in the current case'.

Table 4.16 Discussion of venue decision with others

% of respondents discussing venue with	Sub-sample groups SGU	SGR	SN	Ds	Hs*
Wife	5	1	3	5	7
Parents	0	3	0	7	0
Family	0	1	9	0	0
Friends	0	1	6	14	8
Codefendants	6	6	3	12	6
Others in trouble	0	1	3	2	3
Police	5	5	0	7	9
Lawyers	0	34	44	86	31
Probation officers	2	6	0	2	0
Nobody	81	57	38	12	58

*See note to Table 4.14.

Table 4.16 shows the results for the venue decision, and indicates clearly that for most groups of defendants there is very little advance discussion of this matter. As many as 81 per cent of SGUs, all of whom have to make a choice as to venue, discuss it with no one. The table also demonstrates in a striking fashion the extent to which venue is a lawyer's matter. Defendants may discuss the question with the solicitors (and the interview material shows that this will usually be at the latter's prompting) but seldom with anyone else. In some cases the defendant who is represented will have made the venue decision before he has a solicitor: this is especially true of those in the SGR category, and it explains the relatively low 'score' for lawyers in that group: it is notable that the proportion of SGRs discussing venue with others is almost the same as for the Hs, who have themselves no venue decision to make. The Ds seem an exception to the general rule, with more than average discussion with friends and codefendants; this is largely due to the presence of the student quartet noted earlier.

Venue choice: a right?

We conclude our discussion of the venue issue with a case that raises some important principles:

Case 5024 E, a 17-year-old delivery boy who had never previously been inside any kind of courtroom, was charged with theft of a woman's purse and its contents. He had, in the course of his employment, visited another firm to collect some money. A Mrs D had paid him that money from her own purse, then put the purse on a cupboard while she and E went to another room to write a receipt. Later in the day, the purse was missing when Mrs D went back for it, and it was later found empty in a car park. E consistently maintained (even in our interview, after he had been convicted) that it wasn't him who took the purse, and there was no direct evidence to suggest that he had. He determined on a not guilty plea, and he went to a lawyer (on his parents' strong advice) and got legal aid. The solicitor explained about venue choice (E hadn't known before that, and had expected magistrates' trial), and recommended jury trial. E agreed, feeling that he would like 'to bring everything out clearer with a jury'. Just before the trial, his barrister met him and strongly advised a guilty plea, because 'the evidence is against you'. E refused as he was, he said, quite innocent. The jury convicted. The High Court judge who was trying the case sentenced E to a fine of £15, taking into account his good character and that this was 'a temptation of the moment'. But, he went on, though he could sentence leniently, he could not see why the public should bear the expense of this trial. The young man should have faced up to his offence and had it dealt with by the magistrates months ago; as he had not done so, he must pay substantially towards the cost of the trial. A legal aid contribution order of £70 was therefore made against E, in addition to his sentence.

So E found himself heavily penalised, partly for not pleading guilty and partly for having insisted on Crown Court trial (the costs would have been substantially less in the lower court). No attention was paid to the fact that it was the solicitor who had initiated the venue choice, and of course the solicitor was not penalised by loss of fee.

The case raises dramatically an issue that was also hinted at in some other cases (see e.g. case no. 5013, set out at the start of chapter

1). We have seen that the courts would collapse, administratively speaking, if many more defendants insisted on jury trial; thus there are some subtle pressures to choose summary trial (fear of delay, fear of increased penalty, and, sometimes linked to these, legal advice). But is all this consistent with venue choice being truly a right, available to the defendant to be exercised freely?

It is a problem which recurs in many contexts of the legal process, a problem of conflict between principle and expediency. So far as venue choice is concerned, it might be better if society were to decide clearly on a limited range of offences or circumstances in which venue choice is to be available, and then maintain this as a full right, without penalty, and with full advance notice to the defendant, in that limited range of cases. This could be regarded as more honest than the present system, which notionally offers venue choice across a wide spectrum of cases, but in practice relies on the defendant's bewilderment and/or various kinds of administrative pressure to ensure that the choice is not exercised in administratively inconvenient ways.

5 Plea

The defendant's decision to plead guilty has been described (Bottomley, 1973, p. 105) as 'the single most important aspect of decision-making in the penal process, although typically one of the most under-researched and complex of all'. No one would dispute the importance of an act by which the defendant waives his right to trial, and surrenders the chances of acquittal which the trial procedures offer. But the decision as to plea, although the most dramatic, is only one of a number of related decisions and cannot be isolated from the others. The formal decisions as to venue (which must be taken, or at least announced, before the question of plea arises), the decisions as to legal representation, and especially the whole series of exchanges between defendant and police at the outset of the process, may have such effects that the defendant feels he has little option as to the plea he must make. So, while in some cases all other decisions will be secondary to the overriding resolve of the defendant to plead in a particular way, there are other cases in which events and decisions made in the early stages of the criminal process empty the plea decision of all but formal importance.

It is perhaps understandable, if that assessment of the variable importance of the plea decision is accepted, that criminal justice systems are somewhat ambivalent in their attitude towards guilty pleas. The United States Supreme Court has said that 'a guilty plea is a grave and solemn act to be accepted only with care and discernment' (Brady v. U.S. 397 U.S. 742 (1970)). This is reflected in England by rules such as the one that the question as to plea must be put to the defendant personally, and that a plea of guilty made on his behalf by his barrister or solicitor may be quashed at least if the defendant shows dissatisfaction with the plea (R. v. Wakefield Justices, ex parte Butterworth, [1970] 1 All E.R. 1181; R. v. Ellis, [1973] Crim. L.R. 389; R. v. Gowerton Justices, ex parte Davies, [1974] Crim. L.R. 253). On the other side, it is recognised that the whole system of criminal justice would collapse administratively if defendants exercised their right to plead not guilty in any significantly greater numbers; there is not the manpower or physical resources needed to handle many more contested trials. In various ways, most countries encourage pleas of guilty. In England, quite apart from escaping the delays to which a plea of 'not guilty' may lead, a defendant pleading guilty can expect that fact to be treated as relevant in mitigation of sentence (R. v. De Haan, [1967] 3 All E.R. 618; Cross, 1971, p. 153; Thomas, 1970, pp. 52, 195), though under the formal logic of our sentencing system it does not follow that a plea of not guilty will lead to an increased penalty. Similarly, pleas of guilty are encouraged by the development, especially in the USA, of the practice of 'plea-bargaining' which we shall discuss further below.

Basic statistics: magistrates' courts

It is surprisingly difficult to discover the pattern of pleas in English magistrates' courts. No information is included in the *Criminal Statistics,* so one must look to particular research studies, usually designed for other purposes.

Zander (1969, table 8, p.639) found that 80 per cent of defendants in London magistrates' courts pleaded guilty, 86 per cent of those who were unrepresented and 55 per cent of those who were represented. Dell's sample of women interviewed in Holloway Prison is rather special, but she found that 76 per cent of her women had pleaded guilty at the magistrates' court (Dell, 1971, p.27). If the pattern of pleas in magistrates' courts is similar to that in the higher courts, and we do not know, then the London rate for guilty pleas will be lower than that in the country as a whole.

In our Sheffield study, we observed 1,316 trials in the magistrates' courts. In 93 per cent there was a plea of guilty to all charges, and in a further 2 per cent the defendant pleaded guilty to one or more charges and not guilty to others. Table 5.1 gives a more detailed picture. When subsequently we refer to two groups only, the 'mixed'

Table 5.1 Plea in magistrates' court, by sex and representation

	Unrepresented			Represented			All
% pleading	M	F	All	M	F	All	cases
Guilty	99·2	97·2	98·8	82	75	81	93
Not guilty	0·7	1·4	0·8	14	21	15	5
Mixed	0·1	1·4	0·4	4	4	4	2
Total	100·0	100·0	100·0	100	100	100	100

category has been distributed after individual examination to the 'guilty' or 'not guilty' category on the principles described in chapter 1.

Table 5.1, in line with Zander's findings, shows that there is a greater proportion of not guilty pleas among those who are represented, but the overall level of guilty pleas is much higher than he found, 94 per cent as against 80 per cent. Zander did not distinguish between male and female defendants. In our sample, 95 per cent of the men and 92·5 per cent of the women pleaded guilty (see foot of Table 5.2).

The first two columns of Table 5.2 break down the figures for summary trials by type of offence. There is remarkably little

Table 5.2 Guilty pleas, by sex, venue and offence

% pleading guilty in each offence group	Summary trial M	Summary trial F	Higher courts M	Higher courts F	All
Drugs offences	100	(100)	(100)	(100)	100
Meter-thefts	99	100	—	—	99
Taking car without consent	99	(100)	92	—	98
Arson/damage	98	(100)	(80)	—	96
Other thefts and frauds	95	96	73	(50)	92
Burglary	94	(100)	84	(100)	90
Shoplifting	94	89	(25)	0	86
Handling	86	(75)	69	(100)	81
Sex offences	81	—	75	—	79
Aggressive offences	94	(75)	64	(57)	75
All	95	92·5	73	41	89

variation, only sex offences, handling stolen goods and (among women) shoplifting showing a proportion of guilty pleas of below 90 per cent.

All this suggests that Sheffield defendants regard the magistrates' court as essentially a 'guilty plea court'. Certainly the conviction rate is high: of the 80 defendants (of both sexes) who did not admit all charges, 53 (66 per cent) were convicted on all charges, and 5 (6 per cent) on one or more charge. The other 22 defendants (27·5 per cent) were wholly acquitted and discharged—just over 1·5 per cent of all defendants brought before the court.

Higher courts

Rather more comparative information is available about guilty pleas in the higher courts, though changes in the jurisdiction of the courts must be taken into account in considering the earlier findings. As a whole, the various studies record a proportion pleading guilty of between 55 per cent and 75 per cent (see Bottomley, 1973, pp.105ff).

Taking the studies chronologically, Gibson (1960, table 6, p.9) found an overall guilty plea rate of 75·5 per cent in 1956. The rate had fallen to 64 per cent by 1965, according to a study undertaken for the police (Association of Chief Police Officers, 1966), and Rose in his study of 1967 cases for the Beeching Commission (Rose, 1971, table 22, p.34) found the even lower rate of 57 per cent. There is some evidence that the rate rose again at the end of the 1960s (see Zander, 1974, p.30, note 8), but it was back to just under 60 per cent in 1972 (Lord Chancellor's Department's *Statistics on Judicial Administration,* tables 3.2 and 5.5).

Two findings stand out in the details of some of these studies. The Central Criminal Court has had a consistently lower rate of guilty pleas than other courts, including other London courts. This was found by Gibson (1960, table 7, p.10), Rose (see his table 37 as to uncontested *trials,* which is not necessarily the same as *persons* pleading guilty, p.47) and Zander who made a special study of the London courts in 1972 (Zander, 1974). However, the Lord Chancellor's Department's *Statistics on Judicial Administration* for 1972 (Table 5.5), while confirming that London courts have a lower guilty-plea rate than the rest of England and Wales, indicate that the rate at the Central Criminal Court was marginally higher than in other London courts. The second finding is that burglaries (including breaking and entering offences) have a high rate of guilty pleas, with violence much lower. This is reflected in part in the higher court columns of our Table 5.2, but the overall guilty plea rate for burglaries is almost exactly that for all offences in our sample.

Dell's (1971) study of women prisoners noted a rate of 46 per cent guilty pleas—but this was mainly of London cases, and with a rather special sample. The impression it gives of a low proportion of guilty pleas among women at the higher courts is supported strongly by our figures.

The only previously reported data specifically on Sheffield were in the 1965 police survey described above, where Sheffield had a rate of 55 per cent, rather below the then national average for guilty pleas. In our 1971-2 data, however, we found an overall rate of 65 per cent pleading guilty to all charges, 10 per cent to one or more, and 25 per cent not guilty to all charges. This is clearly at the upper end of the range found in previous studies, and slightly above the national rate at the time of our research. Table 5.2 shows that for men the rate is 73 per cent, but only 41 per cent for women, and this last figure is largely accounted for by the 12 defendants charged with shoplifting, all of whom pleaded not guilty. The offence distribution shows taking cars without consent and burglaries attracting most guilty pleas, aggressive offences and handling stolen goods the least.

From the point of view of the present study the sort of overall figures we have been examining, and which previous studies have produced, are inadequate. It is important for our purposes, and in considering the policy implications of guilty pleas, to distinguish between those defendants whose own election has led to a trial in the higher court (the 'Ds') and those whose case was destined for the higher court by the nature of the offence charged or by a venue decision of the magistrates (the 'Hs'). This is done in Table 5.3, where it is seen that there are very different rates of plea in the two groups.

Table 5.3 Higher court plea, by nature of venue decision

% pleading	Ds	Hs
Guilty	29	74
Not guilty	63	15
Mixed	9	10
Total	100	100

The pattern among the Hs is not unexpected, but the 84 per cent rate for pleas of guilty to some or all charges is a high one. If legislation were to reduce the right of defendants to claim trial in the higher courts, we could expect the pattern of pleas in those courts to be more akin to our Hs figures than to the pattern revealed in general studies such as that by Rose (1971) or in the *Statistics on Judicial Administration*.

Similarly discussion of acquittal rates (on which there has been much acrimonious debate between senior policemen and lawyers) is clouded by the failure to distinguish between the different groups of defendants. The outcome of contested trials in the Hs category is difficult to state because of the high proportion of mixed verdicts. The pattern we found is shown in Table 5.4. It is very important to take the 'mixed' category into account: it is all too easy to assert either that only 33 per cent of contested trials in the H category result in convictions on all counts, implying a failure rate of two-thirds, or on the other hand to say that less than 25 per cent of defendants are discharged without a conviction, suggesting that the prosecution is successful in three-quarters of all cases. Both assertions are correct, but misleading unless attention is drawn to the large middle category.

Table 5.4 Pattern of verdicts in contested trials (for Hs)

	%
Guilty on all counts	33
Mixed verdict	38
Not guilty on all	
jury verdict	21
directed verdict	3
Jury discharged	4
Total	100

The Ds are a most interesting group. We have already examined the decision they made as to venue (chapter 4). The preponderance of not guilty pleas, even after all plea-changing has been concluded, is evident from Table 5.3; and it too has policy implications. If defendants believe that acquittal is almost impossible before

Table 5.5 Pattern of verdicts in contested trials (for Ds)

	%
Guilty on all counts	41
Mixed verdict	14
Not guilty on all	
jury verdict	35
directed verdict	2
Jury discharged	8
Total	100

magistrates, they will see the right to trial by jury as the only way in which their right to plead not guilty can be made meaningful. For them, to reduce the right to claim trial by jury, as has been canvassed by some, would be seen as effectively nullifying the right to a trial of guilt. The outcome of contested trials for the Ds is shown in Table 5.5. The 'mixed' group is smaller than in the Hs group, and the general result is one of rather more acquittals for the Ds.

The minority of Ds who pleaded guilty have already been partly discussed in chapter 4. As seen there, most of them are late 'plea-changers' but a few for special reasons opt for the higher court while all along intending to plead guilty. We consider the plea-changers more fully below.

Characteristics of defendants pleading guilty

We mentioned in chapter 1 that the 'guilty' sample groups were more likely to be younger, and of lower social class, than the others. Table 5.6 shows these trends more systematically; the data on age are taken from the court sample, but on social class from the interview sample. (Cf. Willett, 1973, table 9, p.82: in his sample of serious motoring offenders, guilty pleas were associated with low

Table 5.6 Plea, by age and socio-economic group (males only)

	% distribution of those pleading G	NG	Proportion of group pleading guilty
(a) Age			
17-20	27	15	93·8
21-29	39	35	90·7
30-39	18	18	89·5
40-49	9	16	83·5
50 plus	7	15	79·8
(b) Socio-economic class			
I, II	4	13	78·0
III	41	53	89·6
IV	23	20	92·1
V	27	11	96·7
Students, unclassifiable	5	2	96·0

social class, but there was no age effect.) The same tendency for the guilty pleas to come from the younger defendants was to be seen in the data for women (not reproduced in the table) but this time it was not statistically significant.

The clear overall picture is that the younger and less advantaged are more likely to plead guilty. It is difficult to know what interpretation to place on this. Some might hail it as further evidence of the inherent bias of the criminal justice system against the young and poor. Equally one can say that decisions as to plea are bound up with those as to venue, legal representation and bail, and that our interview data show a bewildering variety of reasons and types of response to decisions which precludes any clear-cut interpretation. We shall discuss this further below; the evidence is against any simplistic explanation.

Information about previous convictions has already been set out (Table 1.7). Of the male defendants, 34 per cent of those pleading guilty and 37 per cent of those pleading not guilty had no previous convictions; for women the corresponding proportions were 58 per cent and 57 per cent. Clearly for neither sex is this an important distinguishing factor as to plea.

We should record that we suspected that those living outside Sheffield would be more likely to plead guilty to avoid, for those on bail, repeated journeys to court. In fact this was not supported by the court sample data: there was no significant relationship between these factors.

Reasons behind guilty pleas

Defendants in our interview sample who pleaded guilty were asked to give their reasons for making that plea. A summary of the main reasons is set out in Table 5.7; it will be seen that the major reasons given were simply that the defendant *was* guilty, or that events at the scene of the crime or in subsequent investigation were such that the defendant felt little alternative but to plead guilty. This finding reinforces our earlier point that the final, formal decision as to plea is often little more than an official acknowledgment of processes already completed.

We examined the incidence of the two main types of reason given for the guilty plea in the different groups of our defendants' typology (see Table 5.8). The reason 'I was guilty' was most often given by the passive (other than dissociative) respondents, by the respectable first-timers and (more surprisingly) by those whose cases were

Table 5.7 Reasons for pleas of guilty*

	% of all defendants
Because I was guilty	41
Police had good case	27
I was caught redhanded	20
I had confessed to the police	11
To get it over with quietly with less fuss	10
On lawyer's advice	7
To get a lighter sentence	5

*Average number of reasons per respondent: 1·4. Reasons not listed here were also given, but no one reason by more than 5 per cent of respondents.

dominated by external circumstances. The respectable first-timers included those pleading guilty while still asserting their innocence; if these are excluded and we confine ourselves to the sub-type of 'remorseful one-time losers' (as identified in chapter 3), the proportion saying 'I was guilty' rose to 60 per cent. Those least likely to give this reason were the strategists and the dissociative defendants (both of which groups tended to plead guilty mainly because of the

Table 5.8 Reasons for guilty pleas, by defendants' typology

	% answering*		
	'I was guilty'	Crime/police events	Other
Recidivist strategists	29	64	47
Other strategists	22	67	72
Respectable first-timers	47	44	31
Right-assertive	(100)	(—)	(—)
Ordinary respondents	41	67	16
Dissociative	27	60	32
Other passive	53	57	18
Other-dominated respondents	26	39	95
External circumstances	51	62	35
Miscellaneous	77	10	44

*Rows do not necessarily total 100 as some respondents gave several reasons.

pressure of earlier events); also the 'other-dominated respondents' who as usual, because of their reliance on advisers, scored very heavily in the 'other reasons' column.

To give a fuller flavour to the important issue of reasons for guilty pleas, we set out below the detailed replies of 30 respondents—10 each in the SGU, SGR and HG categories, each set of 10 being a chronologically continuous series which has been selected by choosing an initial random number.[1] Readers should recall, of course, that differing sampling fractions were taken of each of these three categories, and that 10 forms a different proportion of each category.

(*a*) *SGU category*

1 'I denied it at first but they had fingerprints—there was too much evidence against me.'

2 'I was caught redhanded in the street, passing pot [cannabis].'

3 (Shoplifting of postcards) 'I was caught with the postcards on me and I knew it was wrong. No point in pleading not guilty.'

4 'I kicked the window in—it was my fault' (an ex-mental patient who immediately after the crime walked up to a policeman, confessed, and asked to be locked up).

5 (Shoplifting) 'I was obviously guilty; it was a very silly thing to do.'

6 (Assault on bus driver) 'Well, I was involved, and I pushed conductor away from this lad, so I'd decided to plead guilty. There were so many others involved, I didn't realise I'd be the only one to finish up in court. Was amazed at what was said in court—made me out to be really vicious, when actually I got involved because trying to help—and anyway I didn't hit the bus driver. But I wasn't given a chance to explain, and was so amazed I couldn't say anything. I wish now I'd pleaded not guilty.'

7 (Shoplifting) 'I decided to plead guilty as you have no chance against the police. When asked if I was guilty, I said yes I must be as it was in my hand: but it was a mistake, I am very ill and I didn't really know what was happening.'

8 (Meter-theft from lodgings) 'I had done this, I was fed up, so I went to the police station and told them.'

9 'Didn't tell them at first, then the other bloke made a statement implicating me, and no point in denying it after that.'

10 (Seen by policeman taking a road sign and putting it in his

car) 'I was caught redhanded, and I didn't want to cause trouble and get myself breathalysed.'

(*b*) *SGR category*

1 'Pleaded guilty to get two others off; the police said they'd release them if I admitted it, so I did. I wish I hadn't now, because of sentence [15 months].'

2 'The police got proof from a forensic test. I knew then there was no chance of getting off, and was afraid of a heavy sentence if I pleaded not guilty.'

3 'I find it difficult when talking to police to tell lies. I wanted to get it over and take my punishment.'

4 (Took cistern from house rented from council) 'I had done it—the Housing Department found out and were going to prosecute, so I went to the police and confessed.'

5 (Charged with stealing watch and possessing cannabis) 'The watch I admitted straight away. The cannabis I still deny, but forensic tests [on jacket pocket] positive. It would have meant going to the Crown Court for trial—and I'd have had difficulty refuting police evidence—it would have meant saying they'd planted it. Solicitor advised a guilty plea in the circumstances, although I wasn't guilty.'

6 'Well, if you plead not guilty you get remanded and it wastes time. Also you have to make up a story and so on.'

7 'Denied both at first, but then they searched the house and X grassed on me, they had enough evidence after that.'

8 'Someone [witness] had seen me taking the stuff. No chance of getting away with it.'

9 'I was caught on the job—no chance. I always *think* about not guilty plea—but they had evidence.'

10 Originally denied, then 'after talking to solicitor, felt I was guilty and didn't want to deny it.'

(*c*) *HG category*

1 'There's no use pleading not guilty—if you've done it, plead guilty. With my record, I had no choice.'

2 'Had made a statement that amounted to a confession: case was cut and dried. But I wish now I'd pleaded not guilty—I could have cross-examined witnesses and made the facts seem less bad.'

3 'I had done it, and I told them so.'

4 'I denied it at first, then I came to my senses and made a voluntary statement of guilt.'

5 'I did it, it was obvious I had, everyone saw me.'

6 'It's best to admit it and get it over and done with.'

7 (Assault case: limited English) 'Was going to plead not guilty: self-defence. But barrister told me to plead guilty—he said, it's better for you to plead guilty straight away.'

8 (Theft of lead and taking lorry without consent) 'Yes, I did the lead. About the lorry, pleaded guilty because the police said that what I did was an offence—I didn't think it was. Wish now I hadn't, I still don't think it was an offence. Am thinking of appealing.'

9 'No point in anything else—they'd found the radio in my mum's house.'

10 (Assault on police) 'There's no point in denying an assault of a cop. They all come and give evidence and no one believes you.'

The importance of the early police-suspect encounters is made very obvious from these extracts: we were able to explore them a little further from our data. In all, some 70 per cent of our respondents said that they had told the police right from the start that they had committed the offence. (In the SGU category the proportion was significantly higher at 80 per cent.) Nineteen per cent of all respondents volunteered the information, unprompted, that they had been caught redhanded, a proportion confirmed in the (later) answers recorded in Table 5.7.

Another 24 per cent admitted their guilt to the police at a later stage, and it is in this area that police interrogation practice is relevant. This is an important and sensitive area because of the allegations so often made of police brutality or trickery, or of 'verbals', confessions falsely attributed to the defendant by police officers over-anxious to secure a conviction. The absence of legal representatives at the time of police interrogation leaves the suspect with the somewhat thin protection of the Judges' Rules which require cautions to be administered and place some restrictions on police questions.

We avoided direct questions in this area, but asked simply why it was that the respondent came to admit his involvement to the police (as opposed to the subsequent formal decision to plead guilty in court). In about half the cases the reasons were that it had become clear (sometimes after the defendant had seen a solicitor) that the police had a good case, that the defendant's actions were criminal which he had doubted, or that it was stupid to deny the charge. Of all the defendants confessing at this later stage, 6 per cent said they confessed to cover up for someone else, and 17 per cent claimed that the police had in some sense 'forced' them to confess. We thus get these last allegations in 17 per cent of 24 per cent, or approximately 4 per cent of the whole guilty plea sample.

Like another author (Dell, 1971, p. 30) we debated whether to include this material, since we have no means of checking the allegations. From the defendant's point of view, however (and it is this that, inter alia, we are seeking to reflect in this study), the material is often crucial; so we think we must record it, even though we have only one side of the story.

The allegations of 'forcing' fall roughly into four categories. First, there are allegations of physical assault; second, of various kinds of verbal trickery such as saying that a cosuspect has confessed when he has not; third, pressure by saying they will add other spurious but more serious charges if a confession is not forthcoming; and finally, that they will ensure a remand in custody if no admission is made. The following three cases are illustrative:

> Case 2043 The defendant, aged 17, grabbed a woolly cap off a 13-year-old boy in the crowd going away from a football match. He said it was in fun, but a policeman had spotted him and he was taken to the station to be charged with theft. He claimed that the police had used violence on him and forced him to sign a statement, after which he had no choice but to plead guilty.

> Case 1034 (See also chapter 2 above.) 'I admitted possession. If I hadn't, they would have charged me with supplying. I had no choice: they threatened me and knocked me against the wall. I admitted having the stuff as I was so scared.'

> Case 2080 (Charged with attempting to siphon petrol from a car in garage forecourt.) 'They were going to keep me in all night, and it would have been remand in custody next day. Also they said they'd accuse my friend, who's on suspended sentence—so I admitted it.'

We reiterate that we cannot vouch for these allegations. In one sense, this is in itself disturbing: one gets similar allegations from any sample of defendants, yet it is impossible to know, because of the non-visibility of the police interrogations, how far the allegations are to be believed. We return in chapter 8 to the specific question of custody as a threat.

We have said that 70 per cent of guilty pleas admitted their guilt to the police straight away, and 24 per cent made a confession later on. That leaves 6 per cent of such pleas where no admission to the police had ever been made: the proportion was rather higher for HGs (13 per cent) and much higher for DGs (29 per cent), which suggests that this group is particularly to be found among the 'plea-changers' (see below).

Finally, we asked all guilty plea defendants the question 'Did you ever seriously think of pleading not guilty?' A quarter replied that they had, and their explanations mirrored the reasons given for the eventual plea of guilty: 30 per cent had believed that no offence had been committed; another 30 per cent that the police had no evidence. In the DG category, 30 per cent advanced a belief in 'exonerating circumstances' including drunkenness.

In the whole of this area of inquiry the DG category is very special. Eighty-two per cent had seriously considered pleading not guilty; in giving their reasons for pleading guilty 52 per cent gave 'lawyer's advice'; we explore the nature and timing of that advice in chapter 6.

Guilty pleas and sentence expectations

A series of questions was asked about sentence expectations, partly to discover how these expectations influenced the plea decision. Respondents were asked if they thought it would have made any difference to their sentence if they had pleaded not guilty, with the results shown in Table 5.9.

Table 5.9 Sentence expectations (defendants pleading guilty)

	%
Not guilty plea would have led to	
heavier sentence	49
lighter sentence	5
'different' sentence	1
Not guilty plea would make no difference	31
Don't know	14
Total	100

In line with these answers, 51 per cent said that sentence considerations had been taken into account in deciding plea. The proportion in the SGU category was only 42 per cent; from what we know of the SGU defendants' record and current offences there was in fact a fairly restricted range of possible sentences.

Advice as to plea

We asked the interviewed guilty plea defendants with whom they had discussed the decision as to plea. Table 5.10 contains a summary of the answers received, and there are striking differences in the pattern for the different sub-sample groups.

It is clear that plea decisions are of great concern to the DG category. Every respondent in that group had discussed the matter with others, and this is true of both official and unofficial advisers—but it must be recalled that the group of 4 students contribute heavily to the 'discussed with friends' and 'codefendants' entries. SGUs and HGs were much less likely to discuss the question with unofficial advisers: SGUs relied on police advice to quite an extent (for a similar finding in respect of serious motoring offenders, see Willett, 1973, p.79), but a majority talked to no one. HGs usually talked to their lawyers.

The advice received was predominantly to plead guilty: 72 per cent of unofficial advice and 98 per cent of official advice was to that effect. Respondents were asked whether they were influenced by the advice they received. Eleven per cent said they were strongly influenced by advice from unofficial advisers, 31 per cent by advice from officials; the latter figure rose to 62 per cent among the DGs, yet more evidence of their reliance on legal advice. No HG respondent was willing to say that police advice had any influence at all!

'Innocent' guilty pleas?

Much public concern is rightly aroused when a man or woman is found to have been wrongly convicted through mistaken identification, etc. Equally, many in high places have become alarmed at the number of professional criminals who are not being convicted because, it is said, the rules of criminal procedure are weighted in their favour.

Another group where the outcome of the trial may be unjust, but which has occasioned little public discussion, are those who plead

Table 5.10 Discussion of guilty pleas with others

% of defendants pleading guilty discussing plea with	Sub-sample groups SGU	SGR	DG	HG
Wife	9	10	18	7
Parents	3	5	0	7
Family	3	8	12	4
Friends	9	11	41	9
Codefendants	13	16	35	13
Others in trouble*	3	4	6	4
Police	25	20	12	11
Lawyer	0	52	94	57
Probation officer	1	9	6	2
No one	53	21	0	22

*For meaning of this term, see discussion of Table 4.16 in chapter 4.

guilty although they claim innocence. In the nature of the case, this group—having pleaded guilty—is in a weak position to make subsequent protest; but if it exists, we should clearly know about it.

In the academic literature there are at least two previous examinations of this issue. In the USA, Blumberg (1967, pp.90-4) examined the statements made by guilty plea defendants in response to the probation officer's opening question (in a social inquiry interview), namely, 'Are you guilty of the crime to which you pleaded?' According to Blumberg's classification of the answers (and assuming, as he is unprepared to do, that 'fatalistic' answers represent guilt), then no fewer than 51·6 per cent declared their innocence after pleading guilty. Subsequent questioning indicated that the defence lawyer, and not the police, was the agent most responsible for this astonishing result.[2]

As we shall discuss shortly in relation to plea-bargaining, there are special features of the American criminal justice system which make 'bargain justice' more probable, and we certainly cannot transplant Blumberg's findings to England without careful investigation. The only English work to consider 'innocent guilty pleas' systematically is Dell's (1971) rather special study of inmates of Holloway Prison.[3] She found 56 cases, or 12 per cent of women in the prison who had been tried at magistrates' courts, who were 'inconsistent pleaders' in the sense that they pleaded guilty while believing themselves innocent of all the charges preferred against them. But one would be unwise to generalise from this sample: apart from the special features of the population (female, incarcerated, with a high proportion there on remand for psychiatric reports), one-third of the 'inconsistent pleaders' were charged with soliciting, a rather special offence against which (as Dell notes) it is peculiarly difficult for a professional prostitute to defend herself, however innocent she may be.

In our sample we separated off those who had pleaded guilty to any offence for which their statement of the facts in the interview seemed to us to raise a credible possibility of a not guilty plea. This is a wider definition than Dell's since she excluded both (i) 'those who denied some offences while admitting to others', and (ii) all those who believed themselves (even if wrongly) legally guilty although morally innocent.[4] It is arguably also a wider definition than Blumberg's, since his defendants seem (he is regrettably unclear on the point) definitely to have asserted innocence, and some of ours did not go as far as this.

We have to make clear that we have excluded those cases where the defendant's statement rules out any hope of a legal defence (e.g. taking milk off a step and drinking it, where the defendant knew it was wrong but didn't think it was theft). We must also make plain that we are not saying we would ourselves, as legal advisers, have counselled a not guilty plea in all these cases, e.g. where the defendant had signed a confession which he now disowned, or where police and complainant's evidence seemed to be heavily against the defendant. We are saying, however, that these are cases which, if the defendant's post-trial version is correct, are quite possibly mistaken convictions.

Using this definition, 18 per cent of our guilty plea defendants had at least one charge which came into the category of 'possibly innocent'. This is well below Blumberg's figure, but higher than Dell's. Taking our results by category, the highest proportion came in the DG group (47 per cent), and the lowest in the SGUs (14 per cent), with HGs and SGRs intermediately placed (20 per cent, 23 per cent).

Dell found that lack of legal representation was associated with 'inconsistent pleading', but our results give no support to that view—it will be seen that the only unrepresented category, the SGUs, have the lowest rate of 'possibly innocent'. It may be thought surprising that lawyers will acquiesce in this kind of plea, but the following cases illustrate the kinds of reasons why they do (see also extract 5 in the series drawn from the SGR category, above):

> Case 1043 (handling charge) 'I didn't know the goods were stolen—the evidence showed I should have known. It wasn't till later I knew they were stolen, though I suppose looking back I realised they were cheap—cheaper than they should have been. On solicitor's advice I pleaded guilty.'

> Case 1069 B's brother had bought a house, and they went to look at it together. A three-piece suite had been left behind in it, and B's brother said B could have it. He took it, and then the police came round and accused him of stealing it from the original owners. Frightened, he denied having the suite, and later hid it, though it was found. The solicitor strongly advised a guilty plea—he said hiding it would look as if B had stolen it, and this couldn't be explained away.

We calculated the reasons why our 'possibly innocents' had pleaded guilty to the particular charges in question, and these are shown in Table 5.11. It will be seen that the foremost reason is legal advice, and in this respect our findings are similar to Blumberg's. It

Table 5.11 Reasons for pleas of guilty among 'possibly innocent' defendants

	% of defendants
On lawyer's advice	34
Thought it was legally wrong	16
Get it over/avoid delay	14
Police pressure/induced confession, etc.	9
Not worth challenging police	8
Too trivial to fight	5
Would be found guilty, get heavier sentence	5
Others	12

is apparent that English lawyers like American ones sometimes consider that the best interests of their clients are to be served by submission to a guilty plea rather than by fighting the charge; and in doing so they are undoubtedly partly motivated by the knowledge that heavier penalties may follow an unsuccessful plea of not guilty based on relatively weak foundations. By this deterrent threat, the bureaucracy of the legal system is enabled to keep not guilty pleas to an administratively acceptable level.

It will be recalled that those pleading guilty are on the whole younger and of lower social class than the not guilty pleas. We hypothesised that among our 'possibly innocents' there would be an unusually high proportion of young and of lower social class, and that the difference between them and those who actually pleaded not guilty was one of greater social confidence in pressing their innocence. The data showed no support whatever for this hypothesis; the 'possibly innocents' were not significantly different from other guilty plea defendants on either variable, and what trends there were were not in the direction hypothesised. We also found no difference between the groups in the proportion previously convicted; our negative findings in all these respects are similar to Dell's (at p.31).

There were differences, however, in the typology of defendants. Because of the strong influence of legal advice and of external events 'forcing' these defendants to plead guilty, there were many more 'other-dominated respondents' and 'external-circumstances dominated response' among the 'possibly innocents' than among other guilty pleas (45 per cent as against 16 per cent). Correspondingly there were fewer 'strategists', fewer 'ordinary respondents' and, perhaps surprisingly, fewer 'dissociative' defendants.

Finally, a word of caution. It may be that an ideal legal system would want all these 'possibly innocents' to plead not guilty without fear of sanction, so that their legitimate claims may be fully tested. But at least in present circumstances, it should not be assumed that defendants will want this, as the following case makes clear:

> Case 5043 L was charged with 2 counts of obtaining by deception, and 1 of burglary and theft (or, in the alternative, of handling). He pleaded guilty in the magistrates' court to everything except the burglary and theft, concerning which the prosecution accepted a not guilty plea and withdrew the charge. L was then sent to Crown Court for sentence on the 3 charges to which he had pleaded guilty. There, his barrister refused to plead in mitigation of sentence, saying that L's story amounted to a not guilty plea, certainly on the obtaining charges. There was some legal argument, with the judge showing reluctance to accede to defence counsel's request for the case to be remitted to the magistrates so that the case could begin again at the lower court with a not guilty plea; but this course of action was eventually agreed. The prosecution then altered the charges: the

obtaining counts were withdrawn and L was charged again with burglary and with 2 charges of theft, with 3 handling charges as alternative charges to these 3. The defendant elected (through his solicitor) Crown Court trial, and eventually appeared again in the Crown Court with the same barrister, where he pleaded guilty to the 3 handling charges, but not guilty to the burglary and thefts. This was accepted by the prosecution, and L was sentenced to 18 months' imprisonment. The defendant was utterly disgusted with his barrister: 'If I hadn't had him, I'd have pleaded guilty as I wanted, and might have got less time . . . all this messing around, and I'm worse off in the end. It's OK for him—but I have to wait in Leeds all that time.'

Plea-bargaining and plea-changing

The essence of plea-bargaining is that the defendant agrees to plead guilty to at least one charge in return for some concession by the prosecution. The system benefits the prosecution because there is no contested trial with the expense, delay and uncertainty that it produces. It benefits the defendant in so far as he also avoids delay and uncertainty, and may escape conviction on some charges and end up with a lighter sentence.

The system is highly developed in the USA where the agreements entered into between prosecution and defence will be enforced by the appellate courts. An example is Santobello v. New York (404 U.S. 257 (1971)). Santobello was charged with 2 felonies, both gambling offences. He agreed to plead guilty to the minor charge of 'possessing gambling records in the second degree' in return for the prosecution dropping the other charges and agreeing not to make any recommendation as to sentence. Owing to a misunderstanding caused by a change in the prosecution lawyer, the prosecution did in fact make a recommendation, of the maximum sentence of 1 year. That sentence was imposed despite the protests of the defence, the judge saying that he had not been influenced by the recommendation. The US Supreme Court set aside the sentence, saying that plea-bargaining was 'an essential component of the administration of justice'.

The American system of criminal justice has features which encourage plea-bargaining. Congested court lists threaten to overwhelm the judiciary and negotiated settlement of cases eases the pressure. There are established prosecution agencies and 'public defenders' with permanent staff which makes for ease of communication between the two 'sides'. Minimum sentences are common, so that if a prison sentence is to be avoided so must conviction for certain 'degrees' of crime. The prosecution in many jurisdictions is accustomed to make recommendations as to sentence, which gives added bargaining power. In England, almost all these features are absent (heavy court calendars are an exception, but on nowhere near the American scale); thus the whole plea-bargaining system is correspondingly ill-developed (see Davis, 1971; and Newman, 1966).

So, in England the conduct of the trial in the higher courts is in the hands of the Bar who usually come to the case at the last minute, and belong to no permanent agency. Minimum sentences and prosecution recommendations as to sentence are both unknown. There is neither the structure nor the bargaining-power to nurture the system.

This may be all to the good. Plea-bargaining has its critics in the USA. It is argued that the existence of the procedure encourages malpractices such as the listing of unsubstantiated charges, or charges of a higher degree than can be justified, to increase the prosecution's bargaining-power. The criminal process is reduced to a 'fixing' operation between lawyers, the interests of the defendant and the public being neglected. Inappropriate sentences may result because the eventual bargain does not reflect the true facts. The system is open to political pressures, or at least the suspicion that they exist (see Alschuler, 1968; Arcuri, 1973; Blumberg, 1967; Casper, 1972, chapter 3).

The legal position in England is set out by the Court of Appeal in R. v. Turner ([1970] 2 All E.R. 281). The court made some observations which will certainly act as a brake upon any tendency to develop plea-bargaining on the American model. Lord Parker, CJ, stressed that the judges should not be brought into plea discussions to any great extent; there were cases, for example when the defendant was suffering from an incurable disease and did not know that fact himself, when a private word with the judge was appropriate, and it was proper for both counsel to attend. It was sometimes appropriate for a private discussion to include the question of reducing the charges, but judges should hardly ever discuss likely sentences except perhaps to indicate that, in any event, the sentence would take a particular form, e.g. be non-custodial. The Lord Chief Justice emphasised that the defendant must have freedom of choice; the matter must not be taken out of his hands by the lawyers. But

> counsel must be completely free to do what is his duty, namely, to give the accused the best advice he can, and if need be advice in strong terms. This will often include advice that a plea of guilty, showing an element of remorse, is a mitigating factor which may well enable the court to give a lesser sentence than would otherwise be the case.

The only study of the plea-bargaining phenomenon in England is that by the Oxford University Penal Research Unit (McCabe and Purves, 1972). This was a study of 90 cases, involving 112 defendants, in which the defendant had been sent for trial in the higher court and had been listed as likely to plead not guilty but at the last moment changed his mind and entered a guilty plea. Of the 112 defendants, 48 pleaded guilty to all charges, and 64 'had an arrangement of pleas accepted by the court'. In these cases there would be discussions with prosecuting counsel and usually with the judge, but the study gives no indication of the extent of such discussions. Its finding is that in most, if not all, cases, a change of plea

> followed after the defendant received 'certain good advice' from his legal representatives. This is especially the case with late or last-minute changes of plea where counsel, after reviewing his brief and assessing the evidence, speaks urgently to solicitor and defendant in a conference held, in all too many cases, immediately before the trial is due to start (ibid., p.9).

The Oxford study did not interview defendants, but felt able to say from its data (mainly prosecution papers) that the typical defendants involved were those with previous criminal experience, who 'generally approach plea-bargaining with much the same spirit of realism and practicality which characterises the approach of the police, the lawyers and the judge' (ibid., p.45).

Our definitions of terms, and our scope of study, differ a little from those of McCabe and Purves. They distinguished two kinds of plea-bargaining: (i) involving a judge's intimation as to sentence, which they regarded as virtually dead since R. v. Turner, and (ii) 'discussions and negotiations which culminate in the defendant's decision to plead guilty . . . defence counsel, having examined his brief, conferred with his instructing solicitor and sometimes with the prosecution, gives the defendant the advantage of his advice'. We prefer to distinguish between 'plea-bargaining' (as defined in the opening paragraph of this section), embracing their first category and such of their second category as involve bargains or negotiations with the prosecution; and on the other hand 'plea-changing', or late changes of plea, usually but not always induced by the lawyer, but without apparent consultation with the prosecution. All our data in both these respects are restricted to the interview sample.

In considering 'plea-bargaining', we excluded cases of 'alternative charges', for example theft and handling stolen goods in which charges are of approximately equal gravity, and represent different interpretations of the same facts. In such cases the defendant minded to plead guilty will usually select the lesser charge, and the prosecution is very ready to accept that plea and the not guilty plea to the other alternative. This is not a situation in which the double charge puts any pressure on the defendant to bargain; it seems not to require further examination in that connection. That leaves us with 3 cases of apparently 'real' plea-bargaining in our interview sample, but only in the first of these was the defendant openly offered a bargain by his counsel:

> Case 7034 T was a company director, aged 47. He was active in his social life, a Freemason (he complained that one prosecution witness gave evidence 'in Masonic form, to lend more credibility to his answers'), and lived in a comfortable suburb. He faced 15 counts alleging theft, forgery of cheques and falsification of records, part of a complicated series of steps involving tax evasion, false accounts, deception of shareholders in his company, etc. His first interviews with the police were five months before his first appearance in court; he was not tried in the Crown Court until a further eleven months had elapsed. On the morning of the Crown Court appearance he was offered what he described as a 'deal': if he would plead guilty to 2 counts, 13 would be dropped. He refused—'I wasn't prepared to do any deal and I told my counsel so.' He was convicted (after a five-day trial) on 13 charges, and received a total of 21 months' imprisonment; he subsequently thought that if he had accepted the deal he might have got a suspended sentence.

> Case 4042 W was charged with (i) burglary, (ii) assault occasioning actual bodily harm and (iii) an alternative charge of

assault. Right up to the morning of the Crown Court trial (i.e. ten weeks from his first appearance) he had every intention of pleading not guilty to the second and third charges on the grounds of self-defence. Just before the trial, his barrister came into the cell and according to W said he 'had to' plead guilty: 'your statement says you are technically guilty and there's no point in pleading self-defence.' W agreed, reluctantly; the prosecution then dropped the 'actual bodily harm' charge and W pleaded guilty to the lesser charge of common assault.

Case 4041 The defendant was charged with theft of steel, and obtaining by deception, both charges being in respect of mis-management of his own business affairs. His barrister came to see him a week before the trial and said he would make a bad witness, there was not enough evidence, and he should plead guilty and 'cut his losses'. He saw him again just before the trial and said 'if you plead guilty you will get 18 months, if you plead not guilty you're bound to be found guilty and will get 3 years'. In sentencing the defendant to a total 18 months' imprisonment, the judge said 'you are a wise man to plead guilty and have been soundly advised. If you had been convicted by a jury you would serve your suspended sentence (12 months) plus 2 years. But I take heavily into account your plea of guilty. . . .' The defendant noted that the barrister's and the judge's statements were identical and strongly believed that his trial was 'a charade, with plea and sentence already decided'. He noted that although he had not finally decided on a guilty plea until 10 a.m. on the morning of the trial, no prosecution witnesses seemed to be available, and one such witness who had previously been his employee said that he had not been called.

In none of the 3 cases do we have firm proof of plea-bargaining, but in each case there seem to be strong hints of the phenomenon.

Turning then to plea-changing, we could monitor this matter only at the higher court level (there are formidable difficulties in doing so at the magistrates' court level in view of the small time involved in many cases). Unlike McCabe and Purves, we did not have access to lists of court business specifying cases as 'likely not guilty pleas'; we must therefore construct the plea-changing sample from retrospective interview material. This we may not have done with complete success, especially among the Hs: the Ds are easier because one can discover easily what the intended plea was at the time of venue choice.

In all, we identified 12 of the 17 DGs as plea-changers, and 11 of the 46 HGs (we have included the last two 'possible plea-bargaining' cases above among the DG plea-changers). Making appropriate allowances for the differential sampling fraction, we get a pattern of reasons for plea-changing as shown in Table 5.12.

Table 5.12 Reasons for plea-changing (higher court cases)

	%
Barrister's last-minute advice	68
Solicitor's advice during remand	14
Own last-minute decision	11
Influence of girlfriend or probation officer	7
Total	100

Not surprisingly, it is legal advice which is dominant. The last-minute, 'own decision' cases are interesting, and worth recording briefly. Two of the 3 cases involved 'recidivist strategists', one who admitted that he had done the offence but was hoping that he might avoid getting it pinned on him; the other decided to 'spring' a late change of plea partly as a strategy to reduce his sentence, and partly because no not guilty pleas were being taken at the last Sheffield Quarter Sessions, and he didn't fancy having to face X (he named a High Court judge) in the New Year! The third case involved a man who actually faced a full jury trial, but the jury sent a note to the judge which revealed part of the jury-room deliberations; the judge stopped the trial and ordered a retrial. In the meantime, the defendant got a new job, and then decided to plead guilty (although still believing himself innocent) to avoid losing time and jeopardising his job: 'a job is more important than a conviction', he said, though it was in fact his first conviction.

This last case, of a plea-change after an inconclusive first trial, was surprisingly not unique in the sample. There were 2 other cases, involving three defendants, where this occurred, in both cases on the advice of the barrister:

> Cases 4030/4031 The defendants, G and R, were charged alternatively with (i) taking a motor vehicle without consent and

(ii) allowing themselves to be carried in a taken conveyance. The police had come upon G, R and another pushing a car which had been reported stolen. G and R's story was that they had been walking into Sheffield town centre when a friend stopped to give them a lift; later the car broke down. They said they had not known the car was taken; if true, this would be a defence to either charge. They pleaded not guilty and opted for Crown Court trial; things were going well for them with conflicting police evidence, etc. when the judge stopped the trial as he had to go to Doncaster for another case. A retrial was ordered. Their barrister advised them that the police would now be ready for the defence case, having had a 'dress rehearsal'; he advised them to plead guilty to the second charge which he apparently described as a 'technicality'. The prosecution then accepted the plea of not guilty on the first charge. One of the defendants said in interview that they had agreed, under the 'very unusual circumstances', to change their plea, 'but only on the technicality of being carried in a stolen car—we were, but we didn't know it was stolen'. Both defendants seemed unaware that knowledge of the conveyance being taken is an essential element in this offence (see s.12, Theft Act 1968).

Case 6046 L, aged 18, was charged with causing grievous bodily harm with intent, and committed for trial at the Crown Court; his defence was one of accident, arguing that the victim had intervened in an unfortunate way in a fight L was having with a third party. At the original Crown Court trial, the jury could not reach agreement, and a retrial was ordered. On the morning of the retrial, the barrister (one of the most senior counsel practising in the Sheffield area) saw the defendant and advised him to plead guilty, because the judge he was to face was a very lenient one, and he (counsel) would be able to bring out the facts of the first jury being unable to agree. Counsel apparently said he would not advise this course if the defendant had been scheduled to appear in Court Two, where a much harsher judge was sitting, but in Court One it was the best policy. L was sentenced to borstal training; counsel apparently told him that had he pleaded guilty at the outset of the first trial, he would have probably received 3 years' imprisonment.

These cases illustrate the decisive effect of legal advice in most plea-changing. In this connection, we noted one feature of special interest. Fifty-four per cent of the plea-change defendants (as reweighted) were represented by one particular barrister, who had only 16 per cent of the total caseload of the Bar in our interview sample. This barrister often seemingly gave last-minute advice in very strong terms: cases 4041 and 4042, above, are examples of this, while in another case he is said to have told a defendant that if he stuck out for a not guilty plea he could get 7 years' imprisonment and his family (who were to give evidence for him) could be convicted of perjury. It is true that leading cases have stressed that counsel's duty is to press a plea-change on his client in strong terms if he deems this necessary (see R. v. Turner, above; R. v. Hall, [1968] 52 Crim. App. R. 528); but it is obvious from the Sheffield experience that different counsel may interpret this duty in different ways. It may be relevant to record that the particular barrister in question had a 100 per cent record in contested trials during the research period, i.e. he won all those cases where he did not persuade the defendant to change his plea.

Finally, we have to record that defendants—including defendants with previous convictions—do not always respond to plea-changing advice as happily and as 'realistically' as McCabe and Purves have suggested from their documentary study. True, in the majority of the cases the defendants were satisfied with having accepted the advice. But in just over a quarter of the cases they remained in one way or another unhappy about it, and in one or two cases felt very bitter indeed. Nor is this particularly surprising. Remembering the figures on the delay in handling Crown Court business (see chapter 2), one realises that these defendants have for many weeks expected to plead not guilty. This intention has been supported by their solicitor—after all, a trained professional. Then, out of nowhere appears a barrister, usually on the morning of the trial, strongly suggesting a change of plea. It is hardly surprising if defendants acquiesce, faced with this predicament; it is also hardly surprising if some of them subsequently resent having acquiesced to last-minute pressure. The Bar could do its image some good if it resolved to see defendants some time in advance if any question of plea-changing arises, so that a calmer decision may be made by the defendant.

Not guilty pleas

'Why did you plead not guilty?' almost comes into the category of silly questions—but not quite. Almost all replied, as expected, that they had not committed the offence, either not having done anything or not in a criminal way, or that there were excusing circumstances. Only 3 of the 83 defendants interviewed gave other answers: these were very obviously 'strategic' not guilty pleas in which the defendant regarded himself as guilty but was looking for a possible loophole:

> Case 5001 G, a grocer, was indicted on 2 charges of handling stolen foodstuffs. He was found guilty, but was sure his sentence would have been heavier had he pleaded guilty, as 'the judge might have thought I dealt in stolen goods full-time'. 'In a way, although the judge found me guilty, I think I showed I was not guilty to being a big dealer. Also it was my own fault; I lied and was found out.'

> Case 3016 A very similar case, in which the main motivation for pleading not guilty on a handling charge was to establish that T was not a big dealer. (Details have been given in note 10 to chapter 4).

> Case 7026 B was charged with burglary of a shop, or alternatively with handling the proceeds of the raid. He admitted in interview that he had been there, but he was a lookout outside the shop. He had been going to plead guilty in the magistrates' court, but the magistrates refused summary trial and when B saw the committal papers he realised the police had a very weak case against him. He pleaded not guilty, and secured a directed acquittal from the judge on the grounds of lack of evidence: 'he might have been present but there is not enough evidence to conclude that he definitely was; and it is dangerous to leave the case to the jury on such a flimsy prosecution case.'

To these 3 cases we might perhaps add another, in which the defendant was on his own admission substantially guilty of shop-lifting, but where although he had taken goods he had not yet passed through the supermarket checkout point. He believed he had not committed the offence because one could not be convicted without leaving the shop, a point he repeatedly stressed during our interview in 'barrack-room lawyer' style. In fact this point is legally incorrect (see R. v. McPherson, [1973] Crim. L. R. 191), passing the checkout being merely possible evidence of intent to steal.

In seven further cases our interviewers thought that the defendant's account in the interview was sufficiently unconvincing to make it likely that he was offering what amounted to a 'strategic' not guilty plea, although the defendant himself did not admit this. We do not place too much weight on this figure, which is necessarily conjectural; but if the figure is right, and if we add in the 4 cases specified above, then we get 11 cases or 13 per cent of not guilty pleas which were of a strategic nature.

Although only a minority of such pleas could apparently be called strategic, a clear majority of the defendants pleading not guilty had given serious thought to the possibility of pleading guilty: 71 per cent of those who pleaded not guilty but were convicted, and 59 per cent of those actually acquitted, had done so. Furthermore, a decision to plead not guilty did not imply the expectation of acquittal: 26 per cent of those convicted and 21 per cent of those acquitted had expected to be found guilty. The basis for this pessimism was usually an assessment of the strength of the case against them, but a number of convicted men said that 'the courts always believe the police' or pointed to their own previous record.

Table 5.13 sets out the extent of discussions with others, and that table can be compared with Table 5.10 (guilty pleas). Generally, and as one would expect, those pleading not guilty engaged in more

Table 5.13 Discussion of not guilty pleas with others

% of defendants pleading not guilty discussing plea with	Sub-sample groups		
	SN	DN	HN
Wife	19	16	28
Parents	3	12	4
Family	16	0	8
Friends	22	20	16
Codefendants	6	12	20
Others in trouble*	3	4	12
Police	19	36	28
Lawyer	62	44	64
Probation officer	3	0	0
No one	12	16	16

*For meaning of this term, see discussion of Table 4.16.

extensive discussion of the plea question than was the case in the corresponding guilty plea groups, the Ds being exceptional. The increased discussion was principally with family and friends, and this reflects greater opportunities: those pleading not guilty were much more likely to be on bail during the early stages of the process than those pleading guilty.

Eighty-seven per cent of 'unofficial' advisers and 53 per cent of 'official' advisers recommended the plea of not guilty. As in the guilty plea group, the official advisers were less willing to give that advice. Their advice was regarded as having influenced the final decision by only 17 per cent of this group of defendants, and one can speculate that official advisers who suggested a not guilty plea did so with less force and confidence than those supporting a guilty plea.

Respondents who pleaded not guilty were asked about sentence expectations. They were asked if they thought that a guilty plea would have made any difference to their sentence. Their replies are summarised in Table 5.14.

Table 5.14 Sentence expectations (defendants pleading not guilty)

	%
Guilty plea would have led to	
lighter sentence	26
heavier sentence	12
Guilty plea would have made no difference	37
Don't know	25
Total	100

Although the numbers are small, it is interesting to find that 12 per cent felt that a guilty plea would have led to a heavier sentence. The reasoning was usually that a full trial gave better exposure of the mitigating factors than would have been possible in a plea of mitigation after a guilty plea, a point of view also sometimes expressed in retrospect by dissatisfied guilty plea defendants. Cases 5001 and 3016, above, are very clear illustrations of this particular position, and in both of those cases the defendant was satisfied that the strategy had paid off and that a lesser sentence had definitely been achieved. But of course the formal legal system does not recognise this as a valid reason for pleading not guilty and one can get a clash between the defendant's and the court's perspective on the matter, as a final case example shows:

> Case 7030 E had been charged with theft of £500: the facts were very complex but basically E denied the offence because he said he had not realised the money belonged to a particular sports club. Although he was denying the offence as his main reason for a not guilty plea, E also thought that this plea was advantageous from a sentencing point of view: 'when you plead guilty, you don't get a fair hearing, and the judge doesn't hear all the case. You get a better deal if you plead not guilty.' He was convinced that had he pleaded guilty he would have received an immediate sentence of imprisonment; as it was, he got a 6 months suspended sentence. But the Crown Court judge had taken a very different line in sentencing E: 'you took advantage of Mr S——and there is no mitigation in your case, because you did not confess to your crime.'

6 Legal representation

> 'The right of one charged with crime to counsel may not be deemed fundamental and essential to fair trials in some countries, but it is in ours. From the very beginning, our state and national constitutions and laws have laid great emphasis on procedural and substantive safeguards designed to assure fair trials before impartial tribunals in which every defendant stands equal before the law. This noble ideal cannot be realised if the poor man charged with crime has to face his accusers without a lawyer to assist him.'
>
> (Justice Black, US Supreme Court, Gideon v. Wainwright (372 U.S. 335 (1963))

Justice Black's statement (in which the word 'counsel' is used in the American sense of 'a trial lawyer') would be assented to by the great majority of English commentators on the legal system, who would blushingly overlook the belated development of English law and practice in this matter.

The present English position is that in all cases the defendant is entitled to be represented by a lawyer if he so wishes. But of course many defendants cannot pay for legal services, and one has to look beyond the formal position to consider how far the State will give financial assistance (or 'legal aid') in this matter. In criminal cases, the position is now governed by the guidance laid down by the Widgery Committee in 1966 (Home Office, 1966). The statutory framework of a new criminal legal aid system based on the Widgery Report was set out in the Criminal Justice Act 1967, part IV (now replaced by identical provisions in the Legal Aid Act 1974). The extent of courts' intended use of legal aid orders is not specified in the Act (save for some general words in s.75), but was spelt out by the Committee. So far as higher courts (now the Crown Court) were concerned, under the new arrangements, 'the only accused persons who will appear . . . without legal representation will be persons who are not financially eligible for legal aid and have not made private arrangements, and persons who, although financially eligible, did not apply for legal aid' (para. 152).

Thus, virtually all those below certain means levels going to the higher court would receive legal aid. This is not intended to be the position in magistrates' courts. Here, assuming financial eligibility, legal aid was to be granted only in five specified sets of circumstances; 'if a case exhibits none of these features, then, *prima facie,* it is not a case in which the interests of justice require that the accused should be professionally represented' (para. 180). In practice, the most numerically important of the five specified circumstances relates to 'real jeopardy of [the accused] losing his liberty or livelihood or suffering serious damage to his reputation'.[1] This has been underlined by a Home Office circular (HOC No. 237/1972) which officially commends the 'Widgery criteria' to magistrates' courts and which says in terms that 'in particular [the Secretary of State] thinks it highly desirable that legal aid should be available to any accused person where there appears to be a real likelihood of his being sentenced to imprisonment if convicted'.[2]

But even if the Widgery criteria were fully implemented by all magistrates' courts, it is probable that the majority of defendants tried summarily for indictable offences would fall outside the criteria and would thus be unrepresented unless they made private arrangements.

Representation in the magistrates' court

Our court observations produced data in respect of 1,672 defendants who passed through the Sheffield magistrates' court. Table 6.1 indicates the extent to which they were represented. It shows that 59 per cent of defendants were wholly unrepresented, and that a further 14 per cent were represented for only part of the time. These overall figures mask very important differences between cases ultimately dealt with summarily by the magistrates and cases going via committal proceedings for trial in the higher court.

In cases dealt with summarily the pattern is that 19 per cent are represented when they first appear in court, a proportion which rises to 25 per cent before the case is finally disposed of. In cases which are ultimately sent to the higher court, the majority (55 per cent) are already represented at the time of the first hearing and virtually all are represented before committal proceedings are complete.

In practice, representation by a lawyer is virtually compulsory for committal proceedings. This is the result of s.1 of the Criminal Justice Act 1967, which introduced a shortened form of committal proceedings in which the prosecution tender written statements of witnesses and the court commits the defendant for trial without reading the statements. This procedure, which is now used in almost every committal case (see chapter 2), may not be employed if a defendant is unrepresented; the reason for this is that the short procedure eliminates the (rather slim) chance of the magistrates, on considering the prosecution case, deciding to dismiss the case and not commit for trial, and it is thought wrong to take away this possibility from an unrepresented defendant. The outcome is that lawyers must attend, and be paid for attending, a wholly uncontroversial ritual; the only role open to defence lawyers is to make applications for bail, and for the extension of the existing legal aid order to cover the higher court proceedings. It is arguable that in many cases, legal representation at this stage could be dispensed with; or more radically, that the whole matter could be dealt with, as legal aid applications are, by the clerk in private and without the attendance of lawyer or defendant, provided that adequate argument had been heard at the previous hearing on the question of bail.

It is very difficult to say how the Sheffield data set out in Table 6.1 would compare with the pattern in other courts. No national figures are available, and it is clear from a study of London magistrates' courts (Zander, 1969) that there are wide variations between courts. Zander found that in one magistrates' court 48 per cent of all

Table 6.1 Representation in the magistrates' court

% of defendants who were	Tried summarily	Committed to higher court	All
Represented throughout	19	55	27
Unrepresented at first appearance, represented at later appearance(s)	5	41	12·5
Unrepresented at several appearances, represented at later appearance(s)	1	3	1
Other mixtures including representation	0·2	0·3	0·2
Unrepresented throughout	75	—	59
Total	100	100	100

defendants in proceedings in that court were legally represented, but in another the proportion was only 13 per cent. The overall rate was 27 per cent, which happens to be the same as our 'represented throughout' proportion, but this is not a meaningful comparison. Zander's study was completed in five days, and he could not study the pattern of appearances at different stages in a case; his sample included the whole range of offences, except minor motoring offences, so that at least one-eighth of his cases, of drunkenness and the like, would be excluded from our sample; and his classification of hearings into 'trials', 'sentence hearings' and all other hearings (apparently brief appearance for remand and committal proceedings) prevents any comparative figures being obtained.

Figures are occasionally produced showing the proportion of legal aid orders made in various different places, with quite wide variations by area. Sheffield tends to fare well in such 'league tables'; in 1969 for example, it granted 96·6 per cent of legal aid applications in cases involving summary trial, as against a national figure of 82·2 per cent (H. C. Deb. vol. 807, cols *369-74,* 1 December 1970). This does not necessarily mean, however, that Sheffield has more represented defendants in summary trials than other areas, since the proportion is given in respect of legal aid applications, and not in respect of all summary proceedings. It is possible that applications, as a proportion of cases, may vary widely with such factors as the extent to which the police and other agencies publicise legal aid, how far local solicitors know the mind of the local court and therefore do or do not put in relatively weak applications and so forth. All that we can say is that there is no evidence to suggest that the Sheffield pattern, as shown in Table 6.1, is likely to be worse than other areas of the country.

The Sheffield magistates' court data were carefully examined for the existence of factors related to legal representation. One obvious difference relates to plea: of those represented at any stage, 81 per cent pleaded guilty, as against 99 per cent of the unrepresented (cf. the figures in Zander's study, 55 and 86 per cent respectively). This reflects a deliberate policy of the Sheffield bench and clerk's department to encourage legal aid and legal representation for the not guilty pleas, in view of the difficulties of an unrepresented defendant in cross-examination of witnesses, etc. (We discuss the 3 interviewed SNUs below.) One ingenious 'strategist' took advantage of this policy, declared to the police he would plead not guilty, obtained legal aid, and then pleaded guilty as all along intended: he pointed out (correctly) that he was by no means sure of getting legal aid as a guilty plea defendant!

Other significant interactions in the data were hard to come by. For example, there was no significant effect of social class on representation. Close analysis of the SGR group in the interview sample showed that 63 per cent of that group in socio-economic classes I, II and III were represented at all appearances as against 44 per cent for classes IV and V, but this was not quite significant, and the difference decreases when account is taken of the fact that classes I, II and III have a higher proportion of police bail, with enhanced opportunities for obtaining a solicitor at an early stage. The proportion represented at all appearances is higher for classes I, II and III both among those granted police bail and among those making their first appearance in custody, but not significantly so.

These findings contrast sharply with those of Willett (1973, p.83) who found that social class had a decisive effect on legal representation in his sample of motoring offenders. He does not explore the matter fully, but it would seem that legal aid would not be available to many of his defendants, so that the expense of legal representation becomes a major factor which it was not in our sample.

There was at first sight an interesting difference in the pattern of representation of male and female defendants. The pattern for all proceedings at magistrates' courts was that both male and female defendants were represented at their first appearance in 27 per cent of cases; 16 per cent of the men, but only 6 per cent of the women, obtained legal representation at a later stage, leaving as wholly unrepresented 57 per cent of men and 67 per cent of women, the difference being statistically highly significant. In fact this difference is almost entirely due to the fact that a greater proportion of the men are charged with offences ultimately tried at the higher court, and obtain a solicitor for committal proceedings. If we look only at cases tried summarily, as in Table 6.2, the difference largely vanishes. As between the sexes, the only significant difference is for shoplifting; not only do many women commit this offence, but they are also significantly more likely than men to be represented at their trial for it.

The study by Zander already referred to (Zander, 1969; see table 11, p.642) did not distinguish between male and female defendants, and uses a very different classification of offences, but his findings are similar to ours in one respect, namely the majority of defendants

Table 6.2 Representation at summary trials, by offence group and sex

% unrepresented charged with	Males	Females
Criminal damage	93	(100)
Meter-thefts	89	91
Shoplifting	88	71
Taking car without consent	74	(100)
Other thefts and frauds	70	69
Aggressive offences	66	(100)
Burglaries	60	(71)
Drugs offences	58	(71)
Handling stolen goods	57	(38)
Sex offences	44	—
All	75·2	74·6

tried summarily are unrepresented even when charged with serious offences, such as burglary, handling or possessing drugs (see Table 6.2 for details).

This absence of representation is also reflected in sentencing. In our court sample 54 per cent of the defendants tried summarily and finally sentenced to imprisonment by the magistrates were unrepresented; as were 75 per cent of those given suspended sentences, and 4 of the 7 sent to detention centres (cf. Zander, 1969, pp.643-4; comparable figures for his rather different sample are remarkably similar at 55 per cent, 74 per cent and six out of six). A report by JUSTICE in 1971 discussed Zander's study and other relevant works (Dell, 1971; Borrie and Varcoe, 1971) and concluded that: 'all the evidence available on this question therefore points in the same direction—a majority of those given custodial penalties by magistrates do not have the benefit of legal representation either on legal aid or otherwise' (JUSTICE, 1971, para. 35).

Our data relate to a later time period than any of these other surveys, but point in very much the same direction. It has to be said that such a policy is contrary to both the letter and the spirit of the Widgery criteria. In a few cases the absence of legal representation is partially compensated for by the presence of a social inquiry report from the probation officer,[3] but by no means necessarily so:

> Case 2014 (see also SGU/4, chapter 5) The defendant kicked a window in, walked up to a policeman, said he had done it

and wanted to be locked up. He had previously been in the local mental hospital 16 times; he was sentenced to 6 months' imprisonment without legal representation or the presentation of a social inquiry report or a psychiatric report.

Case 2018 (see also SGU/8, chapter 5) The defendant broke into the meter in his lodgings, was fed up, and went to the police station and told them. He had been released from prison some six weeks before; he said in court he would like to be given a chance to find work and pay the meter money back. He was sentenced to 3 months' imprisonment without a lawyer or a social inquiry report; he said he would not appeal because 'they were lenient and the sentence is agreeable'.

We must make clear, however, that the situation existing at the time of our fieldwork in 1971-2 has very probably now altered for the better, for three reasons;

(i) the Widgery criteria had not been brought specifically to magistrates' attention by Home Office circular at the time of the research, but have now been so.

(ii) s.37 of the Criminal Justice Act 1972, brought into force on 1 January 1973, prohibited the passing of imprisonment or other custodial sentences (including suspended sentences) on unrepresented defendants who have not previously actually served a period in custody. Unfortunately, our data on previous custody, as revealed in court, are not sufficiently complete for us to calculate how many of our unrepresented defendants would have been caught by the terms of this section.

(iii) since 1973 Sheffield has operated a 'duty solicitor' scheme, whereby a solicitor is available in the courthouse to give advice to defendants on the morning of their appearance and to arrange representation for them where necessary. One of the main purposes of the JUSTICE pamphlet was precisely to argue for such a scheme, and the Legal Advice and Assistance Act 1972 facilitated its introduction. It seems likely that among the benefits of the scheme will be a reduction in the number of defendants imprisoned without representation (for a brief survey of new duty solicitor schemes in England, see Legal Action Group, 1974).

Representation at the higher courts

National figures concerning representation at the Crown Court are published in the *Criminal Statistics.* It is not clear whether they are on precisely the same basis as our own data (the national statistics have a category of 'sentence proceedings' which may include some cases originally committed for trial but adjourned for later sentencing), but the pattern (summarised in Table 6.3) is very similar, with a very high percentage represented. The national figures indicate that the great majority of defendants are legally aided, that is their legal representative is paid for by public funds. Thus the Widgery policy of almost all Crown Court defendants being legally represented is plainly being followed, both nationally and in Sheffield. This represents a very considerable change over the last decade, since in 1965 only 58 per cent of all higher court defendants (for trial or sentence) were legally represented (see the table and comment in Borrie and Varcoe, 1971, p.7).

Table 6.3. Representation in the higher courts

(a) Sheffield data % of defendants		Committed for trial	Committed for sentence
Represented		99	95
Unrepresented		0	5
Observers unsure		1	0
(b) National pattern % of defendants		**at trial**	**at sentence proceedings**
Represented:	legal aid	93	95
	privately	6	1
	total	99	96
Unrepresented		1	4

Source: *Criminal Statistics 1972,* p.212.

Represented defendants and the time factor

There are two closely related questions to examine in connection with the time factor. The first is, 'When did the defendant first obtain the help of a lawyer?' We have already seen that a fair number of defendants are unrepresented at first appearance but are represented later. In some of these cases, the defendant will have obtained a solicitor for the purpose of committal proceedings; in others he will have been unable to obtain a solicitor at the time of his first appearance, having only been arrested a few hours earlier. This prompts the second question, 'When did he first decide that he wanted to have a lawyer?'

We asked all represented defendants in our interview sample the question when did they first decide to have a lawyer. The answers are summarised in Table 6.4. In the table, 'during first appearance', which was the answer given by an unexpectedly large number of respondents especially among those pleading guilty, is unlikely to mean the brief period of time spent in the dock before the case is adjourned. It probably refers to the whole period spent in court, or in the cells, waiting for the case to be heard. Solicitors are to be seen around, and as we shall see, some defendants take the opportunity to make contact with a solicitor who is calling on the man in the next cell.

The striking feature of Table 6.4 is that defendants who ultimately plead not guilty decide to be legally represented at a much earlier stage than those pleading guilty; almost a half of those pleading not guilty have so decided before they are even charged.

Table 6.4 Time of decision to have a lawyer

% answering	Defendants pleading Guilty	(cumulative %)	Not guilty	(cumulative %)
Before charge, while police making inquiries	29	(29)	49	(49)
When charged	22	(51)	25	(74)
Between charge and first appearance	15	(66)	12	(86)
During first appearance	13	(79)	5	(91)
Between appearances before magistrates	16	(95)	8	(99)
After committal to higher court for sentence	4	(99)	—	

The table also shows that of defendants who were ultimately represented 66 per cent of those pleading guilty and 86 per cent of those pleading not guilty had decided to have the services of a lawyer before their first appearance in court. Only about 65 per cent were in fact represented at their first appearance, so there is some delay between the decision to get a lawyer and its implementation.

To explore this further we asked the group of defendants who were unrepresented at their first appearance but represented later why they did not have a lawyer at the beginning. The answers are summarised in Table 6.5.

Table 6.5 Represented defendants: reasons for being unrepresented at first appearance

% answering		
Didn't think about it	13	
Thought a lawyer unnecessary	10	
Didn't realise charge serious	2	total 25%
Hadn't applied for legal aid then	14	
Didn't have time	13	
No real delay; applied at first appearance	10	
In custody, so couldn't	6	total 43%
Couldn't afford	6	
Didn't know about legal aid	4	
Didn't know how to get a lawyer	1	total 11%
Police discouraged me	3	
Other reasons	17	

The replies were rather difficult to classify. They are grouped in the table: the first group (25 per cent) have the common feature that the defendant had not decided that he needed a lawyer; the second group reflect more a lack of opportunity for some reason (43 per cent); and the third group ignorance of procedure (11 per cent).

The second group contains especially those kept in custody before the first appearance. As we explain in chapter 8, defendants come to court either on police bail after a charge (and this may be a several-week gap on occasions), or in custody, in which case they must be brought before a court within 24 hours (or longer if the next day is a Sunday or a Bank Holiday). Those kept in custody are very often remanded (on bail or in custody) by the court, because there has not been time to prepare case papers, etc. Many defendants regard it as impossible to get a lawyer for this first hearing; a lot said they had asked for one but none was available, and some treated it as a fact of life that, as one of them put it, 'you just don't have them the first time round'.

We were actually rather surprised to discover that, overall, as many as 36 per cent of defendants whose first appearance was preceded by custody managed to obtain a lawyer for that hearing. We were even more surprised to find that the corresponding figure for those appearing on police bail was lower (26 per cent), but this is accounted for by a much higher percentage of SGUs among this group. When we look only at those who were ultimately represented, we find that at least twice as many of those first appearing on bail managed to have a lawyer there for the first hearing as of those in custody (the figures were: among SGRs, 85 per cent of those on bail represented from the outset against 42 per cent of those in custody; among SNs, 74 and 29 per cent respectively). These data were also analysed by offence types. There were no significant variations among those in custody, but there were highly significant differences as between three groups of those appearing on bail. The percentage (of those ultimately represented) who were represented at first appearance is shown in Table 6.6.

Table 6.6 Proportion of those ultimately represented who were represented at first appearance, shown by type of offence charged

	%
Aggressive offences, burglary, taking vehicle without owner's consent and criminal damage	61
Sex and drugs offences	70
Thefts (all types), fraud and handling	82

This variation may be related to the magistrates' practice in committing cases for trial in the higher court, and the requirement that a defendant be represented at committal proceedings. This is more likely to have an impact in the earlier groups of offences.

This leads to a related issue, that of access to solicitors within the police station, which has concerned a number of commentators and has been considered empirically by Zander (1972b). The legal position, as set out in the Judges' Rules, is that

> every person at any stage of an investigation should be able to communicate and to consult privately with a solicitor. This is so even if he is in custody provided that in such a case no

> unreasonable delay or hindrance is caused to the processes of investigation or the administration of justice by his doing so.

Zander found that in his sample of defendants, only 12 per cent of those taken to the police station had spoken to a lawyer; of the remaining 88 per cent, 39 per cent had asked to speak to a solicitor and had been refused. Overall, of 57 defendants who asked to speak to a solicitor 15 were able to and 42 (74 per cent) were refused. Zander's study sets out verbatim the responses, and a very gloomy picture of police obstruction, deceit and violence appears. It must be realised that his sample is special, consisting of defendants all of whom had been tried in the higher courts and all of whom had appealed to the Court of Appeal; it may, fortunately, not be representative of the treatment received by all defendants.

Our data show some police obstruction, but the scale is much smaller than in Zander's study. We did not ask specific questions on this point, so the evidence has to be built up from various sources. In Table 6.5, we see that 3 per cent gave 'police discouragement' as a reason for being unrepresented at first appearance; to which might be added some of the 6 per cent who said that they could not get a lawyer as they were in custody. We also know that 42 per cent of those kept in custody before first appearance were able to speak to someone (more often a spouse than a solicitor) during that period (though probably after the completion of interrogation); but 12 per cent said they asked to speak to someone but were refused.

So the element of police obstruction is difficult to quantify from our data. But it seems to exist, as remarks made during interview suggested (see also case 7003 in chapter 3):

> Case 7015 Arrested at 9.30 a.m., appeared in court at 10.30 a.m. next day. During the questioning, said that he asked to see his solicitor. They would not allow him to get in touch with the solicitor: 'they gave me no reason; they said solicitors can't help you in here, only in court.' Eventually they did allow him to contact his solicitor before the court hearing.

> Case 7033 A respectable businessman in the steel industry, charged with four offences of handling stolen metal. He was very much a 'middle-class strategist', and his first instinct was to ask for a solicitor during his initial six-hour interview with the police. He said they refused this, though they subsequently denied it when it was put at the eventual trial. When the defendant did eventually get to his own solicitor, he asked him

to recommend the best possible criminal-law solicitor in the area, and the best barrister: his total legal bill was £2,500, including the services of a QC and a junior barrister. (The resulting array of legal talent did not prevent his conviction.) He was surprised at some of the questions in the interview with us, and had not realised before that it was in fact possible to appear in court without a lawyer.

Reasons for being represented

All defendants who were represented at some stage were asked to 'tell me as much as you can about why you decided to have a lawyer', and the interviewers were instructed to probe for multiple reasons. The replies are summarised in Table 6.7; other answers were given but none was given by more than 5 per cent of respondents. The table distinguishes between defendants tried in the higher courts and those tried summarily; for both, the two dominant reasons were simply a feeling that the lawyer would help, and that the lawyer could put the case more clearly than could the defendant. As with other reasons for defendants' decisions, we investigated how far these two and the other reasons varied by the different groups in the defendants' typology, but on this occasion no marked differences were apparent.

Table 6.7 Reasons for having a lawyer: percentage of defendants giving each reason

(a) Defendants tried in the higher courts	
Lawyer could put the case more clearly than I could	31
Lawyer would help (no further details forthcoming)	24
Case serious, so lawyer needed	12
I needed advice as to procedure/what to do/say	11
I believe I was not guilty	10
I needed his legal knowledge	10
(b) Defendants tried summarily	
Lawyer could put the case more clearly than I could	51
Lawyer would help (no further details forthcoming)	21
I needed advice as to procedure/what to do/say	6

Once again it is helpful to supplement the necessarily simplified quantification of the table with some quotations from defendants about why they chose to have a lawyer. We give below five extracts (selected by random methods) from each of four sub-samples, namely the SGRs, the SNs, the HGs and the HNs.

Group (a): SGR

1 'A lad in [Remand Centre] said I could apply: it would be someone to speak for me, to stand up and talk to the judge.'

2 (A university student) 'We didn't want a record—we were thinking of the university and of future jobs.'

3 'Decided as soon as charged. They can say things better, and advise you.'

4 'The probation officer said we would probably go to prison: he told me to get a lawyer.'

5 'I thought it best—the police were charging me with theft and it was never theft because I bought it for 25p.' (Subsequently the charge was altered to handling.)

Group (b): SN

1 'A solicitor can do the talking better—he knows more about it, especially on a not guilty plea.'

2 'With pleading not guilty, I needed someone with experience to speak for me.'

3 (Limited English) 'I can't explain myself, I need an interpreter in the court.'

4 (No previous convictions) 'I wanted to keep my good name, courts frighten me. Also the police suggested it.'

5 'They talk better than me, can say better what I want to say.'

Group (c): HG

1 'I'm not a good speaker, and I have difficulty writing. I get a lawyer each time.'

2 (Social class II manager) 'It's common knowledge that if you're in trouble, it's best to get a solicitor.'

3 'I don't know why I got one.'

4 'Whatever you've got to say, the solicitor can present it in the best way possible.'

5 'I just wanted someone to speak for me.'

Group (d): HN

1 'The police had remanded me on bail but not brought charges, so I went straight away to see a solicitor.'

2 'He knows more about the procedure.'

3 'I don't know why I got one.'

4 'The solicitor knows laws to represent you in court, in order to get a proper defence and prepare your case before the magistrates.' (A 'recidivist strategist'.)

5 'It's a good system.'

It will be seen that a number of defendants are fairly inarticulate about the reasons for having a lawyer, and this explains the relatively unfruitful coding of their answers as shown in Table 6.7. One or two points do emerge, however. The small minority of middle-class defendants stood out as being most likely to turn at once to a lawyer as a matter of social routine (see case HG/2; also case 7033, above); the only other group so ready to turn at once to a lawyer were the recidivists with a shrewd knowledge of the system. Similarly, the small number of defendants with limited English were very likely to turn to a lawyer largely because of their language difficulties (see case SN/3), though sometimes they would find a better-educated friend who would then often find a lawyer for them for more 'strategic' reasons. Again, some of the not guilty plea defendants mentioned their plea as being specifically important in relation to getting representation (see cases SN/1 and 2).

Another feature of interest, although not quantified in the table because of small numbers, was that a few defendants in the HG sample actually did not particularly want lawyers, but had them because they had been told by the police (following the Widgery policy) that 'you have to have one for the Crown Court'. One such defendant went so far as to say that the police 'virtually forced him' to have a lawyer; another very reluctant client was subsequently pleased he had been coerced, for the lawyer did such a good job.

More generally, two main themes emerge from the replies, and from the collation of them in Table 6.7. The lawyer's primary role is clearly seen as that of a spokesman, an articulate voice in a strange environment. This emerged strongly also in some of the assessments of lawyers' performances, which we discuss further below. A lawyer who had pleaded passionately on the defendant's behalf, or had made a long speech explaining all facets of the defendant's case, was generally applauded: the man who had left things out, or seemed uninterested in the defendant's case, was unpopular. There is a genuine difficulty here for the lawyer, since performances of this type, while bringing applause from many clients, do not always cut ice with the bench—though we do not think that by any means all negative evaluations of lawyers' performances can be neutralised on this account.

The second theme emerging from the question about reasons for having a lawyer is that of procedural expertise: the defendant is unsure, not only whether he could put his own points clearly but whether he would know when to make them, or indeed understand what is going on at all. The lawyer here is seen acting as a reassuring agent, guiding the defendant through bewilderingly strange territory, as some interview quotations made clear:

> Case 1060 'The lawyer didn't help much, but we felt more secure with him there.'

> Case 1058 'He gave advice and reassurance as well as speaking up for me.'

> Case 5039 'They take all the worry out of your hands. He made me sure there was no need to worry.'

Specifically legal expertise, it will be noticed, is not perceived as particularly important by defendants, especially those in the lower courts. This accurately reflects the realities of court life, for the daily round of cases in the magistrates' courts is remarkably free from legal interest.

As with other decisions, we examined the extent of consultation with others. The replies showed some slight but interesting differences between defendants by plea and by venue (see Table 6.8). Not guilty pleas seemed more likely to talk to 'unofficial' advisers than guilty pleas, but the pattern was reversed for 'official' advisers; summary trial cases were more likely to talk to unofficial advisers, but less likely to talk to the police, than higher court cases.

Choosing a lawyer

Overall, 69 per cent of those represented defendants who were interviewed had used the services of a lawyer (not necessarily the same one) before. Of these, 77 per cent indicated the previous use of a lawyer in criminal cases, 23 per cent for civil work (including 9 per cent matrimonial). A defect in the construction of the interview

Table 6.8 Discussion of legal representation with others

% discussing with	Represented defendants Pleading NG	G	Tried Sum-marily	Higher court	Unrepresented defendants
Wife	15	7	14	5	4
Parents	8	9	15	4	6
Family	6	4	5	4	1
Friends	23	16	16	18	3
Codefendants	18	16	23	11	6
Others in trouble*	10	11	10	12	3
Police	20	31	23	33	9
Lawyer	3	2	2	3	1
Probation officer	6	10	11	7	0
Prison officer	5	9	8	9	0
No one	23	29	19	34	81

*For meaning of this term, see discussion of Table 4.16.

schedule means that we are unable to say what proportion had used a lawyer in both criminal and civil cases. On the available data, it is clear that those pleading not guilty are more likely to have used a lawyer in previous civil cases than are those pleading guilty.

For the interview sample cases, we recorded the name of the solicitor in each case, and were rather surprised to discover that as many as 37 different solicitors had represented our defendants during this six-month research period. Our surprise stemmed from the fact that the observer of the Sheffield court scene is aware of the domination of a few solicitors, but not usually of the number of others undertaking small amounts of work. The pattern of the research caseload (weighted) is clearly set out in Table 6.9.

As we have already explained in chapter 4 the three leading solicitors taken together dominated the scene to the extent of taking 60 per cent of the available cases. This proportion was roughly constant across the various sub-sample categories, except that the 'big three' were, largely due to the previously-mentioned policy of Mr C, particularly heavily represented among the 'D' cases.

Table 6.9 Sheffield solicitors' caseload (interview sample)

Cases	Solicitors
60 or more	3
35-60	0
20-34	2
10-19	5
0-9	27

There have been serious allegations from other parts of the country that a few solicitors resort to corrupt or at least 'sharp' practices to obtain and retain a virtual monopoly of criminal legal aid work. We found no evidence of this in Sheffield, though undoubtedly other solicitors in the city were at the time of the research envious of the monopoly of the big three and anxious to obtain more work themselves. (There is impressionistic evidence that the advent of the duty solicitor scheme has enabled them to do this partially.)

We asked defendants in our sample how they came to choose the particular solicitor they had. We received a bewildering variety of replies, from a nightclub company allocating the company solicitor to defend two 'bouncers' charged with exceeding their duties and committing an assault; through 'my grandma used to know his mother'; to a member of a higher recidivistic family who simply said 'he is the family solicitor'! The following ten randomly chosen extracts give a flavour (we have referred to the 'big three' as Messrs A, B and C as in Table 4.13; all others are called Mr X):

1 'I chose Mr C, but he was engaged so I was allocated Mr X from the legal aid list.'

2 'Father asked around at work and they said Mr X was good.'

3 'I wanted Mr A—my cousin advised him—but I was given Mr X of the same firm.'

4 'Mr B—I've had him before.'

5 'Mr A—my wife went to him for me as I've had him before and he's a good talker.'

6 'Mr X—allocated from the list.'

7 'Mr C—I didn't choose him, they [legal aid] just gave him to me.'

8 'I chose Mr C but he was too busy and recommended Mr X.'

9 'I chose Mr B from the police list, but the police said, no, go for

Mr C, he's best for getting bail.' (Since the police were opposing bail, this was rather strange advice!)

10 'Mr X—I had the same firm, but not Mr X, last time.'

The tabulated replies are shown in Table 6.10. The category 'assigned by court, or chosen from list supplied by court', refers to cases where the defendant did not previously know of the reputation of the solicitor concerned (or at least, did not in fact reveal this to us). We see from the table that these 'blind' representations are in the minority (though they are larger among guilty pleas and among higher court trial cases); the majority select because of reputation (including reputation among other prisoners on remand) and because of prior contacts. The monopoly of the 'big three' was thus sustained much more by what clients wanted than through any action of the clerk's office.[4]

Table 6.10 Choosing a solicitor

% of defendants answering	Pleading NG	Pleading G	Tried Summarily	Tried Higher court
Reputation, recommended by family, friend or acquaintance	37	31	40	25
Assigned by court, or chosen from list supplied by court	3	23	10	26
Knew solicitor (previously used him; personal friend)	26	25	29	21
Chance (e.g. first office passed, he visited next cell)	13	2	6	3
Referred by other lawyer	6	7	3	9
Other answers	15	12	10	15
Total	100	100	100	100

Barristers are of course selected by solicitors, and we naturally did not ask our defendants anything about this choice. For the record, we should say that there were 28 barristers representing the clients in our interview sample; once again, there was an imbalance in the distribution of work, and 5 barristers between them accounted for 58 per cent of the cases.

Satisfied clients?

Lawyers are remarkably sensitive about their image. Previous research has indicated some adverse client reactions, especially to the work of barristers. Zander asked his sample of defendants who had appealed after conviction in the higher courts whether they would recommend a friend to use any of their lawyers in the same kind of situation as they had been in (Zander, 1972a, p.155). Only 33 per cent of those replying would recommend their (junior) barrister; only 36 per cent their solicitor. Zander describes the result as 'a considerable vote of no confidence in the performance of the legal profession'.

In our study lawyers can perhaps claim a qualified vote of confidence. We asked all those in the interview sample, and this did of course include acquitted defendants and those dealt with in the lower courts (and only a very small number of appellants) whether they thought the lawyer had helped them. Where appropriate separate questions were asked in relation to hearings in the magistrates' courts (where representation was always by solicitors); and in the higher courts (where only the barrister speaks in court except in a very occasional case—one, in our interview sample—where the solicitor exercises his right to appear under the Courts Act rule discussed below). The replies are analysed in Table 6.11; if we take 'helped a great deal' and 'helped a little' together as a qualified vote of confidence, then we can see that in every category there is a majority which believes that some help has been given.

Table 6.11 Defendants' assessment of lawyer's performance

% of respondents answering	In magistrates' court			In higher court		
	Ss	Ds	Hs	Ss	Ds	Hs
Helped a great deal	65	45	34	43	57·5	47
Helped a little	28	22·5	30	29	17·5	22
Helped not at all	6	27·5	35	24	15	27
Made matters worse	0	0	0	4	10	4
Don't know	0	5	1	0	0	0·5
Total	100	100	100	100	100	100

We need to explore the differences between barristers and solicitors a little more carefully. In cases which are going for trial at the higher court, the solicitor's public role is relatively limited: he can make bail applications, and appears ritualistically at the committal proceedings, but that is all, except in 'D' cases where he very often helps to make the venue decision. Thus in the 'H' and 'D' cases at the magistrates' court level, solicitors are not perceived as having helped nearly as much as in the 'S' cases where they play the full role of participation in the trial and sentence proceedings; typical defendants' comments in committal cases were:

'Not much—there's not much to do.'

'He didn't do much in the magistrates', but he's a good solicitor.'

'He didn't help at all, there was little he could do as they had decided to send me to the Crown Court.'

The barrister, on the other hand, does have a full role in all higher court cases. However, it can be said that he faces an uphill task in those cases sent up from the magistrates' court for sentence, since one bench has already indicated clearly that a custodial sentence is necessary; and this point is reflected in the rather lower proportion of 'helped a great deal' responses among the barristers' 'S' cases.

There remains an important difference in the evaluation of barristers and solicitors. If we take only the S cases for solicitors (for the reasons stated above), and combine the D and H cases for barristers (where they have full scope), we have the pattern shown in Table 6.12.

Table 6.12 Defendants' evaluation of solicitors and barristers

	Helped great deal	A little	None or worse	Total
Solicitors	65	28	6	100
Barristers	49	21	30	100

The difference is quite marked, particularly in the 'none or worse' category; and it is statistically significant. It could be argued, of course, that the difference arises from a different (more criminally sophisticated) clientele rather than from any real differences in the perceived performances of barristers and solicitors. But the SGR group is, it will be recalled, about as recidivistic as the typical higher court group, so there seems little to support such an argument.

We give below fifteen randomly selected opinions of barristers, and fifteen of solicitors.[5] The difference in the number and quality of negative evaluations is clear; the Bar has very satisfied clients, but it has more dissatisfied ones than the junior branch of the profession:

Solicitors

1 'Helped a great deal—very good. Would definitely recommend to a friend in a similar situation.'

2 He 'tried hard' and 'was good', although the end result was the same (borstal).

3 'A great help—he did his best.'

4 'He was good.'

5 'Seventy per cent of my acquittal was due to him, he did a very good job.'

6 'He helped very much—I was having psychiatric treatment, and he got medical reports prepared and so on.'

7 'Helped a lot—the magistrates would have believed [prosecution witness] and not us without him.'

8 'Yes, he helped.'

9 'He has helped me in past cases, told them my home life, etc. I don't think he helped me this time: I would like to have spoken for myself and said I wanted prison, not hospital' (given hospital order with solicitor's support).

10 'Yes, he helped, and gave a very good speech, but it was the probation officer who got me the conditional discharge.'

11 'Yes, he did help, but there were other factors involved [in the result].'

12 'Definitely helped. He put it over much better than me. They must have listened to him, I suppose.'

13 'Yes, he was good.'

14 'Helped a tremendous amount, he gave good advice and reassured me as well as speaking for me.'

15 'He helped a lot, he put over our case in a simplified way for benefit of the magistrates. But he could have done better, especially if we had slipped him a bit.' (This case is an alternative life-style strategist, case no. 1009, described in chapter 3.)

Barristers

1 'He helped a great deal, did all he could.'

2 'Not very much—he didn't do very well, especially at the end [i.e. plea of mitigation]; he said stupid things about me and was very bad.'

3 'I don't think he put up any fight—he wasn't very good—he just wasn't bothered about it.'

4 'He wasn't very good.'

5 'He did the best he could, and the result was a lot better than I expected. He put into words what I could never have said.'

6 'He helped a lot—I wouldn't have got off [been acquitted] without him.'

7 'He was very good in court, he put my case really well.'

8 'He was very good indeed, he did all he could.'

9 'He was terrible—he didn't help at all. He only saw me for two minutes and he knew nothing about the case.'

10 'He did his best but he got confused by the facts.'

11 'He helped to put my case clearly: I can't speak English well.'

12 'He helped quite a lot, but they've not got much time [to prepare case]—the probation officer helped more.'

13 'He did his best—I won't complain.'

14 'It was very good the way he put my case over.'

15 'He helped a lot—the way he brought up my family background and so on.'

This difference in evaluation has some possible policy implications. Under the Courts Act 1971, s.12, the Lord Chancellor may at any time direct that solicitors have rights of audience in the Crown Court in the type of proceedings specified in the order. Directions have been issued granting fairly general rights of audience in some specific towns where the Crown Court sits; more generally a direction covering the whole country enables a solicitor to appear in the Crown Court 'on an appeal from a magistrates' court, or on committal of a person for sentence or to be dealt with, provided that he or a partner in or an employee of his firm appeared on behalf of the defendant in the magistrates' court' (see Cross and Jones, 1972, p.372). As we have noted, this did not lead in Sheffield to any immediate exercise on a wide scale of solicitors' representation in 'S' cases in the Crown Court; and we understand this is still the case. There is no doubt, however, that some of our respondents would prefer solicitors to be bolder in exercising this right of audience, and some of them also would have welcomed a wider use of the Lord Chancellor's power, to allow representation by solicitors in 'H' and 'D' cases in the Crown Court.

Linked with this is the apparent late arrival of the Bar to the case: a sore point with many defendants was that they only saw their barrister for a few minutes just before the final court hearing. We asked explicitly when respondents first saw their barrister. Of those committed for trial and pleading guilty, 96 per cent had not seen him until the morning of the hearing, and another 3 per cent only the day before. In relation to those committed for sentence, the corresponding figures were 87 per cent and 9 per cent. A different pattern was expected for defendants pleading not guilty in the higher courts, but the difference was not as great as expected. Seventy-nine per cent of those defendants waited until the morning of the hearing to meet the barrister, 9 per cent had seen him the day before and another 9 per cent in the week preceding the trial. Although no question was asked about this, a number of defendants added that when they did meet the barrister there was insufficient time to discuss the case.

Many members of the Bar would argue strongly that it is no part of their duty to get to know the defendant, and that it is often better for the defendant that he should not speak at any length to his counsel before the trial. Counsel's task, they would assert, is to master his brief and to make professional judgments upon it, judgments which will often not be understood by the defendant.

From many defendants' point of view, that is no answer at all. The defendant, as we have seen, regards the lawyer as his spokesman, who can put into words what he, the defendant, wants to say. From this perspective, the barrister who does not spend time getting to know his client cannot be an adequate spokesman.

In this area there is an interesting paradox in our data. We have seen (chapter 5) that plea-changing in the Crown Court is not uncommon, and is predominantly due to barristers' last-minute advice. Most of the defendants in these cases have been encouraged to plead not guilty by their solicitors, and we know from private conversations with barristers that solicitors are not infrequently regarded as grossly over-optimistic in this kind of advice. Yet the Bar, priding itself on its greater professional competence, turns out to be more negatively assessed by its lay clients. Almost certainly, an important element in this contrast is the better 'bedside manner' of the solicitors, who have much greater contact with the defendant and are perceived as caring more about his case.

A further related point concerns the advocate's strategy. In connection with pleas of mitigation of sentence, complaints were quite often made against the Bar (but much more rarely of solicitors) that some particular point or other should have been introduced, or some witness called. Such a point was regarded as crucial by the defendant, but was apparently omitted or thrown away by the barrister. It may be that the barrister knows much better than the defendant what is the 'right' thing to say to please the judge, but that point is lost on the defendants—especially as, they complained, barristers often did not come to see them after the case was over. If the Bar wants to improve its image with defendants, it could do worse than ensure it always sees defendants after cases, and explains why particular evidence was not introduced. On the other hand, some of our defendants would want more than this. Not infrequently they complained, in represented cases at both magistrates' and Crown Court (but especially the latter), that they had not been asked what they had to say:

> 'I wasn't asked to make a speech in the Crown Court—I should have been.'
>
> 'When they're about to sentence, they don't ask what *you* have to say.'
>
> 'I wanted to speak for myself—I thought I'd be allowed to do that.'

Under the old law as to trial for felonies in the higher courts, abolished with the demise of the felony/misdemeanour distinction in 1967, the defendant had to be asked before sentence 'Have you anything to say why the court should not give you judgment according to law?' This was meant to enable the defendant to take legal points, but he often responded, if he grasped what was going on at all, by making a personal plea in mitigation. One judge (Glynn-Jones, J, in R. v. Rear, 2 March 1965) described this 'allocutus' as an archaic appendage which dangled uselessly on the body of a criminal trial. His call for its abolition was supported in editorial comment in the *Criminal Law Review* (1965, p. 190) which referred to the empty ritual, and the 'unsurprising appearance in many judges of a lack of interest in the prisoner's response'. All this gives insufficient weight to the defendant's view. A more conversational form of the allocutus, giving the defendant a chance to have a final word could well be helpful to him and perhaps to the court. Some at least of our defendants would have greatly appreciated it. Perhaps consideration should be given to its introduction.[6]

We raised a final few questions about the effects of legal representation. Respondents were asked if they thought that their sentence would have been different if they had not been represented. Overall, 33 per cent replied that their sentence would definitely have been heavier, and 18 per cent thought it possibly would have been. Eight per cent said that it would have been lighter but for the lawyer's misguided efforts. The remaining 41 per cent thought that it would have made no difference, or didn't know.

So far as the actual verdict was concerned, of the 21 respondents who had successfully pleaded not guilty, 11 thought that they would have been convicted if they had not had legal representation, 8 felt that they would still have been acquitted, and 2 didn't know.

A final question was whether the respondent in any way regretted having had a lawyer. Only 10 per cent said 'yes', but the greatest dissatisfaction was among the HGs, those who seem to get the worst service from the Bar.

Unrepresented defendants

The unrepresented defendants in the interview sample were all tried summarily; 69 pleaded guilty, 3 not guilty (but were convicted). All were asked whether they had thought of having legal representation in their present case; 78 per cent said they had not. As the last column of Table 6.8 shows, there was little discussion of the question between unrepresented defendants and others. Of the advice they received, 71 per cent were actually in favour of getting a solicitor, advice which was not followed.

In fact a majority of unrepresented defendants (55 per cent) had used a lawyer in previous cases, 30 per cent in criminal and 25 per cent in civil cases (including 16 per cent matrimonial cases). Although quite high, this indicates a smaller previous use of lawyers, notably in criminal cases, than among the group represented at some stage in their present case.

This information leaves the impression that there is a sizeable group of defendants who would never contemplate making use of a lawyer. Table 6.13 gives some further pointers; it summarises the answers to the question why the unrepresented defendants decided not to have a solicitor. Some of the 48 per cent giving the answer 'it wasn't worth it, no point' may be referring to the triviality of the offence, but this is more likely to be the almost instinctive negative reaction to the idea of using a solicitor. The same may be true of some rather more sophisticated replies, such as one we received that 'a lawyer would have taken time, given a lot of irrelevant information and made no difference'.

Table 6.13 Reasons for not using a solicitor

% of unrepresented defendants answering	
It wasn't worth it, no point	48
I couldn't afford it	21
Offence too trivial	12
No time to arrange it	10
Wanted to get it over with, I was guilty	7

On the other hand it is true to say that we did observe cases where a lawyer manifestly made no difference, e.g. as between codefendants, one represented and one not, where both received the same fine. Some of the shrewder SGUs spotted this, either before or after the case:

> Case 2021 'What's the point? You pay for the lawyer and still get the same fine.'

> Case 2005 'I was working late and had no time to go to a lawyer. Jack [codefendant] did, but he's no better off—he got the same fine and he's got no previous.'

(In some of these cases, of course, an unrepresented defendant will have derived benefit from the plea in mitigation put forward on behalf of a codefendant, for such a plea may draw attention to factors which apply to the offence as a whole and are not personal to the codefendant).

The answer 'I couldn't afford it' needs some further examination. Of all the unrepresented defendants, only 6 per cent said that they had not known of the existence of legal aid. At the other extreme, one defendant had actually applied for legal aid and been refused it; he did not know why. He did actually go ahead and consult a solicitor, but was not represented when he eventually pleaded guilty. As to the remaining defendants, 4 per cent had not applied for legal aid because they thought they would be above the income limit, 66 per cent just did not bother, and the rest gave other reasons.

We investigated the comparative incidence of these two main reasons for lack of representation—'not worth it, no point', and 'couldn't afford it'—by the various groups of the defendants' typology. Table 6.14 shows the results: 'strategist' defendants and unrepresented first-timers never gave 'not worth it' as their reason, while 'passive' (including dissociative) defendants were particularly likely to give this as their reason. Recidivist strategists were much the most likely to give the answer that they couldn't afford a lawyer.

Table 6.14 Reasons for not using a solicitor, by defendants' typology

	% answering		
	'Not worth it, no point'	'Couldn't afford it'	Other
Recidivist strategists	—	50	50
Other strategists	—	25	75
Respectable first-timers	—	29	71
Right-assertive	—	—	—
Ordinary respondents	39	18	43
Dissociative	50	7	43
Other passive	53	10	37
Other-dominated respondents	50	—	50
External circumstances	40	20	40
Miscellaneous	—	6	94

All unrepresented defendants were asked what they thought they might have to pay for a lawyer, had they had one. The answers are shown in Table 6.15.

Table 6.15 Unrepresented defendants' estimates of lawyers' costs

	%
More than £50	3
£20<£50	15
£10<£20	18
£ 5<£10	24
Less than £5	3
Don't know	38
Total	100

Thirteen per cent thought that they would have to pay something even under legal aid. We did not probe further to see if the contributory element in legal aid was understood.

An oddity of design in the interview schedule led to respondents being asked two, closely related, questions: 'Looking back on it now, do you think a lawyer would have helped you in your particular case?' and 'Now that the case is all over, do you in any way regret that you did not have a lawyer?' Thirty-two per cent answered 'yes' to the first question, but only 15 per cent 'yes' to the second. This can be explained in a number of ways: there may well be some defendants who recognise the advantages of having a solicitor but did not want the fuss and bother of getting hold of one. Or it may be that the second question invites the respondent to admit directly that he made a wrong decision, the former asking that only indirectly. As many as 37·5 per cent of the unrepresented, convicted defendants said that a solicitor might have led to a lighter sentence; it is surprising that so many took this view yet did not take steps to realise their expectation.

We attempted to assess the performance of unrepresented defendants in court. The only way we could do this was to note the statement made by the defendant in mitigation and classify it as an extended statement, a very brief statement or nothing worthwhile. This is a purely quantitative assessment; silence may be the best policy, and magistrates sometimes feel, and may even show, irritation at the verbosity of some solicitors. Only 2 per cent of such defendants in our court sample made an extended statement, 28 per cent a very brief statement and 70 per cent said nothing or nothing worthwhile. Women defendants were rather more loquacious than men, with 35 per cent in the 'brief statement' groups as against 26 per cent for men.

It remains to consider briefly four unusual cases. We have seen that virtually no one is unrepresented in the Crown Court; in our interview sample there was only one such case, an SGU sent to the higher court for sentence. He was in fact offered legal aid, and refused it; his grounds for doing so were unusual, to say the least. He claimed he had been made a promise by the police, with his wife there to witness it, that if he pleaded guilty they would put in a good word to ensure that D did not go to prison. The police were said to be most anxious to secure the guilty plea in order not to have to expose a police informer to giving evidence in the witness box. D agreed to the deal, and then consistently refused offers of legal aid from court personnel because he could see no point in a lawyer in view of the police's promise to help him avoid imprisonment. In the event the police said nothing in his favour, at least publicly, and D received 12 months' imprisonment; he was very upset about this, regretted not having a lawyer, and regretted even more not having mentioned the police bargain in his own statement in court. Our court observer, however, thought his own statement very moving and arguably better than a professional plea of mitigation.

The other three unusual cases are the three interviewed SNUs. One of these (case no. 8014) actually pleaded guilty to begin with, but then said in his own explanation to the court that he thought the car (from which he was said to have stolen a car seat) was derelict. The bench said this was equivalent to a not guilty plea, suggested that he should plead not guilty, and then, when he had done so, adjourned the case for six weeks in the usual Sheffield fashion for not guilty pleas. S, the defendant, who had never been in court before, misunderstood the nature of what had happened; he thought he had in effect been found not guilty, and that the second court appearance was to be a pure formality to give him an official acquittal. He was angry and upset when he found this was not so, and even more so that the happenings in the first court were never referred to at the second appearance, which was before a different bench. To make matters worse, much of the evidence he wanted to give was ruled out as hearsay, a rule which (despite being an intelligent and articulate trade union official) he found totally bewildering. He had not taken his witnesses, nor had he got a lawyer, because he had not thought they would be necessary at the 'formal' second hearing. Hardly surprisingly, he was found guilty, but he felt the second hearing was very unfair, and was annoyed about the loss of time and money involved, given that he had begun by pleading guilty.

The other two SNUs were not based on this kind of misunderstanding. One of them, however, said rather similarly that he had not got a lawyer because 'something in my mind told me not to apply for legal aid, I kept thinking the case would be dropped'; the other—a mature student at a local college—gave expense and the fact that 'legal aid takes a long time' as his reasons for not getting a lawyer (he had eight weeks!). Both of them, like the first defendant S, now regretted they hadn't had lawyers: as one of them put it, 'I didn't know what questions to ask'.

All our three SNUs were somewhat bewildered by the role they were supposed to play at a contested trial, with cross-examination and so forth. Under the Sheffield policy of generally granting legal aid for not guilty pleas all three of them would very likely have been granted aid had they sought it. This seems clearly right; it is obvious that an unrepresented defendant has the greatest difficulty in handling the procedural complexities of a contested case. One has to say, however, that such a view, and the Sheffield practice, goes beyond the Widgery criteria for legal aid in magistrates' courts. The Widgery Committee said, in a passage we consider very doubtful, that:

> We do not suggest that the need for professional cross-examination exists in every summary case where the defendant wishes to contest the charge, or indeed in more than a small fraction of such cases. The large majority of cases are straightforward and the facts are uncomplicated and clear-cut (para. 175).[7]

Legal aid

Legal aid is, as already indicated, available in all types of criminal proceeding. Orders are made by the court, which usually means the clerk or a magistrate in private, 'if it appears to the court desirable to do so in the interests of justice' but only if the means of the defendant are such that he requires assistance in meeting the costs of his defence (see Legal Aid Act 1974, s.29(1)(2) replacing identical legislation in force at the time of the research).

Table 6.16 presents information from our interview data about the defendants' actions concerning legal aid, and their sources of information. The very small proportion applying for and being refused legal aid is in line with previous published data for Sheffield. Of those who did not apply, it is interesting that 'too much trouble/not worth it' was a far more common reason than that the defendant thought himself too rich; this is consistent with the reasons for not seeking representation at all, as discussed in the preceding section.

Two comments can be made about the second half of Table 6.16. One is that here, as elsewhere, we have a small but significant proportion of defendants with experience of civil legal proceedings or business in the past. The idea, held in one form or another by many people, that the 'criminal' and 'other' clientele of a solicitor are totally distinct groups is clearly unjustified.

Table 6.16 Legal aid

	Tried summarily	Tried in higher courts
(a) % of defendants		
Obtained legal aid	20	97
Applied and refused	2	0
Did not apply		
too much trouble	50	0
thought too rich	5	2
other reasons	18	1
Total	73	3
Did not know of legal aid	5	0
(b) Source of information		
Own experience of criminal cases	21	21
Own experience of civil cases	7	6
From family	0	2
From friend or acquaintance	6	3
From others in prison/cells	2	2
Police: oral advice	6	8
leaflet	30	18
Solicitor's advice	7	14
Advice from bench in court	1	10
General knowledge	13	7
Other answers	6	10
Total	100	100

The other concerns the police leaflet. In Sheffield all criminal charges are formally made at a central Charge Office, and a leaflet about legal aid is handed to each person charged. We believe that this procedure was followed scrupulously during the research period. That a large proportion of defendants failed to mention the leaflet (they were not prompted on this point) and that some reported ignorance of legal aid to the end of the case, or until the bench itself suggested that legal aid be sought, suggests that here—as in many other contexts—leaflets alone are not enough. It remains to be seen whether 'duty solicitor' schemes will prove fully effective in this area.

In his study of the defendant's view of the criminal justice system in Connecticut, Casper (1972, chapter 4) noted that defendants who engaged their own lawyer were much more likely to express satisfaction with his performance than were defendants represented by the 'public defender's office', the official agency handling the cases of defendants who in England would be entitled to seek free legal aid. The two systems are very dissimilar, but we examined our data on lawyers' performance for any differences between legally aided and other defendants.

In answering the questions about the helpfulness of lawyers (as shown in general terms in Table 6.11), more of those without legal aid said that their solicitor had helped a great deal, and fewer that he helped not at all, than in the case of legally aided defendants. This is in the same direction as in Casper's study, but in our case the difference was not statistically significant. On the other hand, when asked whether they now regretted having had a lawyer, 31 per cent of not guilty pleaders paying their own bills did regret it, as against only 5 per cent of those on legal aid. This was a significant difference ($P<0{\cdot}01$), though it was not replicated among the guilty pleaders: possibly there is among the not guilty pleaders who have been convicted a strong feeling that their own money has been wasted. Overall, then, the results are not clear-cut, but certainly the English legal aid system for criminal cases is not viewed with anything like as much disfavour as that with which American defendants apparently view the public defender system.

One final case about legal aid may be mentioned:

> Case 1031 S appeared in police custody, charged with burglary. The police sought a remand in custody for 3 days. S was asked by the clerk whether he had 'any application to make'. He said yes, he wanted to apply for legal aid. The clerk said 'never mind that, we can deal with that later, we're considering bail now. Do you wish to apply for bail?' S did, but was unsuccessful. The question of legal aid was not mentioned again in open court, but at his second appearance S appeared with a solicitor on legal aid (the prosecution at this point had no objection to bail).

It is appreciated that legal aid is normally dealt with 'behind the scenes' and that it is administratively more convenient that this should be so. It seems scarcely defensible, however, for a court to ignore a legitimate application made in open court, as in this case (and this was not unique in our sample). Perhaps more seriously, the case raises the issue how far legal aid should be granted in bail application cases. The current practice, in line with Widgery criteria, is not to take this matter specifically into consideration. Yet if we are to treat (as the Widgery Committee wishes us to treat) deprivation of liberty as a serious matter, then perhaps deprivation of liberty awaiting trial or sentence is also a serious matter, and possibly the whole issue should be reconsidered. One defendant (not no. 1031) who had been kept in custody then given legal aid and won bail against police opposition summed this up: 'If we'd had a lawyer first time, we might have stood a chance of bail then.' Once again, the advent of the duty solicitor may alter practice in this area.

7 Appeal

The criminal process may be thought to come to an end when the defendant is convicted and sentenced. The finding as to guilt or innocence, and the sentencing of the guilty, are the natural culmination of the process to which the earlier decisions as to venue, plea and legal representation have contributed. The defendant can now look back and consider what, if anything, went wrong. He may regret some of his own decisions. He may be bitter at the actions of the judge or the magistrates or the police. He may nurse recriminations against his lawyers. As one interviewed defendant said, if he is in prison he has all the time in the world for thoughts like that.

In a sense, an appeal is an artificial extension of the criminal process. No author of a courtroom drama would think of adding a fourth act in which appeal judges deliberate on whether the trial judge made an error in his summing-up on a point of law, or whether the sentence was wrong in principle. The play is over. This is how it seems to many defendants, who reject the idea of an appeal as a useless prolongation of the whole business. They might as well serve their sentence, live it all down.

Despite all this, and the inevitable absence of data on appeals in our court sample, we thought it right to include questions as to appeal in our interview schedule. For almost every convicted defendant there is some possibility of an appeal, and the decision whether or not to exercise the right of appeal is basically no different from the other decisions we have studied.

The great majority of defendants convicted in the magistrates' court have the right of appeal to the Crown Court. If the defendant pleaded not guilty, he can appeal against his conviction or sentence or both; if he pleaded guilty, he can appeal against the sentence. (In law, 'sentence' here does not include certain orders, notably probation orders and conditional discharges; it follows that a man who pleads guilty and is put on probation has no right of appeal—see Magistrates' Courts Act 1952, s. 83—though there are other procedures open to him if he wishes to challenge some ruling on a point of law.)

In our interview sample, only 0·5 per cent of defendants convicted in the magistrates' court appealed: which actually means two defendants, both of whom were represented and pleaded guilty (i.e. SGRs). This overall figure is about the proportion one would expect from the national picture, as shown in the *Criminal Statistics*.

Defendants dealt with in the higher courts have more limited rights. Unless they can raise a point of law they must, before being allowed to appeal, successfully seek leave to appeal from the Court of Appeal—and this applies whether they are seeking to challenge their conviction or sentence. Nationally only some 16 per cent of applicants were granted leave to appeal in 1972; leave to appeal against conviction is very seldom granted to a man who pleaded guilty at his trial. If an applicant for leave to appeal is serving a custodial sentence, he runs a special risk: if the Court of Appeal, or the single judge who first examines the application, decides that the appeal is wholly without merit, the prisoner may be told that some or all of the period he has spent in prison awaiting the result of his application for leave to appeal will not count towards his sentence (Criminal Appeal Act 1968, s. 29; Practice Note issued by Lord Parker, CJ, [1970] 1 All E.R. 1119; see, generally, Zander, 1972a). This rule is discussed further below.

Eleven per cent of our Sheffield sample convicted in the higher courts applied for leave to appeal, as against a national figure of 13 per cent (*Criminal Statistics 1972,* table V).

The appellants

We asked all the defendants in our interview sample (and it will be remembered that this was exclusively male) whether they intended to appeal. Eleven said they planned to appeal, and a further 15 were uncertain at the time of the interview. The staff of the courts concerned were able to supply us with information about subsequent action by these 26 men, and with the outcome of those appeals which they made. It is possible that some of those who told us that they had no intention of appealing later changed their minds, but we think it unlikely, and we did not feel justified in asking the court staff to make the necessary searches to trace any such cases.

In the event there were only 12 men (3 per cent of the whole sample) who took formal steps to appeal. Of the 11 who told us that they planned to appeal, 9 did so, though one abandoned his application for leave to appeal before a decision was reached by the

Court of Appeal. Three of those who were undecided at the time of the interview later gave notice of appeal, but 2 subsequently abandoned their appeals.

The striking feature of the appellants is that without exception they had received a custodial sentence. The decision for or against an appeal is overwhelmingly a reaction to the sentence; this is true even of many who pleaded not guilty. In 7 of the 12 appeal cases (63 per cent, as reweighted) it was the defendant's reaction to his custodial sentence which dominated his decision to appeal; in a further 3 cases (20 per cent) it was a denial of guilt which was the principal motivation.

With such a small number of appellants, detailed statistical treatment is obviously inappropriate. It was interesting to note, however, that the appellants were entirely confined to three sub-sample groups, namely the SGRs, the HGs and the HNs. When we 'weight' these three sub-sample groups in the appropriate way, as many as two-thirds of the appellants are from the HG category; but looked at in another way, only 11 per cent of all the HGs appealed, as against 15 per cent of the HNs, with the SGRs well down at 4 per cent. The complete absence of SGUs from the appeal group is unsurprising, but one might have expected some of the convicted SNs to challenge that result; even more so, one might have thought that the Ds (who had after all taken the trouble to insist on a Crown Court trial) might have been more assertive of appeal rights than they were.

In terms of the defendants' typology, no one type was particularly strongly represented among the appellants, though the largest single group was of 'strategists' of one kind or another (3 cases, or 23 per cent of cases as reweighted). Two appellant-defendants were classed as predominantly 'passive'; this may seem strange when they are among such a small group who have made the final protest of an appeal, but in both cases there had been a marked passivity in earlier decisions taken, and this led us to group them as passives despite the subsequent appeal.

We set out below brief details of the 12 appellants; in each case we give in parentheses at the beginning the sub-sample group and the typology category. We begin with the only 2 of the 12 whose appeals were in any way successful:

Case 1036 (SGR; 'recidivist strategist') Pleaded guilty in the magistrates' court to charges of burglary of a shop and of going equipped with tools for burglary. He had been arrested in the shop, not having taken anything, and his solicitor in mitigation gave a full account of his domestic problems which included the eviction of himself, the girl he was living with and their 3-month-old child on account of the non-payment of rent by the girl's father, whose house it was. After a retirement, the magistrates announced sentences of 6 months' imprisonment on both charges, 'to run concurrently'. The chairman then corrected this to 'consecutively', which meant a total of 12 months.

The defendant thought this correction very unfair, and also said that he did not think the magistrates had heard all the circumstances. The Crown Court allowed his appeal to the extent that the original sentence, 6 months concurrently on each charge, was restored.

Case 6043 (HG; other-dominated respondent) This was also an unsuccessful burglary. The defendant, M, ran away from the door of a shop when disturbed by a policeman. He was chased and waved a gun. He was none the less arrested, and the gun was found to be a plastic imitation. M had a long record, having received sentences totalling 10½ years since 1962, and being described as thoroughly institutionalised. He was convicted of attempted aggravated burglary, going equipped with tools for burglary and using an imitation firearm to resist arrest. He pleaded guilty. He received concurrent sentences of 5 years, 18 months and 8 years, the judge explaining the last sentence by saying that the use of firearms, real or imitation, would be heavily punished. He commended the police officer's bravery. M's counsel suggested an appeal, and the 8-year sentence was reduced to 6 years by the Court of Appeal. In its judgment, the Court of Appeal mentioned M's excellent reports from the warden of a hostel for ex-prisoners, who blamed M's further offences on his genuine inability to find work. The court based its reduction in the length of sentence on the fact that M had pleaded guilty; the trial judge 'did not give him any credit for that plea and we are inclined to think that some effect might be given to it'. M also complained to our interviewer that the police had broken his nose, and would not allow him a doctor until his solicitor insisted; he had written to the Chief Constable but had received no reply at the time of our interview. The Court of Appeal noted this complaint of police violence in its judgment, but made no comment.

One other appellant had his full appeal actually heard; he was sentenced in the magistrates' court, so could appeal as of right to the Crown Court:

> Case 1014 (SGR; 'ordinary respondent') G, 50 years old, was convicted on a guilty plea of burglary of a store and the theft of goods worth £186, and sentenced to 6 months' imprisonment. He was very angry at the sentence, describing the magistrates as 'employers and shopowners'. He had a similar conviction but that was ten years previously, and an ailing wife; he had expected a suspended sentence, as had his solicitor. His appeal failed, the Crown Court judge telling him to 'take your sentence like a man'.

All the above cases were dominated by the defendant's reaction to his custodial sentence. As already noted, there were in all 7 cases where this was so; the next 2 we give were ones in which dismay at the sentence was coupled with acute dissatisfaction with the performance of counsel:

> Case 6016 (HG; passive respondent) G, aged 26, received a sentence of 3 years' imprisonment on charges of causing grievous bodily harm to his cohabitee and actual bodily harm to the man with whom she was considering living. During proceedings in the magistrates' court, the girl said that she had provoked G, and now wanted him back. G complained bitterly that his counsel did not call her in the Crown Court, nor was he, G, allowed to say anything. The sentence was more than he expected; the judge was 'a tough one'. He applied for leave to appeal against sentence, but leave was refused.

> Case 1088 (SGR; passive respondent) J, aged 27, lived in a hostel for ex-prisoners. He was on probation and subject to a 2-year suspended sentence. He broke into an office in which he had earlier done some repairs, and stole stamps worth £2. He was ordered to serve the 2 years, with a further 18 months for the latest offence. He told the interviewer that he had not expected that he would have to serve the suspended sentence (though it is difficult to see any basis for such a belief), and was very angry with his barrister who failed to hand in a letter

to the court J had written, did not say what J wanted said, and had 'told J off' in the cells. Speaking of his appeal, J said 'It's pride really. I am bitter about the way the lawyers dealt with my case'. He was refused leave to appeal.

Of the remaining appeals in which sentence considerations are dominant, one is of a young man whose decision to appeal was strongly influenced by his father's advice, the other an Irishman whose case was complicated by the presence of co-defendants:

Case 6015 (HG; alternative-society strategist) Aged 18, the defendant was the son of a well-known local Communist, whose views about the legal system he shared. He was convicted of two burglaries involving theft of goods worth almost £300. He asked for 4 other burglaries to be taken into consideration, and his previous record involved 20 other such offences. He was sent by the Crown Court to borstal. A very assured and articulate man, he told the interviewer that he was not a criminal, but was driven to burglaries because of his domestic responsibilities. 'Law is there to protect capital, to protect those who have, not the have-nots.' His lawyer had advised that there were no grounds for appeal, but his father had urged him to appeal because he thought he should have been given 'a chance'. Later his father had visited the borstal and declared that it was not bad, and the defendant was, at the time of our interview, not bothered if the appeal failed. In fact he later abandoned his appeal.

Case 7004 (HN; 'external circumstances') C, an Irishman aged 22, was given a 2-year sentence for taking a car without the owner's consent and obtaining cash with forged cheques, having found a cheque book in the car. He had previously served a similar sentence and been in borstal. The case was complicated by the fact that C's codefendant, E, who was in the group 'uncertain about appealing' had been convicted on 2 indictments alleging offences ranging from theft to forgery to possessing drugs; C had spent a long time in custody awaiting trial, and the probation officer had recommended a suspended sentence. C did give notice of appeal against sentence, but abandoned it later.

Of the remaining 5 appellants, 3 were primarily motivated to appeal by their belief that they were innocent, though one had actually pleaded guilty:

Case 6035 (HG; 'external circumstances') R, a Hungarian with imperfect English, pleaded guilty to charges of theft (2) and obtaining by deception (2), for which he was sentenced to 15 months. He was sentenced to a further 21 months on charges of taking a lorry without the owner's consent, driving while disqualified, and driving without insurance. He had pleaded guilty to these charges also, but now reverted to his earlier view, which he said some police officers shared, that his conduct in respect of the lorry did not amount to an offence. The point he had in mind was unclear to our interviewer, but he felt his barrister had let him down. He applied for leave to appeal against conviction and sentence, but was refused.

Case 7029 (HN; insufficient data to code typology) S, a Jamaican aged 27, was convicted of robbery and wounding. He was defended by two counsel who made an unsuccessful plea for a postponement of the trial to enable two men to be found. He was convicted after the jury had been out for 2½ hours, and was sentenced to 10 years' imprisonment. He refused to be interviewed except on the question of appeal—the interviewer, who had seen the trial, noted that she had expected that—but he did tell us in no uncertain terms that he was appealing against a wrongful conviction: 'There is no such thing as justice if you are black.' His application for leave to appeal was refused.

Case 7003 (HN; 'right-assertive') (see also chapter 3) E, aged 25, faced alternative charges of burglary and theft and of handling stolen goods. The goods had been found in his house and the prosecution case was that he had taken part in the burglary; a letter stolen from the house in question was found in his pocket. E's counsel advised him to plead guilty to the handling charge; he refused, and was convicted of the more serious charge. His reaction to appeal has been detailed in chapter 3; he was eventually refused leave to appeal against his conviction and sentence.

The final 2 cases are in different ways rather pathetic. They each made a deep impression on our interviewer; the two cases have the common feature that the defendants did not see themselves as criminals:

Case 6013 (HG; respectable first-timer) H, aged 47, had 1 minor conviction 28 years previously. He was an epileptic, a heavy drinker, a gambler, who had several times taken overdoses of drugs. After one such incident he discharged himself from hospital, got drunk, and wounded his wife with a knife. The wound was not serious, and his wife (rather reluctantly, thought the judge) was willing to take him back once more. Medical reports were obtained, but no mental disorder was revealed. The judge imposed a sentence of 3 years' imprisonment to protect his family. At the interview he was obviously ill, shaking the whole time, and said that he had had sixteen blackouts since coming to prison. He said that he deserved to be punished 'but not like this': 'I am completely broken . . . I shouldn't be here in prison. I should be at home working and keeping my wife and children. [He had worked for the same firm for twenty-four years.] I am not a criminal . . . I want to be an asset to my wife and family, not a burden.' He complained that his barrister had not seen him after the trial, but his solicitor approved of his appeal. Leave was refused.

Case 7034 (HN; middle-class strategist) This case has been detailed in chapter 5 as a case where a 'plea-bargain' was offered to but rejected by the defendant. He had been on bail throughout his 16-month wait from first police interviews to final trial, but for the last night of the trial he was kept in custody, in a police cell the walls of which had pictures drawn in human excrement. Despite a moving plea based on that experience and its effect on the defendant, a sentence of 21 months' imprisonment was imposed. This the defendant considered very severe: 'After thirty-two years of service to the community and my firm I get 21 months.' He compared his own case with those of his cell-mates, a 'bully' who got 18 months for pushing a glass into a man's face, and a 'sad case' in for a year for wounding his wife; as against them, his own sentence of 21 months was 'very unfair'. His application for leave to appeal against conviction and sentence was later abandoned, probably on his counsel's advice; counsel was studying the transcript at the time of our interview.

As will have been seen, these 12 cases have little in common with one another. The presence of a custodial sentence in every case has been noted, and in a majority of cases sentence factors are uppermost.

Defendants who considered an appeal

Fourteen interviewed defendants said at the time of our interview that they intended or were uncertain as to appeal, but subsequently made no formal steps towards an appeal. When these cases were examined it was found that the pattern was not quite the same as among the appellants. Six of the 14 (21 per cent as reweighted) were maintaining their innocence (3 of these were in prison, 3 had received non-custodial sentences). Four (39 per cent) were most concerned about the sentence they had received. Two were men in their 50s convicted for the first time in many years, and fined; they were clearly wounded in their pride, and talked of an appeal, but it was no surprise to discover that they did not in fact give notice of appeal. In the remaining 2 cases, one involving an Adeni with limited English, no clear reason for an appeal was given.

Considered by sub-sample group, the 14 cases are more diverse than the appellants: DNs, DGs and SNs are all present, as indeed are all sub-samples except, again, the SGUs. As with the appellants, a majority (57 per cent) of those who considered an appeal but did not make one came from the HG group; but once again, the highest proportion of possible appeals were in the HN category. In all 27 per cent of the HNs, 20 per cent of the HGs, but only 7 per cent of the Ds, considered or made appeals; among the S cases the proportions were generally lower, and the overall percentage for the whole sample was 6 (16 among those in custody).

In terms of the defendants' typology, strategists (29 per cent) and right-assertive defendants (14 per cent) constitute somewhat larger proportions of those who considered appeals than of those who actually made them. This surprising result emphasises further the miscellaneous nature of the actual appeal sample.

Of those who considered but did not make appeals, those who denied their guilt are perhaps the most interesting. Of the 6 cases in this group, 4 made accusations against the police to explain their convictions; the other 2 deserve fuller summaries:

> Case 5033 B was charged with attempted burglary of a shop. He had previous convictions for burglary, theft and indecent assault, but the evidence on this occasion was only circumstantial. Three men were seen running away from a shop by a police officer, and three men, including B, were later found in a derelict house. The most notable feature of [illegible] was the repeated interruption of defence counsel's [illegible] by the

judge who complained of its irrelevance. Our observer described the animosity between judge and counsel as 'open and embarrassing'. This won counsel golden opinions from B, who described his 'fight' as 'terrific'. B was convicted, and sentenced to 9 months' imprisonment. He planned to appeal because he was not guilty, but the lawyers said that there were no grounds. No application was actually made.

Case 7009 This case arose out of a brawl in a public house. The defendant, B, was certainly involved but there was great dispute as to which of the parties started the fight and who intervened to break it up. B was convicted of assault occasioning actual bodily harm on the publican, but only by a majority verdict of 10 votes to 2 after the jury had been out for over 6 hours. He received a suspended sentence. He denied his guilt, said he was 'furious with the case'. His solicitor had promised to write a letter to B advising about an appeal, but had not done so at the time of interview: no appeal was subsequently made.

The two cases show also the importance of legal advice as to an appeal. Of those who were uncertain about an appeal at the time of our interview (including the 3 who did subsequently appeal), over 60 per cent said they were waiting for legal advice and would rely on it: typical comments were:

'Barrister's opinion will decide it.'

'I will decide when I speak to the solicitor and see his reactions.'

'Barrister said no grounds; but solicitor has been fair with us and we want to ask his advice when he returns from holiday.'

'I will rely entirely on solicitor's opinion.'

This last comment came from a recidivist strategist who had previously described his solicitor as 'hopeless' in the handling of bail application. It emphasises the point that many of our defendants saw the appeal process as a somewhat remote affair, a lawyer's procedure where they essentially had to rely on the professionals. Some few brave souls (cases 1088, 6015 and 7003 in our sample) are prepared to appeal despite discouragement from legal representatives, but they are an exception to a general tendency to follow legal advice. Since legal advice is predominantly against appeals, this helps to explain the low proportion of defendants making formal application against conviction or sentence.

Defendants who had decided not to appeal

We asked all those interviewed defendants who had decided not to appeal to give us their reasons. The replies are summarised in Table 7.1.

Table 7.1 Reasons for not appealing (% of respondents giving each reason)*

		Plea		Sentence	
	All	G	NG	Fine	Custody
Defendant accepts situation	50	51	30	51	47
No point, unlikely to succeed	31	30	46	33	28
Fears worse sentence	9	10	5	7	13
Get sentence over with	8	8	8	0	20
Get case over with	7	7	11	12	0·3
Solicitor's advice	5	5	22	2	11
Didn't know appeal possible	4	4	11	6	1
Expense	2	1	8	3	0·3
Family or friends' advice	0·3	0·3	0	0	1
Fear of publicity	0·1	0·1	3	0	0·3
Other reasons	5	6	0	5	6

*Columns do not total 100 because some defendants gave more than one reason.

Half the defendants accepted the situation as it stood. This includes quite a range of reactions from resigned acceptance of the inevitable to astonished delight at having got off so lightly. Another large group of respondents said that they were sure an appeal would fail. Some were like the first group, in having a lenient sentence which could hardly be bettered on appeal; others nursed a sense of injustice but felt, or were persuaded by their friends or their solicitors, that they were unlikely to get better treatment from the appeal court. Sometimes this feeling was quite strong: one intelligent SN defendant who had been convicted said 'I didn't get justice—I don't see how an appeal would help', ignoring the fact that appeals were instituted precisely in order to right injustices.

As with reasons for other decisions, we considered the principal reasons for not appealing by the different categories of the defendants' typology. Table 7.2 shows the results; there were no significant differences, but acceptance of the situation was least common among the right-assertive and most common among recidivist strategists, ordinary respondents and passive respondents. Pessimism about the outcome of the appeal was most common among right-assertive and passive respondents.

Table 7.2 Principal reasons for not appealing, by defendants' typology (% answering)

	Accepts situation	No point, won't succeed
Recidivist strategists	48	19
Other strategists	19	23
Respectable first-timers	35	13
Right-assertive	13	33
Ordinary respondents	58	18
Dissociative	46	28
Other passive	42	26
Other-dominated respondents	28	23
External circumstances	31	31
Miscellaneous	61	13

A further comparison was made of reasons for not appealing by social class. Middle-class defendants significantly more often gave the reason 'get it over with' or 'fear of publicity'; ashamed and embarrassed, the thought of renewed upset and gossip was for them unbearable.

Perhaps most interesting of all differences, there were variations in reason for not appealing by plea and by sentence received, as shown in the last four columns of Table 7.1. Not guilty pleaders were less likely than guilty pleaders to 'accept the situation', but were much more likely to feel that an appeal would fail. Not guilty pleaders were also more likely to refrain from appeal on solicitors' advice, but of course many more such pleaders than guilty pleas were legally represented; more surprising was the high incidence (11 per cent) of ignorance about the existence of appeal mechanisms among the not guilty cases. The major difference found in sentence types was that non-custodial sentence cases were more likely to say 'get the case over with', while those sentenced to imprisonment or other custody gave 'getting the sentence over' as a reason in one-fifth of all cases. These reasons have some similarity, but are in fact identifiably different reactions, and that of the prisoners requires some further consideration.

We have seen that the Court of Appeal may order loss of waiting time in the case of an unarguable, hopeless appeal. Prior to 1966, the general rule was that unsuccessful applicants for leave to appeal almost automatically lost 42 days (in some cases 63 days) waiting time: this rule was considered unfair by the Donovan Committee (Lord Chancellor's Office, 1965) and altered in the Criminal Appeal Act 1966 to a provision that waiting time should be part of the sentence unless the court specifically ordered to the contrary. Until 1970, this power was virtually never used by the single judge considering the question of leave to appeal, but in March of that year Lord Parker issued a Practice Note stating that this practice would now alter, because under the new provisions as to legal aid in the Criminal Justice Act 1967 (based on the Widgery Report) 'provisions for advice on appeals under legal aid were made . . . [and] now no prisoner need be without advice'. It seems that his announcement, which was given wide publicity at the time, halved the number of applications for leave to appeal, and that the position remained constant at this lower level at least until the time of our research in 1971-2 (see Zander, 1972a, pp.132-3). In fact, however, even under the new situation, the court (including the single judge) does not use the power in many cases (ibid., at pp.166-7) and it is quite wrong to think that every unsuccessful appellant pays the penalty as to waiting time. But prison mythology, and the fear of possibly losing time, is very strong: our interviews were full of answers such as 'you lose time while waiting'; 'I want to get time started'; 'it would be more time to serve', and so on. The misconception is very widespread indeed, and may prevent some appellants with worthwhile and arguable cases from exercising their rights of appeal.

Indeed, some defendants actually feared that their sentences could be increased on appeal: 'They would make it heavier for messing them about'; 'I could get an extended sentence, I am eligible'; 'It is best to leave it as it is, I could get more', and other similar remarks were made—but this power of increasing sentence, though it existed until 1966, does so no longer (see Lord Chancellor's Office, 1965, pp.42-7; Thomas, 1972a).[1] That such a degree of misconception should exist is disturbing.

As in previous chapters, we provide below some randomly selected replies on the question of reasons for not appealing, in order to fill out the formal categories of Tables 7.1 and 7.2. In this instance we give eight replies from defendants in custody, eight from those who pleaded not guilty and eight from other defendants.

(*a*) *Defendants in custody*

1 'Got a fairly light sentence' (12 months for possessing cannabis, including 6 months of a suspended sentence).

2 'Waste of time: I deserved more.'

3 'Only 4 months to do.'

4 (A meter-theft) 'The court was lenient. Sentence agreeable: I do these things as I have nowhere to go.'

5 (A recidivist who had served prison sentences totalling 13½ years) 'They can take waiting time off if unsuccessful; I don't intend to make the sentence any longer.'

6 'Very satisfied with sentence: I could have got more on second charge alone.'

7 Solicitor 'said there was no point.'

8 Solicitor 'said it would do no good.'

(*b*) *Defendants who pleaded not guilty*

1 (A 51-year-old shoplifter) 'It wouldn't make any difference. The stigma is the same even if you are found not guilty.'

2 'Not worth it. Solicitor asked me if I wanted to, but no point really. The court only fined me half the cost of a new battery, and only half what [a friend] got when he pleaded guilty.'

3 'I don't want any more to do with it.'

4 'Waste of money. Lawyer said he wished it was worth fighting, but it wasn't.'

5 'Solicitor said it was no good—we'd get nowhere at great expense. Anyway I have no money left.' (This was a case in which the judge hinted strongly at the possibility of an appeal on technical grounds related to the evidence of one witness, a recidivist who later featured in our sample.)[2]

6 'Solicitor advised against it. Said it would be the same result and would be expensive.'

7 'Glad it's all over.'

8 'I want to forget it, all finished.'

(*c*) *Others*

1 Didn't know he could appeal until the interview. When it was explained that he could only appeal against sentence (£20 fine for stealing 20p from employer): 'It would do no good: I wouldn't win.'

2 'Just relieved court decided to be so lenient with [girl co-defendant].'

3 'Never thought about it. A fine is OK.' (£10 fine for 2 burglaries.)

4 'I'd be crazy to: would be laughed out of court.'

5 Had not thought about it; and did not know about appeals: 'Only worried about the endorsements, though.' (Fine and licence endorsed for 2 offences of taking cars without the owners' consent.)

6 'Light sentence: wouldn't get any better.'

7 'No point: got probation which is what I wanted.'

8 (A defendant given a conditional discharge for burglary, and described by our interviewer as 'a pathetic man in very poor circumstances') 'It would only linger the case on.'

The last two answers were given by men sentenced in the Crown Court who were thought at the time to have a technical right to apply for leave to appeal. A subsequent decision of the Court of Appeal (R. v. Tucker, [1974] 2 All E.R. 639) has established that they had in fact no such right.

Finally and more frivolously, we record the sad case of the 18-year-old borstal boy sentenced for obtaining a radio by deception. He had decided not to appeal: 'I was going to, as I thought my wife was pregnant. But then we realised she wasn't, so there was no chance.' Not surprisingly, this defendant appears in the typology as 'dominated by external circumstances'!

Information about appeals

We have already mentioned some of the misconceptions prevalent among prisoners about the appeal process. Prisoners have special difficulties about appealing. One defendant told us that 'Neither courts nor prisons like appeals'. So far as the prisons are concerned there is at least some truth in his observation. Appellants have to be specially treated and have a few special privileges in prison; the process of classification, transfer and 'treatment' can be held up while an appeal is dealt with. This can take a long time—which points to another complaint of the prisoner, that by the time the appeal is dealt with he may have completed the whole of a short prison or detention sentence.

In some of our replies there was a reference to help being offered by the prison staff in preparing appeals. Such staff are, as we have already mentioned, instructed to give advice about available facilities rather than give individual advice to prisoners: though it is perhaps worth mentioning that this function is much more developed in some American prisons, which have small law libraries run by inmate clerks (cf. Zander, 1972a, pp. 146ff—see also Paterson, 1970, section IV). One disturbing interview with a foreign prisoner included his statement: 'I cannot write English. You have to fill in a form to appeal and I cannot read it or write an appeal.' It is difficult to believe that any prison officer would refuse to help such a prisoner to complete his form; but it seems that help was not very actively offered in that particular case.[3]

There has been much discussion of the problem which prisoners face in obtaining legal advice about appealing. Although the prisoner's difficulties are particularly great, the complaint about the lawyers' failure to advise on appeal is a more general one: 'he never came to see me after the case'; 'he said he would write but I am still waiting.' Zander (1972a) has pointed out that legal aid includes advice as to grounds of appeal, and where the grounds exist, assistance in preparing appeal papers (Legal Aid Act 1974, s.30(7), re-enacting earlier provisions). He found that no advice was given in at least 10 per cent (and, if the defendants were to be believed, perhaps one-third) of cases in which notice of appeal was actually given, and in 45 per cent of cases in which advice was given, this did not include help in drafting grounds of appeal.

Our data for appellants are based on small numbers and in some cases the interview took place quite soon after the trial, so that legal advice may have been given at a later stage. But it is clear that our defendants, like those in Zander's group, were dissatisfied with the attention they received after the passing of sentence. Several had completed appeal forms in prison without having had any advice from their solicitors. It is precisely these cases in which the Court of Appeal, acting on the assumption that legal advice is available, is likely to react to an ill-prepared application for leave to appeal by ordering waiting time to be excluded from the time counted as part of the sentence.

Perhaps more important are the data about those who did not plan to appeal. We asked about the discussions which such defendants had had with others about the possibility of appealing: Table 7.3 sets out the results. The absence of any discussion with the police is quite understandable, but the general absence of discussion about appeals and the low 'score' for lawyers are worthy of note. Virtually all those tried in the higher court were in receipt of legal aid, but only 28 per cent reported discussion of an appeal with their legal advisers. This strongly confirms Zander's gloomy findings.

Table 7.3 Discussion of appeal with others (convicted respondents not appealing or considering appeal)

% of defendants discussing with	Tried summarily	Tried in higher court	All
Wife	1	—	1
Parents	0·1	3	0·5
Family	—	3	0·5
Friends	1	2	1
Codefendants	1·5	7	3
Others in trouble*	0·1	2	0·5
Police	—	—	—
Lawyer	3	28	8
Prison Officers	0·5	6	2
No one	93	63	86

*For meaning of this term, see discussion of Table 4.16.

This would not matter too much (ignoring the ethical problem of receiving payment when the work has not been done) if defendants were fully informed in other ways about appeals. A series of questions in our interview schedule tested this, with depressing results.

Only 28 per cent of non-appellants knew how to go about appealing (23 per cent of those tried by the magistrates (Ss); 48 per cent of those tried in the higher court (Ds and Hs)). Sixty per cent were unaware of the time limit for appeals (68 per cent Ss, 32 per cent Ds and Hs). Only 21 per cent could correctly answer the question about where an appeal was heard (17 per cent Ss, 35 per cent Ds and Hs). Fifty-two per cent could not offer any estimate of the cost of an appeal (58 per cent Ss, 33 per cent Ds and Hs). It is true that most of these defendants had no possible grounds of appeal; and also that those convicted of more serious offences were generally better informed. But the overall impression is one of ignorance, which makes the apparent failure of the legal profession to carry out its duties to advise and assist possible appellants all the more serious.

Fortunately, concern over this matter exists within the legal profession. An unofficial group of practitioners, academics and civil servants met to consider the question under the leadership of the late Mr Justice Bean. The result was an official document on appeal procedures (Criminal Appeal Office, 1974), which stressed the role of legal aid, and which was refreshingly blunt in its advice. For example:

> It is essential that the solicitor should remain in touch with the lay client after conviction or sentence. If the client is in custody this can hardly be achieved without a visit while he is still in the precincts of the Crown Court by the solicitor's representative, preferably with counsel. (Para. 2.5.)

The Lord Chief Justice drew attention to this document in a Practice Note of June 1974 ([1974] 2 All E.R. 805); it is to be hoped that this will lead to substantial improvements.

Once again we are faced with fundamental issues as a result of our review and research. Criminal appeal proceedings deal with alleged wrongful convictions or sentence, and from the point of view of a fair and just legal system the importance of such a safeguard needs little emphasis. But most of our defendants knew little about the safeguard, were apparently seriously underinformed by their legal advisers, and very seldom attempted to exercise their rights under the appeal mechanism. (Appeals are, for example, less common than the exercise of the right to be tried in the Crown Court.) Moreover, there are administrative pressures against the appeal, notably the possible deduction of waiting time which as we have seen operates as a more severe deterrent than the facts appear to warrant. All of this may tend to diminish the real effectiveness of the appeal as a safeguard against injustice.

Against this, one may legitimately argue that the administrative structures of the criminal justice system must be protected against the waste of professional time and public money involved in the hearing of hopeless appeals. An extension of this view would be that the appeal is not so much a general right as a special procedure designed to correct the occasional specific case. Arguably, the fact that those convicted in the Crown Court must normally seek leave to appeal is evidence that our legal system supports this view.

The resolution of these conflicting positions is not easy, and raises again the perennial dilemma posed in this volume between the full protection of the rights of the accused and the undoubted need for speed and administrative efficiency in criminal procedure. But the present position, as revealed by our work and Zander's (1972a) earlier article, is not reassuring at least on the specific question of the 1970 Practice Note, the failure of lawyers to act as envisaged by that Note, and the widespread belief of prisoners that powers are exercised under the terms of the Note more widely than they actually are. That specific matter requires further debate and deliberation, but in our view this can only be satisfactorily accomplished in the context of a wider consideration of the role and status of the appeal in the criminal justice system as a whole.

8 Bail or custody

The main focus of our research was on decisions made by the defendant, and on his view of the criminal justice system. At first sight, the subject of the grant or refusal of bail seems to stand rather away from that centre of concern; the decision, after all, is for the magistrates or the judge. How then can we justify the inclusion of this chapter?

One important answer is that decisions by the defendant are very much involved in certain aspects of the matter. It is true that in the public arena of the courtroom, the defendant's only decision is whether or not to raise the matter by applying for bail (or opposing a prosecution request for a remand in custody, which amounts to the same thing). After that he can only react with pleasure or dismay to the decision of others, much as he does to a sentence. This is to overlook the most important stage in the whole bail/custody process, the stage which occurs in the police station. The police have power to grant bail pending the defendant's first court appearance, and we shall show that this initial decision influences the conduct of the case at its later stages. This first police decision is taken when the defendant is without the help of a solicitor, and is often willing to enter into negotiations or bargains to obtain his freedom. 'Bail-bargaining' is a neglected but vitally important aspect of the process.

A second point is that decisions as to bail or custody influence and are influenced by the other decisions we examine. There is some evidence, for example, that a defendant remanded in custody is more likely to plead guilty than one given bail; but equally a defendant who announces his intention to plead not guilty is more likely to be given bail than one who does not.

A third and more mundane, but still respectable, reason for including a study of bail decisions was the opportunity we had to obtain detailed observation records of almost 1,700 cases. We were able to use our court observers to obtain a considerable amount of information about bail decisions made in open court. Our data are not as comprehensive as they could have been if bail/custody were our main subject of study, but they are full enough for meaningful comparisons with the results of earlier, specialist studies.

Legal background: summons, arrest and police bail

There are two legal procedures which may precede the first appearance of the defendant in a criminal court. The first is the summons, which is a notice addressed to the defendant, issued and signed by a magistrate. The summons must normally be served on the defendant personally or by post; moreover

> it must state shortly the offence or offences alleged together with such reasonable particulars as to enable the accused to know what facts are alleged to constitute the offences, and must require the offender to appear at a certain time and place before the magistrates (Cross and Jones, 1972, p.308).

The alternative procedure is by arrest, which may be immediately followed either by custodial detention pending court appearance, or by 'bail'. This requires a little explanation.

To grant bail is to give someone temporary freedom on certain legally binding conditions. The person bailed is told that he may go, but must attend again at a stated time. Before he can go he must 'enter into a recognisance', the effect of which is that if he fails to attend at the stated time, if that is, he fails 'to answer bail', then he must forfeit a given sum of money—£25 in a simple case. Other conditions may be imposed, and he may be asked to find sureties, independent people who guarantee his appearance on pain of a similar penalty.

Bail can be granted after arrest but before court appearance in three different types of cases. The first is where an arrest has been made but further police inquiries are necessary before charges can properly be laid. An inspector or more senior officer, or the officer-in-charge at the police station, may grant bail, requiring the suspect to return to the police station a few days later (Magistrates' Courts Act 1952, s.38(2)).

In the other two types of cases, inquiries are complete, or have at least got far enough to justify a charge. If the suspect is arrested under a warrant issued by a magistrate, the magistrate will have decided whether or not bail may be granted. If it is allowed the warrant is said to be endorsed, or more usually, 'backed for' bail

(Magistrates' Courts Act 1952, s.93). In this situation, the police have no discretion.

In the much more usual case of an arrest without warrant, the police have a discretion to be exercised by an officer of the rank set out above. He may grant bail in any case. If it is not practicable to bring the suspect before a magistrates' court within 24 hours (and in a city with daily courts that really means in cases of weekend arrest), then he must grant bail 'unless the offence appears to the officer to be a serious one' (Magistrates' Courts Act 1952, s.38(1)). There is no statutory definition of a 'serious' offence, and the result is that unless a defendant is arrested on a Saturday night for a very trivial offence, the police will always have a discretion whether or not to grant bail.

In Sheffield, it is the police custom to summons all those charged with motoring offences and almost all those charged with minor non-indictable offences. Equally, it is the custom to arrest all alleged indictable offenders and those charged with those summary offences most akin to indictable offences. The result is that all choice-of-venue cases are arrested, and hence all those dealt with in our sample were arrested rather than summonsed.[1]

Furthermore, in the rest of this chapter we assume that whether the defendant appears in court in custody or in answer to his bail is the result of a police decision. We have seen that there are a few cases in which the police have no discretion, but they are numerically insignificant and we shall not complicate matters by making repeated references to them.

Court bail

The question of bail also arises whenever criminal proceedings are interrupted by an adjournment (other than a short break during a day's sitting) or by the committal of a case from the magistrates' to a higher court. On each occasion the defendant can be remanded in custody or on bail. In our court sample, 58 per cent of cases were disposed of at first appearance (cf. Bottomley, 1970, p.23: 64 per cent in his urban court); the bail/custody question was relevant in the remaining 42 per cent of cases.

The great majority of these cases were such that the judge or magistrates had an unfettered discretion in granting or refusing bail. Statutory rules do exist requiring the grant of bail in certain types of case; some of these, in which the magistrates had agreed to summary trial of indictable offences, fell within our sample. The rules, contained in s.18 of the Criminal Justice Act 1967 are of such complexity and contain so many qualifications and exceptions that their practical effect is very slight indeed. A Home Office research study of decisions as to bail in selected London courts in 1969 (Simon and Weatheritt, 1974) found that only one-sixth of all decisions were within the mandatory bail provisions, and the bail rate in such cases was almost 80 per cent before the passing of the Act. In our court sample, from which cases only triable summarily were excluded (they form one of the major groups affected by the mandatory bail provisions), the direct relevance of the Act was even less. The provision will disappear if the recommendations of the Home Office Working Party on Bail Procedures in Magistrates' Courts (1974) are implemented: it proposed a statutory presumption in favour of bail in all cases, and in view of this believed it would 'not be appropriate to retain a detailed provision applying to a limited category of cases', especially as the provision is 'complicated and confusing' (para. 87).

Accordingly we have not examined the details of the 1967 provisions (set out in summary form in Simon and Weatheritt, 1974, pp.2-3) nor their application to our sample. On the other hand the indirect effect of the Act is important. The Home Office research study found an increase in the granting of bail between 1966 and 1969, no doubt attributable to the greater interest in bail excited in part by the new legislation. The provisions are also relevant as giving a somewhat indirect statutory blessing to certain practices. The rules require the magistrates to grant bail in certain cases, but then dispense with that obligation if certain circumstances exist. These circumstances *enable* the magistrates to remand in custody; that is not to say that bail should be refused whenever the circumstances are present, but it does identify some factors as being at least relevant. They include:

the defendant's failure to answer bail on a previous occasion;
his (alleged) commission of the offence with which he is charged while on bail;
that he has no fixed abode or is ordinarily resident outside the United Kingdom;
that it is necessary to detain him to establish his identity or address;
that he is likely to commit an offence if released;
that detention in custody is necessary for his own protection;

that the offence charged involved certain types of violence or indecency or the use of real or imitation firearms.

We shall see that the reasons customarily advanced by the prosecution when seeking a remand in custody include some which are very similar to those listed.

Case law offers some guidance on the proper approach to bail questions, but the absence of any regular system of appeal from bail decisions (a dissatisfied defendant may apply to a judge, but the hearing is in private and unreported) means that the guidance is fragmentary. The case law that exists is unhelpful in that it tends to consist of judicial statements that it is not improper to consider a particular factor; but it is seldom made clear what weight should be given to that factor, or what inferences are proper (see Zander, 1967; Bottomley, 1968).

There is general agreement in the legal sources that the primary question is whether the defendant, if given bail, would attend at the required time. Lord Russell of Killowen, CJ, in 1898 said:

> It cannot be too strongly impressed on the magistracy of the country that bail is not to be withheld as a punishment, but that the requirements as to bail are merely to secure the attendance of the prisoner at the trial (R. v. Rose (1898), 18 Cox C.C. 717).

The Criminal Justice Act 1967, in authorising the use of special conditions of bail, provides that they must be likely to result in the defendant's appearance at the time and place required or be necessary in the interests of justice or for the prevention of crime (s. 21(1)). Lord Hailsham of St Marylebone, LC, speaking extra-judicially in 1971, gave as the first consideration 'the likelihood or otherwise of the defendant disappearing' (see Zander, 1973, pp.163-7).

It is clear, however, that other factors can be considered. Some, for example the protection of the defendant, or the need for medical reports, are special to particular cases. The others are more general, and raise the question whether they are independent criteria or merely indications pointing to the likelihood of the defendant answering bail. The nature of the offence, the likelihood of conviction, possible sentences, are all capable of receiving either treatment, but the latter view was preferred in R. v. Robinson (1854), 23 L.J.Q.B. 286. The bad record of the defendant, and the chances of his committing further offences or interfering with witnesses while on bail have been put forward as independent criteria (see, e.g. R. v. Armstrong, [1951] 2 All E.R. 219; R. v. Wharton, [1955] Crim. L.R. 565; Lord Hailsham, loc. cit.).

These authorities were examined in the report of the Home Office Working Party on Bail Procedures in Magistrates' Courts, published in 1974. Having reviewed the case law (pp.7-9), the Working Party looked afresh at the relevant considerations (pp.17-24) and in effect endorsed the conclusions reached by the judges. In the Summary of the report (p.70) it is stated categorically that:

> there should be no change in the three established reasons for refusing bail, which are—
> (i) the likelihood of the defendant's failing to attend at the time and place required;
> (ii) the likelihood of his committing serious offences; and
> (iii) the likelihood of his otherwise interfering with the course of justice, if granted bail.

In particular the report commented on the judicial encouragement given to magistrates in burglary cases to consider seriously the risk of the defendant committing further offences on bail (see R. v. Phillips (1947), 111 J.P. 333). The statistics collected by the Metropolitan Police demonstrated that there is a significantly greater risk of offences being committed on bail by persons charged with burglary, and also with robbery, than by those charged with other offences (Report, 1974, p.21).

There remain to be considered two factors which in actual daily practice are frequently and heavily relied upon by the prosecution, i.e. the need for further police inquiries to be made, and the likelihood of further charges being brought. It is clear that these factors can have little bearing on the primary question of whether the defendant would answer bail. Their use is rather the result of the general police attitude, since they

> feel it is their job to keep [the accused] in custody before trial if this helps to protect the community from the risk of further crimes, and enables the police to complete their enquiries as quickly and efficiently as possible. . . . Such a portrayal of police attitudes and involvement in the bail decision naturally raises many controversial issues . . . but many of the common police objections to bail seem to square better with some such picture than with the usual arguments focussing on the risk of non-appearance at trial (Bottomley, 1973, p.97).

We discuss this police attitude further below, but it should be stressed that these additional factors ('further inquiries' and 'further charges') have not received express judicial approval in considered, reported judgments. The Home Office Working Party discussed only the former and indicated that the courts should take a critical view:

> we consider it desirable that courts should question the police closely when they object to bail on these grounds. Although on occasion it may not be possible for the police to say very much about their further inquiries, we think that they should in most cases be able to give some indication to the court of what is involved (Report, 1974, p.23).

Previous studies

Data on English court practice as to bail and custody can be found in a number of studies, but the question received particular attention in Bottomley (1970) and in a Cobden Trust study (King, 1971). There are also two studies of London court practice, one by Zander (1971, in conjunction with the national Cobden Trust study) the other by the Home Office (Simon and Weatheritt, 1974). There are remarkable differences between the results of the two national studies.

Bottomley studied the practice of the courts in two areas during 1965-6. His 'urban court' was in a North of England city of 300,000 people; on the face of it, one would expect the Sheffield practice to be similar (Sheffield has a population of half a million). Bottomley also looked at the practice of courts in a rural area in East Anglia. His findings as to remands before conviction or committal for trial, that is during adjournments in the magistrates' courts, are summarised in Table 8.1 (see his p.28).

The Cobden Trust study in 1970-1 surveyed the practice in London

Table 8.1 Remands during adjournments in magistrates' courts (Bottomley's study)

Defendants (%)	Urban court	Rural court
Always remanded on bail	30	31
Mixed bail/custody experience	9	13
Always remanded in custody	61	56

and 5 provincial centres, and the total sample was of 1,001 cases. For each court selected, the observation period was only five days, so that it was not possible to follow individual cases through to completion; the results are in terms of decisions made rather than of case histories. The courts were urban courts, but the results are not at all like Bottomley's urban court (King, 1971, figure D, p.97): bail granted, 68 per cent; custody ordered, 32 per cent.

The London study which formed part of the Cobden Trust study produced similar results, as one would expect; the proportion of defendants granted bail during an adjournment before conviction by magistrates was 66 per cent. Simon and Weatheritt (1974, tables 3,4 and 7)[2] found that 56 per cent of London defendants were granted bail on an adjournment during the course of proceedings in the magistrates' courts in their 1966 sample, the rate rising to 68 per cent in 1969. Gibson found a bail rate of 61 per cent in her earlier study (1960, p.24), and none of the provincial centres studied by the Cobden Trust fell below 55 per cent.

It is clear that Bottomley's results are very much out of line with all other studies. He indicates (p.28) that at his urban court '30 per cent of those remanded in custody before conviction . . . were detained for 48 hours or less'; it seems likely that his urban court was unusual in that respect, for such short adjournments in custody are not common. Even if some allowance is made for this, his results are still unexpected, especially as the rural court pattern was similar.

Surprisingly this discrepancy is not discussed in the Cobden Trust report. Nor did Bottomley himself, in his original study, draw attention to the discrepancy between the performance of his courts and the national average in the matter of committal for trial,[3] though in a more recent work (Bottomley, 1973, p.86) he has noted without comment or explanation the different figures in his own and the Cobden Trust study.

The only possible conclusion is that Bottomley, through sheer bad luck, selected two separate areas of the country in which the courts' practice in bail/custody decisions was radically different from the national pattern. We can say at once that the Sheffield pattern was found to be close to that found in the national studies already referred to; but Sheffield magistrates were less ready to grant bail than the national figures lead one to expect, and some regional effect, showing itself in a more extreme form in Bottomley's urban area, cannot be altogether ruled out.

One feature common to previous studies is the critical importance of the police role to the question of court bail. In cases in which the police objected to bail when it was applied for in court, the magistrates overruled their objections and granted bail in only 8·3 per cent of cases in Gibson's sample (1960, p.31), 4 per cent of Bottomley's cases (1970, p.59); but the Cobden Trust figures were much higher (20 per cent in cases before lay magistrates, 24 per cent before stipendiaries) and also reveal wide variations between individual courts (King, 1971, pp.17-19). All studies, and ours (in which the corresponding figure was 13 per cent) is no exception, find police recommendations followed in the very great majority of cases.

The Home Office Working Party on Bail Procedures felt driven to comment on the fact that bail is granted against police advice in a comparatively small proportion of cases. Their report declares that 'a high correlation between the views of the police and the decisions of the courts is to be expected, since the considerations which each should have in mind are in many respects similar' (para. 91). This may be the case, but we show below that there are grounds for doubting whether the considerations are in fact similar. Unfortunately the Working Party decided that police bail decisions were outside their terms of reference (para. 179).

It is indeed the matter of police attitudes which seems to explain the discrepancies between some of Bottomley's results and those of other studies. In his cases, the police opposed bail in 64 per cent of all cases (1970, p.59). All other studies record objection in less than half that proportion: 28·5 per cent in Gibson's sample (1960, p.31), 28 per cent in the Cobden Trust lay magistrates' cases, 21 per cent in their stipendiary cases (King, 1971, p.18). In Sheffield, the number of contested applications was higher—as we shall see it was 37 per cent—and fewer cases ended in a grant of bail. So it seems that Bottomley's misfortune was in his choice of police forces, not his choice of courts, and this would also explain why he found no obvious inconsistencies within the group of courts contributing to his 'rural' sample, as all shared a common police force. His forces, and the Sheffield police to a lesser extent, took a hard line in opposing bail; magistrates everywhere generally accept the police view, and so discrepancies in court practice arise.[4]

Before first appearance

This conclusion suggests that researchers should give attention to the decisions made by the police as to bail or custody, an area of police discretion which has been wholly neglected hitherto. We know from studies of arrest practices, such as that by LaFave (1965), that individual police officers may be influenced in their initial decision to take a person into custody by a variety of factors. A lot may turn not just on the nature of the offence, but on the offender's attitude towards the policeman: the man who flaunts his guilt, or abuses the police officer, increases his chances of arrest. Are similar factors operative at the police station when the question of police bail arises? How far is the charge officer guided in making a decision by the arresting officer himself?

Our study was not designed with this area in mind, but we do have two sources of data which enable us to get closer to the answers. The court sample contains information about the defendants' first court appearance, whether this was in custody or on bail. (There are some defendants who are arrested only hours before the court hearing; they will appear in custody, the question of bail being virtually irrelevant. To that extent our data can give only a partial view of the police decisions.) We also have a good deal of material from our interviews about the way in which the police handled defendants in the police station, and in particular about police reactions to questions as to bail. We set out first the data based on the court sample.

Of our defendants, 73 per cent were on bail at first appearance, 27 per cent in custody. The custody rate is much lower than Bottomley found. In his sample (of cases in which there was at least one adjournment), 80 per cent appeared after spending at least the previous night in police custody, and 13 per cent appeared on bail or summons (Bottomley, 1970, p.26: what happened to the remaining 7 per cent does not appear from his report). Taking Sheffield cases directly comparable with his, i.e. excluding those cases disposed of at first appearance, the custody rate was still only 52 per cent.

What factors determine whether or not a defendant is kept in custody before his first court appearance? Leaving aside the time of arrest, on which we have no clear information, the main statistical factors appear to be:

(i) the sex of the defendant;
(ii) the nature of the offence with which he is charged;
(iii) the gravity of the offence within its particular offence category; and
(iv) the defendant's previous criminal record.

The sex factor is clearly indicated in Table 8.2. Altogether 95 per cent of women defendants appeared on bail, as compared with 68 per cent of men. A woman defendant has a better chance of bail even if she is charged with an offence triable in the higher courts; but it must be admitted that the male and female data are not comparable because of the different offences committed by members of each sex.

Table 8.2 Percentage bail before first appearance, by sex and venue

	M	F
Case ultimately tried summarily	77	97
Case tried in higher court		
defendant's election	68	93
without defendant's election	35	63

Our list of factors refers to both the nature of the offence and to its gravity. By 'nature' we refer to the legal label which is applied to the offence: for example, a burglar is much less likely to be given bail before first appearance than is a handler of stolen goods. Within these offence categories there are of course offences of greater or lesser severity. Handling stolen goods may involve buying a packet of cigarettes knowing it to have been stolen, or it may involve arranging the disposal of valuable jewels stolen by a professional gang. In Table 8.3 we use venue as a somewhat crude measure of gravity, analysing separately those cases committed for trial to the higher court otherwise than as a result of the defendant's own choice. In terms of our sub-sample groups, the H category is the more severe, the D and S groups the less severe. This is a very imperfect device, for the choice of venue is influenced in at least some cases by the defendant's criminal record, another of the factors we have to examine; but it is the best we can do.

It is perhaps rather surprising that criminal damage cases, especially those in our less severe category, are so high in Table 8.3. This may of course reflect a large number of early-morning arrests on the day of first appearance. At the other end of the scale, handling offences are in a surprisingly lowly place, for some would regard handling as a more serious offence than theft. The table seems to reflect the realities of practice, that handling charges are used against those on the fringe of a group of thieves, against those suspected of theft but against whom there is insufficient evidence to

Table 8.3 Percentage in custody before first appearance, by offence category and 'gravity' (male defendants only)

	Hs	Ss + Ds	All
Burglary	78	63	68
Arson/damage	75	48	50
Aggressive offences	61	15	40
Taking car without consent	84	33	37
Frauds	(38)	26	28
Sex offences	67	6	26
Thefts (not shops, meters)	55	18	20
Drugs	(83)	10	20
Shoplifting	(100)	8	11
Handling stolen goods	13	5	9
Meter-thefts	—	9	9
All	64	24	32

bring a theft charge, and—in Sheffield especially—against 'respectable' scrap metal dealers who are unlikely to abscond.

The proportion in custody is consistently higher for the more severe, Hs, category; it is significantly higher for burglaries, aggressive offences, and thefts (other than shops, meters) where the numbers sent to the higher court are appreciable.

The fourth important factor is previous record. We divided the cases into those in which the defendant had previously served a custodial sentence, others with previous convictions, and those with no previous convictions. A number of cases had to be omitted as the previous record was unclear. Each offence category was examined to see whether there was any significant difference between cases in the H category and others; this was so only for burglaries and aggressive offences; these are listed separately in Table 8.4.

There are seen to be consistent trends in the proportions kept in custody, which is more likely for defendants with a previous record, and more likely again if there has been previous prison experience. If burglary and aggressive offences are omitted, the custody rates for other offences, which do not differ significantly, are 58 per cent where there is previous custody, 24 per cent for others with previous convictions and 14 per cent for others.

We can thus demonstrate statistically the importance of sex, offence type, offence nature and previous record in helping to

Table 8.4 Percentage in custody before first appearance, by offence and previous record (male defendants only)

	Previous custody	Other previous convictions	No previous convictions
Burglary			
H cases	89	69	(0)
others	88	61	31
Aggressive offences			
Hs	80	71	42
others	60	19	0
Arson/damage	(50)	37	67
Taking car without consent	78	29	29
Frauds	40	23	17
Sex offences	(100)	27	12
Thefts (not shops, meters)	56	26	8
Drugs	(100)	29	6
Shoplifting	50	16	16
Handling stolen goods	(17)	9	9
Meter-thefts	(100)	27	(12)
All	73	34	16

determine the police attitude to bail before first appearance. What we cannot adequately quantify, but which emerged with disturbing clarity and consistency in quite a number of the interviews, was that the natural police wish to secure a conviction apparently very much enters into the bail-granting process. What we can legitimately call 'bail-bargaining', that is the bargaining of the police power to release against the defendant's reluctance to capitulate, certainly exists, as a considerable number of cases made clear (see also case 2080, set out in chapter 5):

> Case 1001 E was arrested at 10 p.m. on a Saturday night, having been found in a warehouse by a police-dog patrol. He said he was then interrogated until 3 a.m. on the Sunday morning, and held in custody until court on the Monday morning (when he was dealt with straight away and sentenced

to imprisonment). During this interrogation period, 'They told me if I told them of anyone who had "knocked off stuff", they would release me on bail'.

Case 1093 A police constable saw two men pushing an old pram; it contained lead. At the police station: 'They said, if you don't tell us the truth you can't have bail. Then I made a statement admitting it, then I got bail'.

Case 2075 (See also chapter 6) As part of the 'bargain' entered into with this defendant (as explained above, i.e. to plead guilty so as not to expose a police informer to the witness box, in exchange for recommendations against imprisonment), the police also apparently agreed not to oppose bail. J was on bail throughout, even for his committal to Crown Court for sentence, although he had a very long record of previous convictions and had previously served a total of 13 years in prisons. J was not in the least surprised about being granted bail (although in the past he had normally been refused it) because of the agreement: 'plead guilty, get bail.'

Case 6044 D, a scrap metal dealer, accustomed to a middle-class life-style, was charged with 4 counts of handling stolen metals. He was interviewed by the police, made a statement, and was then released on bail: 'They only released me when I made a statement, and they weren't going to release me until I did. The police wrote the statement for me.'

Case 6046 L was involved in a fight outside a working men's club, which was broken up by the organisers. He went home, fetched a dagger, and waited for his adversary. When he came out, L made stabs at him and with one stab cut off the finger of his adversary's girl friend, who had attempted to intervene. He was picked up an hour later and (in the words of the prosecution) 'made a voluntary statement'. L's version was: 'They told me if I admitted it, I would get bail. So I made a statement but they still refused to give me bail.' (L eventually pleaded not guilty but changed his plea at a retrial: see chapter 5.)

Case 2028 E was charged with theft of lead from derelict houses due for demolition. He had only recently been released from prison, and was found in a house. At the police station: 'I kept denying it, and the police said they'd lock me up, and that it'd be easier for me to plead guilty as I'd just come out of prison. They said I'd only get a fine anyway.' Eventually E did make an admission 'to get out of the station': he was given bail, and didn't bother to contact a lawyer because 'the police said I would get a fine'. At his trial he was given 3 months' imprisonment.

Case 7002 M and his companion were out in the early hours of the morning, having had rather a lot to drink. They took a short cut across some private property, and two men came out of a house to investigate the noise. There was a fight, the details of which were disputed, and M and his friend were eventually charged with malicious wounding. They had been taken to the police station, where 'they said we had to make statements if we were going to get bail. At first we didn't say anything. Then I made a statement as the police said [my friend] had. If I hadn't made that statement, I'd have got off' (he had pleaded not guilty unsuccessfully).

One could multiply case examples, but there is little point in doing so. Quite clearly this kind of 'bail-bargaining' is important in some cases, and we were able to identify a specific complaint of it in a total of 7 per cent of all the cases, without having asked a direct question about it. In a considerable number of other cases, other threats of custody (not allied to a specific bargain) were identified; and from some of these cases it would seem that even where the police have in fact no real intention of using custody, they will nevertheless use the threat of custody in a veiled way, by light-heartedly joking about it, to establish mastery over the defendant in the charge-office situation. One 'entrepreneur strategist' was able to see through this strategy and deal with it: 'they kidded me about keeping me in custody, but I told them to stop acting like Morecambe and Wise.'

Obviously ours is a very indirect study of the bail-bargaining phenomenon, and for an adequate piece of research one needs to get inside the charge room itself. Yet what little we have established raises important issues of policy. We have seen that it is the police view which tends to dominate court decisions as to bail, and that this explains geographical variations such as the high rate of custodial remands in Bottomley's study. We have seen also that the dominant official legal view is for bail to be determined principally on the question of appearance or non-appearance at trial. Clearly, this is very often not the dominant matter in the police mind, though it is obviously a consideration. The police view and the legal view of bail may be poles apart in many cases, but it is the police view which in practice tends to dominate in the courts. This adds weight to the argument against courts' attaching importance to the objection that 'further inquiries have to be made'; at worst, this could degenerate into 'further pressure needs to be put on the defendant to get him to sign a statement'.

The bail-bargaining allegations are by far the most important data to emerge from our interviews about police bail. But a number of specific questions were also asked, the results of which should be noted.

Of those who first appeared at court in custody, 60 per cent had asked unsuccessfully for police bail. We asked whether any reasons were given by police for refusing such requests: 37 per cent of those asking were apparently given no reason; of those who were given reasons, the most common reasons stated were (predictably) factors such as the defendant's lack of a settled address, his likelihood of absconding and the possibility of further offences. One or two replies hinted at the existence of informal policy rules within the charge office, which emphasises further the importance of a direct research study of police bail:

> 'The police told me it was compulsory to oppose bail in all burglary cases, but they would help all they could to get me bail as I had co-operated with them—but later they didn't.'

> 'The police were going to release me on bail, but they rang through to the charge office, and they said "no" because I was on detention centre licence.'

As many as 16 per cent of those held in custody before the first appearance claimed not to know of the existence of police bail.

Of those who had been granted police bail, 13 per cent had not realised it existed before it was granted. In fact only 19 per cent had actually asked for police bail, the rest being granted it before any request: a third of those who had asked were released at once, while the rest had to wait a little for the completion of inquiries. A number of those who were on police bail (sometimes for quite extended periods) expressed apprehension about the situation, feeling that any time the police might revoke the bail and revert to a position of requiring custody:

'All the time we were on [police] bail we thought they might just drop [bail].'

'We were to make accusations against the police [in a not guilty plea]; we thought they might try to intimidate us and get us in prison, but Mr A [solicitor] said there was no chance of custody as we'd already had police bail.'

'I didn't know what to expect, though it crossed my mind I might be kept in custody. Then after the charge [and release on police bail] the police came to my house and asked me who had sold the [goods] to me. I said no, I wouldn't tell. They said, "We'll make sure you get a week in Leeds"' (though bail was not subsequently opposed).

Not surprisingly, a number of defendants expressed feelings of helplessness about the police bail situation. One defendant was arrested at 1.30 a.m. and kept in custody until the next morning's court, when bail was not opposed; but during the night no hint was given of this outcome: 'They said I'd be in for a long time. They seem to have such power—I felt completely helpless.'

Consequences of custody before first appearance

We have already referred to the significant relationship between bail/custody at first appearance and subsequent court decisions as to bail or custody during adjournments. An analysis of the data relating to male defendants is given in Table 8.5 (cf. Simon and Weatheritt, 1974, table 11, p.55, with very similar findings for a group of defendants roughly equivalent to our Ss and Ds).

Defendants whose first appearance was on bail are much more likely to have their cases finally disposed of then and there than those in custody. The overall figure—68 per cent compared with 28 per cent—is affected by the different types of case included in the two categories; but as the table shows, a breakdown into SGUs, Hs and others reveals a consistent trend although the figures are less dramatic. Aggressive offences and burglaries are much less likely to be dealt with at once than other offences; these offences are those most likely to be sent to the higher courts.

This may also explain why among those defendants making their first appearance in custody significantly fewer charged with these offences (14 per cent as against 2[illegible] per cent of others) are granted

Table 8.5 Bail/custody related to bail/custody at first appearance

	Aggressive	Burglary	Others	All offence types SGU	Others	Hs	All
On bail at first appearance							
no adjournments (%)	39	50	73	88	33	—	68
In cases with adjournments							
always bail (%)	98	89	97	96	99	92	96
mixed (%)	0	5	1	0	1	4	2
always custody (%)	2	5	2	4	0	4	2
In custody at first appearance							
no adjournments (%)	11	20	41	72	13	—	28
In cases with adjournments							
always bail (%)	14	14	23	38	22	11	18
mixed (%)	12	17	13	7	16	15	15
always custody (%)	74	70	60	55	62	74	68

court bail. (There is no significant variation by offence in the outcome for those who are on bail at their first appearance.) Also of interest is the fact that among the custody cases there is a decreasing proportion given bail by the magistrates as one moves from SGUs to Hs—38 per cent, 22 per cent for others, 11 per cent.

Another important effect of custody before first appearance is on the legal representation of the defendant. As we saw in chapter 6, of defendants who are ultimately represented, a much larger proportion of those making their first appearance on bail were represented at that stage than of those appearing in custody.

We also examined the use of lawyers for the prosecution. The proportion of cases in which the prosecution in the magistrates' court was always conducted by a solicitor was lower among defendants making their first appearance in custody than among those bailed. The figures are in Table 8.6(a); for custody cases, the proportion with solicitors for the prosecution at all appearances is significantly lower for the 'H' category than for the others.

These findings can readily be explained. The custody cases include the early-morning arrests, and a solicitor may not have been called for at that early stage in a case; when a number of appearances are expected in the type of case destined for committal proceedings leading to trial in the higher court, the early appearances

Table 8.6 Percentage prosecution by solicitor

(a) By custody and sub-sample group

	SGU	SGR	SN	Ds	Hs
Appearing in custody	59	40	(14)	26	14
on bail	87	87	88	88	78

(b) By custody, sub-sample group and offence

	SGU	SGR	SN+Ds	Hs
Burglary				
Appearing in custody	55	29	10	9
on bail	95	(100)	(57)	67
Other offences				
Appearing in custody	60	48	31	17
on bail	87	86	91	81

will be largely formal and can be handled by the police. But Table 8.6(b) is more puzzling, revealing a significantly lower use of prosecuting solicitors in burglary cases (except in the SGU category). We are at a loss to explain this finding.

Equally surprising was the high proportion of solicitor-conducted prosecutions in cases involving women. Eighty-one per cent of those in custody, and 96 per cent of those on bail were prosecuted at all appearances by a solicitor. We supposed that this was the result of a policy decision, perhaps dictated by the source of the complaints, with gas and electricity boards and retailers strongly represented, many women committing meter-thefts and shoplifting. Those with whom we discussed our results ruled out any such policy decision, and were frankly surprised by our findings.

Adjournments during magistrates' proceedings

There are no national statistics on bail/custody decisions. The best information we have is a table published in the report of the Home Office Working Party on Bail Procedures which analyses decisions in relation to the remand immediately before the defendant's last appearance in the magistrates' court. This is a somewhat eccentric basis, but the table does reveal a trend to a greater use of bail, the bail rate rising each year, from 66 per cent in 1967 to 80 per cent in 1972.

In the Sheffield court study, we observed 892 decisions by magistrates before the completion either of summary trial or committal proceedings. The bail rate was 54 per cent, lower than the rate in the Cobden Trust's national sample (68 per cent: King, 1971, p.97) and in Zander's London sample (66 per cent: Zander, 1971, p.193).

In line with the point we have already made about the importance of police attitudes, the Sheffield figures would seem to reflect local police views, as shown in the number of contests between prosecution and defence. The pattern was: 49 per cent uncontested applications for bail; 13 per cent uncontested applications for remand in custody; 37 per cent contested. The magistrates granted bail in only 13 per cent of the contested cases.

Comparison with other studies is not easy. Bottomley recorded police opposition to bail in 64 per cent of his cases (1970, p.59), but it would seem that this would include almost all uncontested applications for a remand in custody as well as contested cases (see his p.44). Gibson's study found 'police opposition to bail' in 28 per cent of cases (1960, p.31) and the Cobden Trust the same figure (King, 1971, p.18, lay magistrates' cases). Our findings (37 per cent contested; police opposed to bail in a total of 50 per cent) are intermediate between those of the other studies.

Another way of looking at the data is to analyse cases rather than decisions, that is to examine the pattern of decisions experienced by individual defendants. We found the following: 57 per cent (330) on bail throughout; 8 per cent (47) had a mixed history of bail and custody; 35 per cent (207) were always remanded in custody. The last group included 51 defendants who never applied for bail. If the recommendations of the Home Office Working Party on Bail Procedures are implemented, there will be a presumption in favour of bail, with the procedural consequence that an application for custody would be made by the prosecution with the defendant being invited to add any arguments in favour of bail in addition to those considerations available to the court on a standard bail information form with which it would be supplied (see further below). The result would be that the court would have to consider bail in every case, including those who (like our 51 defendants) would not otherwise apply for it.

Other studies have reported a higher proportion of defendants who are on bail throughout. Gibson (1960, p.24) found 61 per cent; Simon and Weatheritt (1974, tables 3, 4 and 7, pp.49-51) 56 per cent for 1966, 68 per cent for 1969.

One special sub-sample group of magistrates' court defendants deserves detailed attention. We have seen (chapter 2) that in Sheffield there are specially long delays associated with a plea of not guilty in the magistrates' court (the SNs). It would be truly intolerable if to the pressure of an 8-week delay was added the burden of this period having to be spent in custody. The police, in fact, seem well aware of this, and temper their policy on bail objections accordingly: there was only 1 case (where the defendant was said to be of no fixed abode) where the police objected to bail for the long SN-type adjournment, and even here they were unsuccessful. Other cases illustrate how the courts and the police are aware of the special features of the local SN situation:

> Case 3003 The defendant was charged with 2 counts of burglary, one of which he denied, saying he was drunk at the time and couldn't remember anything about it, though he had been picked out at an identification parade. (He admitted in interview that it was a rather weak defence, although he stuck to it.) The police opposed bail and K was held in custody for 9 days during which the identification parade was held. After 9 days, police objections to bail were suddenly lifted, and K was bailed for the 64-day adjournment before the summary trial.

> Case 3006 The defendant, Y, was charged with obtaining property by deception, which he denied, and the case was adjourned on bail for 10 weeks. Three weeks before the date set for the trial, Y was arrested for taking a car without consent; he was held overnight and brought before the court in the morning, but no objection to bail was made, although he had broken bail.

As with police bail, so for court bail we examined the data for significant statistical interactions. This topic was very fully examined by Simon and Weatheritt (1974, pp.15ff). They found that there was a significant relationship between the grant of bail and a number of factors including police bail and type of offence (see our Table 8.5, which agrees with Simon and Weatheritt's finding of a low bail rate for defendants charged with burglary), and also previous criminal record and number of charges. In our sample there were significant interactions between (i) bail and the defendant's married state, with married defendants being more likely to get bail at all stages (this is one factor in Simon and Weatheritt's social stability score; see below); and (ii) an absence of previous criminal record (significant for SGUs, SGRs and HGs).

Of special interest, however, is the relationship, not examined by Simon and Weatheritt, between bail/custody decisions and legal representation. This relationship has been considered twice by Zander in his studies of practice in the London courts. One study (Zander, 1969, at p.640) examined 297 cases in which defendants were remanded on first appearance. He ignored later remands, on the rather questionable basis that the bail issue would be most carefully considered the first time it was raised. Seventy-six per cent of represented defendants secured bail, 75 per cent of unrepresented defendants. This suggested that legal representation had no effect.

His later study (Zander, 1971, at p.194) with a sample of 585 cases, this time looking at all remands in the course of a case, supported this conclusion: bail was obtained by 69 per cent of those represented, and 65 per cent of the unrepresented. On closer analysis he found that legal representation was much more important in contested cases. Taking those cases only, 37 per cent of those represented get bail at first appearance but only 20 per cent of the unrepresented; on later adjournments the proportions were 29 per cent and 9 per cent.

Examination of our 892 decisions supports Zander's earlier view. Table 8.7 shows that there is an almost identical pattern of decisions for unrepresented and represented defendants. The only significant difference was in our SGR group, many of whom are unrepresented in the early stages. They later obtain legal representation, and later

Table 8.7 Percentage bailed, by representation

	All defendants		SGR group only	
	Unrepresented	Represented	Unrepresented*	Represented*
Bail				
uncontested	45	43	23	53
after contest	5	5	7	3
Custody				
after contest	36	37	47	36
uncontested	13	14	23	8

*I.e. at time of decision as to bail/custody.

obtain bail—but as the table shows, not generally after a contest. Whether the prosecution agree to bail later because the police inquiries are complete, or because they see that the defendant is now represented and wish to avoid a contest, it is impossible to tell.

Bail/custody on committal for sentence

There are once again no official statistics on bail/custody decisions made by magistrates when committing a defendant to the higher court for sentence. The official view is that this will almost always be a committal in custody, 'because the whole purpose of the committal is to have the accused sent to prison, and have him sent to prison for a longer period than the justices could impose'. (Lord Parker, CJ in R. v. Coe, [1969] 1 All E.R. 65; see Home Office Working Party on Bail Procedures, paras 33 and 157.) That view seems to be borne out by the bail rate of 3 per cent found by Simon and Weatheritt (1974, table 9, p.51). On the other hand Zander's study (1971, p.193), also in London courts, found a bail rate of 21 per cent and the national Cobden Trust study 38 per cent (King, 1971, p.97).

In our Sheffield court sample, the bail rate was 30 per cent. We were able to examine the rates for defendants who were represented at this stage separately from those who were unrepresented. As Table 8.8 shows, there is more likelihood of a contest when a solicitor is present but his efforts make little difference.

Table 8.8 Bail rate of represented and unrepresented defendants on committal for sentence

		Unrepresented (%)	Represented (%)
Bail:	no contest	23	21
	after contest	0	9
Custody:	after contest	15	48
	no contest	58	21

Bail/custody on committal for trial

Official statistics are available on bail/custody decisions made when it is decided to commit a defendant for trial. They form part of the *Criminal Statistics* (table I), and the figures for the period 1966-72 are conveniently reproduced as appendix E of the report of the

Working Party on Bail Procedures. The bail rate has risen from 62 per cent in 1966 to 78 per cent in 1972; Simon and Weatheritt's London study reflects the same trend, showing 51 per cent for 1966, 72 per cent in 1969 (tables 6 and 8, pp.50-1). Neither the Cobden Trust nor Zander's (1971) study contains clear results.[5]

Our Sheffield study found a bail rate of 61 per cent (see Table 2.7). Here as at some other stages, the Sheffield magistrates are less generous in granting bail than might have been expected.

Adjournments for reports

In our Sheffield sample there was an adjournment for reports (usually probation reports) after conviction in the magistrates' court in 160 cases, divided equally between male and female defendants. So far as the men are concerned this represents 8·5 per cent of cases proceeding to sentence in the magistrates' court, but 28 per cent of women defendants. Reports will, of course, be available in many more cases, either having been prepared in anticipation of a conviction or obtained while a case is 'stood down' for an hour or so; we are here speaking only of adjournments.

The Sheffield bench are much more generous in granting bail at this point in the proceedings than other courts studied. Zander's London courts granted bail for reports in 52 per cent of such cases (1971, p.193), a finding confirmed by Simon and Weatheritt: 33 per cent for 1966, 51 per cent for 1969 (table 5, p.50). The Cobden Trust found a 60·5 per cent bail rate in their national study (King, 1971, p. 97). It is astonishing to find that in Sheffield, bail is given in 92 per cent of these cases. There were only 13 defendants who were remanded in custody for reports, and 4 of those were special cases: 3 had previously been on bail for reports which had not been obtained (presumably because of the defendant's non-co-operation), and 1 had previously during the present case failed to answer bail and a warrant for his arrest had had to be issued.

A probable reason for the Sheffield practice is that custody means Leeds Prison, which is overcrowded and distant from the Sheffield agencies.

Prosecution reasons for opposing bail

Our court observers noted the arguments advanced in connection with any application for bail or for a remand (or committal) in custody. All cases were included, whatever stage had been reached and whether or not there was any contest. In general the findings were similar to those of other studies (e.g. Bottomley, 1970, p.60; King, 1971, p.19; Zander, 1971, p.196). Tables 8.9 and 8.10

Table 8.9 Prosecution reasons for seeking remand in custody by magistrates (all cases; and cases ultimately tried in the higher court)

Reason	All cases*	Higher court cases
Previous record	152	116
Nature of present offences	150	119
Further inquiries to be made	126	77
Likely to commit further offences	103	77
Likely to abscond	101	75
Further charges likely	84	57
No fixed abode	59	38
Fear of interference with witnesses/evidence	53	35
Offence while on bail	43	33
Failed to keep bail before	15	13
Others	22	14

*In this table and in table 8.11, 'all cases' includes a few cases which for one reason or another never reached trial in any court, but were dropped.

Table 8.10 Prosecution reasons for seeking remand in custody by magistrates (cases ultimately tried summarily)

Reason	No.
Further inquiries to be made	48
Previous record	34
Further charges likely	27
Nature of present offences	25
Likely to abscond	24
Likely to commit further offences	23
No fixed abode	18
Fear of interference with witnesses/evidence	16
Offence while on bail	7
Failed to keep bail before	1
Others	8

indicate the number of applications in respect of which the prosecution used a particular argument. There was, of course, no means of telling what reasons influenced the court, and it may be that some reasons are advanced as a matter of routine, adding little to the one really persuasive argument.

We have seen that the official legal view is that the likelihood of the defendant absconding is the primary factor in bail decisions. The table shows that it is only the fifth factor in order of popularity with the police officers or solicitors conducting prosecutions. In the more serious cases, they rely on the nature of the offence charged—'this is a serious offence'—or on the defendant's record—'and the defendant's record is not a good one'. In the less serious cases, the need for further police inquiries and the threat, or promise, of further charges, are more to the fore; we have already noted that these arguments, so commonly heard, have no express judicial approval.

Defence reasons for seeking bail

A similar exercise was carried out to record defence arguments in favour of bail. It was expected that defence reasons would be more varied and less predictable than those advanced by the prosecution, and the relevant part of the court observation form was not pre-coded. In fact a standard list of arguments soon emerged, and the pattern is much the same for all types of offence. It is set out in Table 8.11.

The fact that the pattern is similar for the various types of offence is itself of some importance. The prosecution talk in terms of the offence, the record, the state of the police inquiries. The defence talk much more about the defendant—his family, his job, his record of answering bail in the past. Most commentators agree that the strength of a defendant's 'roots' in the community is a valuable test of the likelihood of his answering bail. In particular, a number of American jurisdictions in which the administration of bail has developed many abuses and injustices from which England has escaped (see Katz et al., 1972, chapter 4) have adopted 'release on recognizance programs' based on an assessment of the defendant's stability in the community. (See Institute on the Operation of Pretrial Release Projects, 1965; Wice, 1974. A summary of these schemes, originating with the Manhattan experiment, is contained in the report of the Working Party on Bail Procedures, 1974,

Table 8.11 Defence reasons for seeking bail

	All cases*	Higher court cases	Summary trial cases
Has fixed address/address to go to	183	134	42
Offers surety, prepared to accept special conditions of bail	158	116	30
In work/has job to go to	112	79	27
Intends to plead not guilty	63	31	31
Answered bail in the past	45	31	13
Particular family problem	35	26	7
Length of time before Crown Court hearing	30	26	2
Police inquiries now complete	9	8	1
Others	67	50	17

*See note to table 8.9.

pp.44-6.) In Sheffield it is the defendant's arguments which are in accord with this modern approach, rather than the prosecution's.

The Home Office Working Party on Bail Procedures (1974) recommended the introduction of a version of the American schemes into the English system. A member of the court staff would prepare in relation to each defendant a bail information sheet with details of his marital status, domestic circumstances, address (with length of residence), employment and income, and this would be before the court in making a bail/custody decision. There is little doubt that the availability of this information in a standard form would very considerably affect the submissions by the two 'sides' in a bail/custody application, and probably also the decisions which would be reached.

Bail/custody and subsequent events

It is commonly asserted that to detain a man in custody before his trial, quite apart from subjecting a man who is presumed innocent to a prison regime, makes it more likely that he will plead guilty, more likely that he will be convicted despite a plea of not guilty, and more likely that if convicted he will receive a custodial sentence. Gibson's data (1960, p.9; discussed by Zander, 1967, p.30) indicated that of those committed for trial in custody 82 per cent pleaded guilty, but only 71 per cent of those given bail at that stage. A study by Davies (1971) in which samples of defendants given or refused bail were matched as to offence and previous convictions found that 88 per cent of those in custody pleaded guilty, but only 69 per cent of those given bail.

By a remarkable coincidence, the Sheffield figures correspond exactly with Davies's, though our sample was not selected in the way his was. Looking at male defendants only, the proportion of defendants pleading guilty was: remanded in custody at all times, 88 per cent; remanded on bail at all times, 69 per cent; with mixed bail/custody experience, 85 per cent. We would not base any conclusions on these figures. This is because a defendant may well decide on his plea at an early stage; if he resolves to plead not guilty he, or his solicitor, will use this as an argument for the grant of bail. It stands both as an argument in its own right, and also lends added weight to the point that there will be a considerable delay before trial; we have already seen that those pleading not guilty experience very considerable delays.

Much the same points can be made when discussing the relationship between bail/custody and verdicts after a not guilty plea. A number of studies have found that the acquittal rate is higher for defendants who have been on bail. They include Gibson's study (1960, p.9; see Zander, 1967, p.26) and that of Simon and Weatheritt (1974, pp.24-5), in which the apparent effect of custody persisted after the previous convictions of the defendants in each group were taken into account, and also studies in the USA and Canada where the framework is very different (e.g. Foote et al., 1954; Friedland, 1965). Bottomley (1970, p.33) found the opposite at his urban court: of those committed for trial in custody and pleading not guilty, 46 per cent were acquitted as against 43 per cent of those on bail.

In fact the matter is very complex. Bottomley points out that we must look at the distribution of not guilty pleas as well as acquittals, and all studies are plagued by the 'mixed' cases, the large proportion of defendants who experience remands on bail and remands in custody, or who are convicted on some counts only, or whose case is 'mixed' in both respects. It would be expecting too much for a general study like ours to have anything new to offer. We merely record that 38 per cent of those who pleaded not guilty after experiencing custody at some stage in the course of the case were acquitted on all charges, and that 43 per cent of those without custodial experiences were so acquitted.

One measure of bail/custody decisions is the proportion of defendants who experience custody during an adjournment or on committal to the higher court who do not return to prison under sentence. In our sample, 33 per cent of such defendants did not so return: 5 per cent were acquitted, 9 per cent given a suspended sentence and 19 per cent a non-custodial sentence (such as probation or a fine).

Although the numbers involved are small the SGU category merits closer examination. Only 13 male defendants in this category (2 per cent of the total) experienced custody; as many as 9 of these did not receive a custodial sentence. The point is that the criteria for bail/custody decisions are not the same as those relied on in sentencing. Of the 13 defendants, 12 had previous convictions, 9 faced more than one charge, 5 had no fixed abode; these are all matters likely to be urged in support of a police request for a remand in custody but are less central at the sentencing stage for minor offences. At that stage, the time already spent in custody may of course be taken into account.

Of all male defendants in our sample, 79 per cent were given a non-custodial sentence or were acquitted (suspended sentences being treated as non-custodial). Taking only those defendants who had experienced custodial remands, the corresponding figure was 33 per cent (cf. Simon and Weatheritt, 1974, tables 17 and 18, p.61; although not readily comparable with our data, their findings lead to the same conclusion). Some would argue that this discrepancy demonstrates the disadvantages suffered by those detained in custody, but one must be beware of trying 'to have it both ways'. If the latter figure were higher, it would feed the alternative criticism that there was an excessive amount of pre-trial detention.

Bail/custody in the higher courts

There were only 37 cases in which the defendant had to make two or more appearances in the higher courts. In 33 of these 37 cases, the decision as to bail during the adjournment followed that of the magistrates' at committal, with those committed on bail having their bail renewed, and those committed in custody remaining in custody. In 1 case a man committed on bail was remanded in custody, having come into custody on fresh charges in the meantime; 1 defendant committed for trial in custody was granted bail in the higher court; the other 2 cases involved several adjournments and the defendants had bail for part of the time, one having been committed on bail, the other in custody.

Two cases illustrate the complexity of events. One involved 3 charges, 2 of driving while disqualified and 1 of taking a car without the owner's consent. The defendant admitted the first two, which he regarded as minor matters, but protested his innocence of the third charge. He was committed on bail to stand trial at Quarter Sessions. His case was reached on 21 December, just as Quarter Sessions were preparing to adjourn for the last time before their abolition. He was told by the Recorder that in view of his not guilty plea his case would be adjourned to the Crown Court, and that the remand would be in custody. The defendant applied to the judge in chambers and was given bail. The Crown Court dealt with his case in mid-April, and he was acquitted. To his great surprise the defendant was then given two concurrent sentences of 9 months' imprisonment on the charges of driving while disqualified, which he had admitted 5 months before.

The second illustration is rather disquieting. The defendant appeared before the magistrates in late November with codefendants. He was charged with aiding and abetting their driving while disqualified—in effect, being a passenger, not on the face of it a desperately serious offence. He was however remanded in custody on two occasions. He would have been given a summary trial, but his codefendants were committed to the higher court for trial, and so was he, still in custody. He applied for bail to the judge in chambers, who granted it but required sureties; he was unable to find acceptable sureties and appeared at Quarter Sessions in custody. Quarter Sessions confirmed the existing terms of bail and he later found sureties. At his trial in late February, his plea of not guilty was accepted by the prosecution, but a fresh indictment alleging obtaining by deception was signed and he was convicted on that count. One is left with the feeling that his earlier detention in custody was not justified by the charges he faced, but was thought desirable because of his criminal associates and suspected activities. And that is not what pre-trial custody is for.

Judge in chambers

These last two cases both applied to the judge in chambers, a high court judge sitting alone and in private, who may hear representations against a remand in custody by a legal representative (or by the Official Solicitor if the case is unrepresented). Under the Courts Act 1971 (which came into force on 1 January 1972, during our research period) an appeal against remand in custody is also possible in certain circumstances to the Crown Court judge.

Because these hearings are in private, they were impossible for us to monitor except with our interview sample. In this sample, as many as 40 per cent of those defendants always remanded in custody by the magistrates had applied to the judge in chambers, or the Crown Court judge, or both. There are no readily accessible national figures, but the report of the Working Party on Bail Procedures suggests a high proportion of applicants: some 30,700 defendants were remanded in custody at their last remand by magistrates (see para. 32) and about 8,000 applications were made to the judges in chambers, with perhaps another 2,000 applications to Crown Court judges (see para. 162). So far as the fate of the applications is concerned, the Sheffield figures suggest a meagre success rate; only 12 per cent of those who applied were granted bail by the judge, but even this is marginally higher than the national rate of 10 per cent in 1968-70 (see King, 1971, p.67).

The high figure for judge in chambers appeals may be thought to be because this is almost the only occasion in the present criminal justice system where there is no sanction against attempting to assert one's rights. We have seen that there may be sentence penalties against not guilty pleas and against Crown Court choice of venue, and that appeals against conviction or sentence are often not pursued because of the fear of loss of waiting time from a custodial sentence. There is no such sanction against a judge in chambers application, and it thus becomes the more interesting why applications are not pursued.

The answers, from our data, seem to be threefold. First, a large number (about a quarter) did not apply simply because they did not know the procedure. Second, there is the question of time: as one defendant put it 'they remand for a week at a time, and it takes ten days to get to the judge in chambers'; the hope of bail at the next magistrates' court hearing (in cases which have not yet reached the committal stage) may seem much more real than the somewhat ghostly figure of the unseen judge in his chambers. Third, there is especially among more experienced prisoners a well-developed sense of cynicism about the chances of success (partly based on the informal information available in the prison about the high failure rate): so, as various prisoners put it, they hadn't applied because there was 'no chance', it was a 'waste of time' or (in more sophisticated versions) 'I was already convicted, and it's very rare for convicted prisoners to get JIC bail'; 'the police were opposing it and the judge has your previous record'. One or two who in the result had been kept quite long periods did however subsequently regret not having applied.

A source of disquiet among some applicants was that no reason is ever given for the refusal of the application; and one or two objected to the purely written nature of the application: 'If you could see the judge on appeal it would be better instead of just writing it down.'

'Inconsistent' bail decisions

We have analysed, perhaps at tedious length, court bail decisions in various different stages of proceedings—magistrates' hearings before a finding of guilt, committals for trial, committals for sentence, post-conviction adjournments for reports, higher court bail. It is easy, in the statistical complexity of all this, to lose sight of the actual processing of an individual defendant.

Here, we look at one aspect of 'sequential' court processing, that is those cases where courts made apparently inconsistent bail/custody judgments in the same case, ordering bail at one hearing and custody at another (we ignore police bail for this purpose). The analysis is restricted to the interview sample.

If we leave aside the very few cases where an application to the judge in chambers was successful (and where later courts naturally followed the judge's lead), there were a total of 4 per cent of the interviewed cases in which 'inconsistent' decisions were made. These fall naturally into four different categories. The first, which requires no further comment, consists of those originally released on bail, but who committed further offences while on bail, or broke a condition of bail, and were thereafter remanded in custody. The second category is of cases where two different benches, faced with virtually identical arguments reach differing conclusions, sometimes with the aid of fresh facts:

> Case 7028 K and his wife had a history of domestic troubles. On Christmas Eve, K went out to visit a relative, and returned at 10.30 p.m. to find his wife gone out and his children being looked after by a neighbour. He put them and himself to bed; his wife returned at 1.30 a.m. and an argument developed

while toys were being placed in the children's pillowcases. K's wife called the police, and eventually had herself to go to hospital with facial injuries. K was taken into police custody forthwith, and held there until the next court sitting on 28 December. At this hearing the prosecution objected to bail because of K's previous record, and the likelihood of further attacks on the wife; the defence said K had only 2 previous convictions, neither for violence, and he was willing to go to his mother's house and not see his wife pending the outcome of the case. The magistrates remanded in custody until 4 January. On that date, all the same arguments were repeated again, the only difference being that this time the wife was in court and said she was prepared to have him back. Bail was granted.

The third category, a small one, is of those who are on bail throughout magistrates' court hearings and are then committed to the Crown Court for sentence (under ss 28, 29 of the Magistrates' Courts Act 1952), such committal being ordered in custody. Until the Criminal Justice Act 1967, custody was compulsory in such cases; although it is now discretionary, some courts often prefer to commit in custody since they have, by definition, already decided that a custodial sentence of more than 6 months is necessary.

The fourth and final category of 'inconsistent' bail decisions is the most interesting one, and also the most numerous, accounting for exactly half of all 'inconsistent' decisions. It consists of cases where the police object to bail at one or more early court appearances, and the magistrates uphold the objection; then later the police withdraw their objections and the case proceeds to unopposed bail. What is especially interesting is that in every such case, a main reason for bail being opposed at first was that 'further inquiries have to be made', or that 'further charges are to be brought'. Three illustrative cases give an impression:

Case 6015 C, an intelligent and articulate 18-year-old, was charged with burglary. At his first appearance the police objected to bail on the grounds that (i) the present offence was serious, (ii) C was likely to commit further offences, (iii) further inquiries had to be made, (iv) C was thought likely to interfere with evidence and (v) that he was likely to abscond. The defence solicitor said C was needed at home, where his father was sick, and that he was anxious to co-operate with the police. C was remanded in local custody for 3 days; when he reappeared, the police had no objection to bail. Asked why he thought he had been given bail, C replied (in our interview) 'I presume bail is for giving a person a chance—you can see his reaction to being given a chance, with his attitude to work, etc. I did well on bail'. (Significantly, C describes bail here in terms similar to probation, rather than as a legal right.)

Case 6032 E was charged with burglary of a shop. The alleged theft was of only £6 value, and E's only previous conviction was in the juvenile court fourteen years previously. Bail was nevertheless opposed because (i) the modus operandi of the present offence suggested that he was responsible for other offences, (ii) further inquiries were to be made and (iii) further charges were likely. E protested that he lived with his wife and three children and had a regular job, but he was remanded in custody. Three days later, the police withdrew all objections to custody, although at a later hearing another charge was added. E said the reason for the change was that in the 3-day interval the 'police were satisfied with what I had told them'.

Case 7027 Y was charged with attempted burglary and going equipped for stealing. His codefendant was charged with aggravated burglary (which has to be tried at the Crown Court) so the magistrates decided to commit for trial. An adjournment was sought for the preparation of committal papers: the police opposed bail because of (i) the defendant's previous record, (ii) the nature of the present offence and (iii) the likelihood of further charges. This was opposed by Y's solicitor who stressed his fixed address, the fact that the charge was only attempted burglary and could have been dealt with summarily, and the minor nature of Y's previous record. Bail was refused. At the committal proceedings eight days later, the prosecution made no objection to bail: no further charges were ever brought against Y. In interview, Y said: 'I could have had bail the first time round—nothing happened while I was in custody. It was just a waste of time all round.'

These cases again raise disturbing issues. Prima facie, at least, they suggest that the initial police request for custody was made much more in terms of police convenience in pursuing inquiries than because of a real need for custody to ensure attendance at trial, or other compelling reasons associated with the administration of justice. (If not, why did the objections disappear?) And once more, we have to say that police convenience is not what pre-trial custody is for. One defendant in our sample told us that—'I said to the police—what further inquiries could they not make if we had bail?' This is a question that magistrates could usefully ask police officers more often, and it is encouraging that the Home Office Working Party has recommended that they should do so (para. 75).

Court bail: the defendant's view

It remains only to consider the defendant's views about court bail as expressed in our interviews. Our questions in this area were necessarily rather restricted by the large number of possible patterns of courts' decisions and by the relatively inactive role of the defendant; and one or two groups of decision patterns had so few defendants that no statistical treatment is possible.

One group was of those on bail throughout. Only 18 per cent of this group said that they were surprised that the police did not oppose bail; these defendants had sometimes (35 per cent of the cases) been led by the police to expect opposition, and sometimes based their pessimism on their own criminal record (19 per cent). The great majority who had not expected police opposition regarded their own trustworthiness and the triviality of their offence as justifying their optimism.

At the other extreme are those who had been in custody throughout. Of these, there was a proportion (18 per cent of the whole 'custody only' group) who had never applied for bail.[6] The majority of these cases (56 per cent) said they had not applied because they knew they would not succeed, and usually gave cogent reasons for this belief, e.g. that they were of no fixed abode or had already jumped bail on another charge. Twenty-five per cent said they had not applied for bail because they wanted to get started on serving the custodial sentences they knew they would receive; the rest had special reasons such as lawyer's advice, unwillingness to disclose a relative's address, etc. It was very interesting that this small number of 'no application' cases was entirely confined to two sub-sample groups, namely the SGRs and the HGs; also of importance was that in terms of the defendants' typology, most of them were either passive (including dissociative) respondents (38 per cent) or else recidivist strategists (25 per cent).

All those who had been in custody at any stage (other than simply overnight police custody), and who had applied unsuccessfully for bail were asked why it was they thought they had failed. The results are given in Table 8.12. Comparing this with official prosecution reasons for opposing bail (see Tables 8.9 and 8.10), there are some interesting differences. 'Further inquiries to be made' and 'further charges likely' do not feature at all in the defendant table (except as an occasional answer under 'other'), despite their prominence in the prosecution table. The two top-scoring defendants' answers, the likelihood of absconding and the possible interference with witnesses, are both well down the prosecutors' table of frequency of reasons given; yet paradoxically in the official legal literature it is these two reasons which feature most prominently. It would seem that defendants are attributing to police and prosecution a degree of adherence to official criteria which they themselves are willing to dispense with; or, alternatively, that defendants are able to identify the 'real' reason, and ignore those arguments customarily advanced by the police to fill out their statement.

Table 8.12 Defendants' perception of reasons for failure of court bail applications

	%
Thought likely to abscond	16
Thought likely to interfere with witnesses	14
Lawyer made bad job of application	12
Charge too serious	12
Previous record	12
No fixed abode	8
On suspended sentence	1
Other	10
Don't know	15

On the other hand, this should not be interpreted as a vote of confidence in the bail system by defendants, for this clearly does not exist. Only 22 per cent of those who had been remanded in custody and made application(s) for bail thought that their application had been handled fairly. There was a widespread view (not without foundation, as we have seen) that the police dominate the court bail decision pattern, and that opposing the police is, while worth trying, not very likely to bear fruit. Allied to this was a view that magistrates often did not seem to give bail cases adequate careful deliberation, but simply endorsed the police view. The following are some representative quotations:

> 'If the police oppose bail, you have no chance.'

> 'You have no hope against the police.'

> 'Magistrates always believe the police. The bail system is unfair—they [police] shouldn't be allowed to try this issue, it should be independent. They keep people in custody and hinder their defences.'

> 'Getting bail depends how helpful you are to the police.'

> 'Only one in a hundred get bail, and if you're in lodgings you can't get it.'

> 'I was asked if I wanted bail. I said yes and was remanded in custody. I didn't get a chance to say anything.'

A final quotation comes from a wholly unrepresentative case, one of our most sophisticated 'recidivist strategists' (case no. 4022, above, chapter 3):

> 'I was very disappointed in the solicitor's application for bail; my mates [codefendants] certainly deserved bail. A was only involved with one offence, he had a wife and kids and a house; though he had a suspended sentence, and that would have gone against him. B had only very minor offences. As for myself, I realise I had less reason to expect bail—I was NFA (so far as the police were concerned), unemployed, and I'd committed an offence while on bail; but it depends what legal principles are involved in granting bail. Is it all these things, or is it just the likelihood of absconding? I've always been known to keep bail before, and would never skip bail: but is that the legal principle?'

It is a very good question, and, especially in view of the role of the police and their very different view of the whole bail issue, one that the legal system should urgently clarify. The Working Party on Bail Procedures in Magistrates' Courts had an opportunity to resolve this point, but sadly failed. They recommended, as we have noted, a presumption in favour of bail, but the courts would still be free to remand in custody: what is crucial is the criteria the courts would use. The Working Party rejected (see para. 88) proposals which would spell out detailed rules in new legislation: the circumstances of individual cases are so variable that, in the Working Party's view, the courts' discretion should not be further restricted. In the new scheme, a court ordering a remand in custody would have to state its reasons for refusing bail but 'the reasons need not be elaborate; it should in general suffice simply to refer to one or more of the relevant factors which we have set out' (para. 89). In other words, the new procedure would give a clearer picture of the ways in which the existing criteria are applied, but there is no reformulation of those criteria, and so no new answer to our respondent's question.

9 Conclusions and implications

Models of the criminal process and the defendant's perspective

There is one truth which is seldom revealed in the literature of the law or in studies of the administration of criminal justice. It is a truth which was made evident to all those involved in this research project as they sat through the cases which made up our sample. The truth is that, for the most part, the business of the criminal courts is dull, commonplace, ordinary and after a while downright tedious.

Of course that is not the picture presented by the writers of fiction or of its near-relation, the legal memoir. A layman spending a few days off work to serve as a juror in the Crown Court is excited by the novelty of the experience, by the wigs and gowns and legal language; and he is by definition involved in a contested case in a higher court. Many researchers, too, concentrate on the areas of special interest such as 'victimless crimes'—prostitution, gambling and drugs—which certainly raise real questions of policy and of practice but also provide astonishingly good 'copy' for the writer; a brave few write of motoring offences or petty thefts.

This is more than the self-pitying cry of the researcher reflecting on hours on the hard seats of the magistrates' courtroom. It is important for a number of reasons to remember that our cases were typically of unexciting offences handled in the ordinary routine way by court personnel who had seen it all before many, many times. There were moments of drama—the haunting picture of the middle-class first offender experiencing his first night in a cell gazing at pictures in human excrement on the walls—but most defendants pleaded guilty, said little, and were quietly given an average sort of sentence, the case leaving little impression on the observer's memory.

One reason for stressing all this is that it contrasts sharply with the picture of the criminal process advanced by Packer at the commencement of his much-cited presentation of two models of the criminal process (Packer, 1969, p.149):

> People who commit crimes . . . ordinarily take care to avoid being caught. If arrested, they ordinarily deny their guilt and

> otherwise try not to co-operate with the police. If brought to trial, they do whatever their resources permit to resist being convicted. And even after they have been convicted and sent to prison, their efforts to secure their freedom do not cease. It is a struggle from start to finish.

That description cannot be applied with any accuracy to the situation we observed. No doubt Packer, like many other writers, was thinking primarily of serious crimes and superior courts; but he also falls into error in treating 'people who commit crimes' as forming a homogeneous group.

If we use our findings as to the distribution of defendants on the typology developed in chapter 3 (see Table 3.1), those who could possibly be described as 'struggling from start to finish' comprise the strategists (15 per cent of the whole sample as reweighted); those 'mistakenly indicted citizens' who pleaded not guilty (1·4 per cent); the right-assertive defendants (1·3 per cent), and some of the 'other-dominated respondents' who were guided by their lawyers or families (up to 7·6 per cent). To these groups, which total only 25·4 per cent of the whole, might be added some of those whose response is dominated by the triviality of the offence (5·8 per cent), who would perhaps have 'struggled' if faced with a more serious charge. Overall we could say that at the very most one-third 'struggle' in the Packer sense; another third we group as passive respondents, leaving another third in a central or miscellaneous group. (For a critique of Packer's approach on other grounds, as basically a 'battle model', see Griffiths, 1970.)

Why do many defendants not 'struggle'? As we have suggested in chapters 1 and 3, to develop adequate explanations of the differing ways defendants approach court proceedings would require sophisticated discussion of (inter alia) personality, cultural background and upbringing, and the defendant's personal ideology—and that is beyond the scope of this work. But we must not overlook the possibility that the present structure and operation of the legal system might itself contribute to the apparent passivity and acceptance of so many defendants. Social scientists have recently shown a marked interest in developing explanations of individual action not so much in the traditional terms of culture, personality, etc., but in terms of the operation of societal systems and structures upon the individual. Is such a possibility plausible in this case?

A useful approach to this question is again through Packer's work. He has very usefully highlighted two very different ideal-typical concepts of the criminal process, which he terms the 'Crime Control Model' and the 'Due Process Model' (Packer, 1969, part II, passim). The Crime Control Model emphasises the importance of the repression of criminal conduct; it requires that primary attention be paid to the efficiency of the system, the aim being to produce a series of routinised operations which pass the case along to a successful conclusion—the rapid exoneration of the suspect if he is really innocent; otherwise his rapid conviction, preferably on a plea of guilty, since the fact-finding endeavours of the police are just as efficient, and possibly more efficient, than those of formal adjudicative agencies. The Due Process Model, on the other hand, stresses the possibilities of administrative errors by police and others, and erects an obstacle course of formal, adjudicative, adversary processes, which take time but which the prosecution authorities must complete before a conviction can be obtained: only thus, it holds, can a just system be maintained.

A conventional lawyer's account of the English system of criminal justice would stress those aspects which accord with the values underlying the Due Process Model. A suspect is protected at the stage of pre-trial interrogation by the restrictions which the Judges' Rules place on police questioning and by his right to seek the advice of a solicitor before answering. If charged he has, for all cases falling within our sample at least, the right to trial by jury, with the right to legal representation, legal aid if he needs it, and the advantage of having the prosecution case disclosed to him at the committal proceeding stage, thus ensuring that he can exploit to the full the undoubted advantages of the adversary mode of procedure at the trial itself.

But the system as seen in our study is very different. To understand it adequately we have to introduce a third paradigmatic model of the criminal process, not discussed by Packer, which we shall call the 'Liberal Bureaucratic Model'.

The Liberal Bureaucratic Model is the model of the criminal justice process typically held by humane and enlightened clerks to the justices and Crown Court administrators in this country—as well as by many others. It differs substantially from the Crime Control Model, the model typically held by the police, since it dissents from its underlying central value-position: 'The value-system that underlies the Crime Control Model is based on the proposition that the repression of criminal conduct is by far the most important function to be performed by the criminal process' (Packer, 1969, p.158).

The Liberal Bureaucratic Model holds, rather, that the protection of individual liberty, and the need for justice to be done and to be seen to be done, must ultimately override the importance of the repression of criminal conduct. The liberal bureaucrat here joins with the advocate of Due Process in agreeing that formal adjudicative processes are very important, and moreover that—in the conventional phrase—'it is better for ten guilty men to go free than for one innocent man to be convicted'.

But the Liberal Bureaucratic Model also differs substantially from the Due Process Model. For

> the Due Process Model looks very much like an obstacle course. Each of its successive stages is designed to present formidable impediments to carrying the accused any further along in the process. . . . [It] resembles a factory that has to devote a substantial part of its input to quality control. *This necessarily cuts down on quantitative output* (Packer, 1969, pp.163, 165; italics added).

It is precisely this restriction on quantitative output which offends the liberal bureaucrat about the Due Process Model. The liberal bureaucrat is a practical man; he realises that things have to get done, systems have to be run. It is right that the defendant shall have substantial protections; crime control is not the overriding value of the criminal justice system. But these protections must have a limit. If it were not so, then the whole system of criminal justice, with its ultimate value to the community in the form of liberal and humane crime control, would collapse. Moreover, it is right to build in sanctions to deter those who might otherwise use their 'Due Process' rights frivolously, or to 'try it on'; an administrative system at State expense should not exist for this kind of time-wasting.

Throughout this study, from the two shoplifting cases with which we began, we have in various places drawn attention to the conflicting arguments of 'lawyers' rhetoric' and 'administrative efficiency' when discussing aspects of the court processes. These we can now more precisely define as the arguments of the Due Process and the Liberal Bureaucratic Models. Moreover, we have shown at various points the crucial role of the police in determining defendants' decisions—and the police typically operate on a Crime Control Model. It would seem helpful, therefore, to re-examine the English criminal justice system from the defendant's point of view, and bearing in mind the possible operation and application of the three models of criminal justice which we have outlined.

Packer (1969, p.162) argues that in the Crime Control Model, 'the focal device . . . is the plea of guilty; through its use, adjudicative fact-finding is reduced to a minimum'. We agree with this assessment. In our sections on guilty pleas (above, chapter 5) we repeatedly saw how the final, formal decision as to plea was little more than an official acknowledgment of processes that had been already accomplished in police-suspect transactions. There is little doubt that the police know this, and that they consciously work towards a position where the suspect's confession, or that of his companion(s), leaves him little alternative but to plead guilty. Towards this end, we have seen in chapter 8 that a suspect may be subjected to pressures from the police to make a confession statement: if he refuses he is told he will remain in custody. Similarly, data presented in chapter 6 show that the right to legal representation is limited in certain ways: few defendants saw their solicitors in the police station, and at least some of them had sought to exercise their right to approach a solicitor and apparently been fobbed off by the police. In short, the police, operating mainly but not exclusively on a Crime Control Model, effectively control the early stages of the criminal justice process; and through this early control—especially in its influence on pleas of guilty—they are able (as we shall see more fully below) to influence powerfully the remainder of the criminal justice system.

At this stage, the defendant enters the court system. There is here less scope for informalities such as the police seem to practise, and the system cannot be said to operate with Crime Control as a dominant value.

But the values of the Liberal Bureaucratic Model are everywhere to be found in the actual operation, and even in some of the formal rules, of the English courts. Thus in chapter 4 we noted the pressures on a defendant to elect for the administratively simpler summary trial rather than opt for the full 'due process' of jury trial—fear of delay, fear of a heavier sentence at the higher court, and even costs penalties specifically against the defendant who chose to go to the Crown Court. Similarly in chapter 5 the same pressures of sentence were seen to operate vis-à-vis the basic question of plea; and delay was also again a factor, at least in Sheffield at the lower court level (see chapter 2). Again in chapter 7, we saw how the rules about loss of waiting time for 'frivolous' appeals operated as a deterrent (much stronger in practice than the formal content of the rule warranted) to defendants considering an appeal. All these rules help to smooth the administrative operation of the system, while leaving open to the defendant his formal rights—a classic statement of the Liberal Bureaucratic position.

But what about defence lawyers? Packer (1969, p.172) says that 'questions about the right to counsel . . . become absolutely central if one's model moves very far down the spectrum of possibilities toward the pure Due Process Model'. The formal English system, recognising this, makes generous allowance for legal aid in Crown Court cases, and at least some provision of the same kind in the magistrates' courts. But what sort of advice do lawyers provide? We have seen (Table 5.11) that of those who are 'possibly innocent' but who nevertheless plead guilty, one-third do so primarily on their lawyer's advice; also barristers' last-minute advice is the dominant reason for late plea-changing in the Crown Court (Table 5.12). Lawyers do not provide this kind of advice (at least usually) for their own convenience, nor because of any commitment to a Crime Control ideology, nor because they are the subservient hacks of the court system (as some American evidence on public defenders suggests). They provide it because they are operating within a system heavily imbued with Liberal Bureaucratic rules and values, and they know that their clients might indeed receive heavier penalties if they are found guilty rather than plead guilty. The same goes for other advice given, such as the advice not to appeal—though we have seen that in that particular connection there is some apparent dereliction of duty by lawyers (chapter 7). Indeed, even where lawyers take a stricter Due Process view their clients can, given the importance of the Liberal Bureaucratic Model in our existing system, have cause for considerable dissatisfaction (see case 5043 discussed in chapter 5).

Thus the provision of defence counsel, sacred tenet of the Due Process Model, is no guarantee of the operation of the values of Due Process where the dominant structure of the court system is Liberal Bureaucratic; for lawyers must and do work within that system. The same applies to the other Due Process rights formally available under our system. Hence the legal system is able to maintain the formal semblance of a Due Process Model, while in fact being largely committed to a Liberal Bureaucratic Model.

Moreover, and perhaps most importantly of all, the Liberal Bureaucratic Model powerfully reinforces the Crime Control Model —which as we have seen is dominant in the pre-court processes. The linchpin of the Crime Control Model is the plea of guilty, and various processes take place to assist in the fulfilment of a substantial proportion of such pleas. At the court level these processes are often actually reinforced by the rule that guilty pleas may receive lighter sentences; and defence counsel, working as they have to within this and other Liberal Bureaucratic rules, tend further to buttress the position. Moreover, there is no provision (as in inquisitorial legal systems) that the court satisfy itself that the statement of guilt is entered into with full-hearted consent by the defendant—to examine the defendant's story carefully in each case would (it is thought) take too much time, and create administrative blockages, although of course if the defendant inadvertently indicates a story which amounts to a denial of guilt after a guilty plea, then the court's liberal ideology usually requires it to suggest a change of plea (e.g. case no. 8014, discussed in chapter 6). So, despite the superficially apparent similarity of the value-systems underlying the Liberal Bureaucratic and the Due Process Models, in practice the Liberal Bureaucratic Model offers much stronger support to the aims of the Crime Control Model than the Due Process Model.

From the defendant's point of view, this convergence of the Crime Control and Liberal Bureaucratic Models is of great importance. Our defendants were typically realistic about the extent to which the early police-suspect encounters had compromised what chances they had of 'struggling' in Packer's sense; and more often than not, despite the negative views some of them had about barristers they were willing to accept lawyers' advice as to plea, venue and appeal, including the quite frequent advice not to 'struggle', but to plead guilty, abandon ideas of appeal, etc. In short, we can indeed explain at least part of the absence of 'struggle' in our sample by the way in which the system operates through the intermeshing of the Crime Control and Liberal Bureaucratic Models.

We must be careful not to overstate this conclusion. It must be remembered that an important minority did do a certain amount of 'struggling', and as we have said already one needs detailed information on individuals' cultural background, personalities and ideologies before being able adequately to explain individual differences in approach to the courts. But there can also, we think, be no doubt that part of the total explanation of defendants' behaviour in court and in decisions taken before court lies in an understanding of the constraints placed upon them by the values and operation of the police and court processes themselves.

Implications for policy

In discussing future policy, we must begin by declaring our values, since clearly these affect the kind of reforms we would wish to see. Briefly, then, in terms of the three models discussed above, we are not much impressed with the Crime Control Model, although recognising the need for any coherent society to enforce bans against certain behaviours. We are much more sympathetic to the Liberal Bureaucratic Model, for we have done enough administration in universities and elsewhere to recognise the importance of smooth administration; but we think that there has been insufficient recognition of the extent to which the Liberal Bureaucratic Model has in our legal system formed an effective alliance with the Crime Control Model. Hence we think there is a strong case for the Liberal Bureaucratic Model at present operative to be given a decisive push in the direction of Due Process, but without taking Due Process itself to such an extreme that viable administration becomes impossible. In this context also, we would agree with Packer (1969, p. 154) that 'a person who subscribed to all of the values underlying one model to the exclusion of all of the values underlying the other would be rightly viewed as a fanatic'.

How can this 'decisive push towards Due Process' be taken in the English context? A first point concerns the basic issue of the defendant's knowledge or ignorance of his rights. 'No system of criminal justice', wrote Justice Goldberg in his opinion in the leading United States case of Escobedo v. Illinois (378 U.S. 478 (1964)), 'can, or should, survive if it comes to depend for its continued effectiveness on the citizens' abdication through unawareness of their constitutional rights'.

We discovered that our defendants had, as one might expect, a patchy and limited knowledge of their rights. One defendant might not know that the police could give him bail; another might not know that he would be given a choice of venue; another again might suppose that legal aid did not apply until after first court appearance; yet another that there was no right of appeal.

We also found that on many of the decisions we set out to examine, defendants more often than not made decisions for themselves, discussing the matter with no one else. So, a majority of unrepresented defendants pleading guilty in the magistrates' courts had not discussed their plea with anyone else (see Table 5.10); 81 per cent of unrepresented defendants had not discussed the possibility of obtaining legal help (see Table 6.8); only 14 per cent of convicted defendants talked with anyone about appeals (Table 7.3).

To us, these findings suggest that the criminal justice system is at fault in failing to take positive steps to inform defendants of their rights. Duty solicitor schemes may help where they exist, but they will never cover the whole country, and there seems a real need to increase the provision of information to defendants about the courts and their procedures, perhaps especially in the areas of venue and appeal. We have pointed out in chapter 3 and again in this chapter that to the court official or habitué much court business is familiar to the point of being 'second nature', and the oppressive ordinariness of most cases is a standing discouragement from making too much of the procedural decisions. Yet to the defendant the case may be a unique crisis; in retrospect a particular decision made quickly and almost uncomprehendingly may seem to have been a turning-point.

But even a well-informed defendant may plead guilty although believing himself innocent; or fail to appeal because of his knowledge of the 'waiting time' rule although he and perhaps even his counsel think an appeal has some merit. This raises the whole issue of the 'penalty clauses' which are built into the Liberal Bureaucratic Model. The prime example is the rule of sentencing practice allowing lower sentences for guilty pleas. The possibility that this rule might encourage spurious pleas raises a strong case for its abolition, but on the other side of the argument are the undoubted advantages of the rule: a recognition of genuine contrition, a saving of court time, and a saving also of the time of witnesses who may be spared the ordeal and embarrassment of a court appearance. A way of securing these advantages while discouraging false guilty pleas would be a rule of practice requiring the court to ensure that it obtains the defendant's own story of the incident and that that story is consistent with the plea. Such a rule would not eliminate the possibility of spurious pleas, but it would be a useful check. It might also serve to identify the cases of unrepresented defendants who plead guilty, not realising that a legal defence might be open to them.

There remain the 'penalties' attached to venue choice and appeal. If venue choice is to remain open to the defendant, we think that no penalty in terms of sentence or costs should attach to a choice of Crown Court trial. If this created administratively impossible work-loads, then the only equitable solution is some restriction on the range of offences or circumstances where the defendant is offered the choice; we discuss below a possible solution which yet retains the importance of most defendants' clear perception of the Crown Court as offering superior justice. As to appeal, as we have suggested at the end of chapter 7, society must choose whether appeal is a general right or a special procedure designed to correct the occasional specific case. If the former, then the 'waiting time' rule must clearly be abolished (especially in view of the widespread overestimate of its effect by defendants); if the latter, then we must make it clear that appeal is not a general right, and indicate more specifically the kinds of case for which it is intended. The difficulty with the latter approach is the task of establishing criteria which identify in advance the meritorious appeal, but this difficulty, however, is not insuperable.

We have placed much stress throughout the book on 'lawyers' versus 'administrators' arguments, on Due Process versus Liberal Bureaucracy. It is an issue which has been insufficiently faced in our legal policy, and central to the issue are these various 'penalties' as to pleading not guilty, opting for Crown Court trial, and appealing, to which we have drawn attention. The resolution of policy concerning these 'penalties' is a central ideological and administrative matter for the English criminal justice system, and one to which there are few easy answers. We recognise that our own answers, as given above, are contentious, but we hope they will begin a serious debate not just about any single rule, but about the general issues which underlie each of the rules in a similar way.

Another crucial issue relates to practices in the police station, and the dominance of the Crime Control model at that point in the procedure. Various important suggestions have been made in recent years to introduce some independent element (such as magistrates, solicitors or tape-recorders) into this early questioning (see e.g. the discussion of various proposals in Criminal Law Revision Committee, 1972). This is not the place for a detailed discussion of such suggestions, though we are in general sympathy with the philosophy behind them. Assuming, however, that no such independent element is introduced, is there any way in which the courts can monitor more carefully what has gone on in the police station? We think there is. We have suggested in chapter 8 that police objections to bail on the grounds that 'further inquiries have to be made' should be much more carefully scrutinised by magistrates. Similarly, our suggestion above that guilty pleas should be carefully examined by the court before being accepted, would at least go some way to mitigate any possible malpractices in the way in which such pleas are encouraged by the police.

Turning to less central but still important issues, we noted one aspect of criminal procedure in which due process almost disappears. It is probably inevitable that the defendant in a summary trial should be at a marked disadvantage as against the defendant in the higher court in having only the most limited information about the case against him (cf. Napley, 1966a); to interpose a preliminary stage would be wholly impracticable. But there are special problems at the sentencing stage after a guilty plea. The police officer or prosecuting solicitor gives a short statement of the offence, as seen by the prosecution. We have seen in chapter 3 that some defendants feel that this statement of their offence has been unfair and misleading. They have felt unable to challenge it; they feel amazement, surprise and uncertainty. Even a represented defendant can be at a serious disadvantage at this point; he has pleaded guilty and has no witnesses, and how can he correct a false emphasis in the police account? Some defendants do in fact plead not guilty simply to avoid this problem.

We believe that this problem is a serious one, and can be remedied quite easily. When a defendant in a motoring case is invited to plead guilty by post, he is supplied with an advance copy of the statement of facts to be relied upon by the prosecution in case of a guilty plea. He has time to consider that statement, and when pleading guilty to the charge can write to the court expressing his dissent from some aspects of the statement. It would not be difficult to supply a similar statement in more serious cases. The defendant would still have the problem of speaking out in a strange environment, but the element of surprise would be eliminated.

There remains the important question of the delays described in detail in chapter 2. As we saw in that chapter, official inquiries have concerned themselves primarily with delays in the higher courts, and this has tended to obscure the very considerable delays in dealing with the more mundane cases in the magistrates' courts. Research studies of the business of magistrates' courts have tended to be sited in London where the presence of stipendiaries produces a wholly different pattern of business. In other cities a bench of three magistrates will normally sit for only a half-day, giving way to another bench for the afternoon session, and this leads to the practice of postponed fixed dates for considering contested cases. As we have seen, the dates are often unacceptably far in the future. There are also delays in processing other sorts of case, including those destined for the higher courts.

We believe that there should be adopted for the magistrates' courts the system used by the Streatfeild Committee in 1961 for the higher courts, and in the USA by the Administration of Justice Task Force of the President's Commission on Law Enforcement. For each type of business a maximum acceptable time should be declared, for example that committal proceedings should normally be completed within 28 days of first appearance. There would be exceptions, of course; full committal proceedings in complex fraud cases can take many months to prepare and many days or weeks to hear. None the less this sort of 'target' has great value and would lead to closer inquiry into the reasons for delays.

We were especially disturbed by the delays in the SN cases in Sheffield, and the evidence that in some cases defendants were pleading guilty rather than face a two- or three-month wait for a contested trial. Since not guilty cases will always take longer to prepare than guilty cases, we think there are strong grounds for court administrators exercising 'positive discrimination' in favour of not guilty cases in the lists, so that the discrepancy in waiting time between guilty and not guilty pleas does not grow unacceptably large. As a reserve power we think there may be grounds for introducing a Statute of Limitations at least for magistrates' court cases, securing automatic acquittal for the defendant if his case is not brought to trial within a stated period after the charge.

One method of generally reducing delay is to reduce the number of cases which have to be sent to the higher courts. We point in chapter 2 to the large proportion of Sheffield Crown Court business resulting from local practice in refusing summary trial in numbers of cases. Local variations no doubt exist, and we would like to see statutory criteria developed—such as value of property stolen, degree of personal injury, etc.—to reduce inconsistency and perhaps reduce the overall proportion of cases handled in this way.

We have also raised one small point about the form of committal proceedings, asking whether the attendance of legal representatives at short-form committals (which is productive of some delays) is really necessary. At present it is mandatory, but we question whether this rule is justified.

To make any real impact on the problem of delay in the higher courts more radical reforms are needed. The transfer of business from the Crown Court to the magistrates' court, the favourite device of official committees examining the pressures on the higher courts, can do little but increase the pressures on the magistrates' courts, shifting without solving the problem. Major reconstitution of the magistrates' courts by the appointment of stipendiaries, magistrates sitting alone on a permanent basis, would have a great effect, but seems impracticable.

A strategy which we would commend would be the reduction of that part of Crown Court work which consists of guilty pleas. Under present arrangements, the choice of venue is made before, and therefore independently of, the decision as to plea. If this order were reversed a wholly new situation would be created.

So, a defendant pleading guilty before the magistrates would never reach the choice of venue. The bench would decide either to sentence him themselves or to commit him for sentence to the higher court.[1] If he pleaded not guilty, the venue question would arise and both bench and defendant would have the right to insist on the trial being in the Crown Court; we have already commented on the need for criteria to guide the bench in its decision.

This change would reduce the overall burden of work by eliminating the need for committal proceedings in those cases which now become guilty pleas in the Crown Court—some 70 per cent of Crown Court cases in our sample. Yet it would not erode what the defendant typically regards as his most important right and safeguard, namely the right to claim trial by jury in a contested case. We have seen that magistrates are seen by some defendants, especially those with the greatest experience, as offering second-class justice. The magistrates are seen as incurably pro-police, 'amateurs' unable to give the case full, fair and careful consideration. The change we suggest would leave open the route to the 'first-class' justice of the Crown Court for the man who wished to plead not guilty: it would be much more acceptable to defendants than the recently heard suggestions from Lord Hailsham and others for restricting the range of offences for which jury trial may be claimed.

In chapter 4 we examined the special group of DGs who opted for higher court trial with a view to securing not trial by jury, but a Crown Court sentence rather than a magistrates' sentence. The reform we have suggested would preclude that particular strategy, but the great majority of defendants in our sample would choose to be sentenced in the magistrates' court, and this is especially the case among those with wide experience of the criminal justice system, so that our proposal would cater for the majority 'consumer' view for guilty as for the not guilty plea cases (assuming that a defendant is a consumer for at least some purposes).

These last questions emphasise the importance of the defendant's view in the development of policy in this area, as well as in the problem of explanation considered in the previous section. Consumer views of the legal system have been typically ignored by official committees investigating the system, but we hope that this will not be so in the future.

Our policy prescriptions, then, are largely in the direction of requiring greater Due Process in our system. (Reduction of delay is a part of the Due Process ideology, but is less contentious since it is also shared in general terms by both the Crime Control and Liberal Bureaucratic Models, though for different reasons.) That is not to say we are insensitive to the available Due Process routes of our system, not shared to the same extent in a number of other countries; nor is it to say we are unaware of the need for administrative efficiency. But our research has revealed a number of areas where from the defendant's point of view, adequate Due Process is not available—and we agree with him that it should be made more freely available.

Implications for future research

There has been nothing less than an explosion of interest in empirical research in the criminal justice process in England over the last decade. Prior to 1965, such studies scarcely existed, though Gibson's (1960) early Home Office study was a notable exception. Since then, there has been a whole spate of studies: half a dozen from the pen of Zander, and others which we have cited from academics such as Bottomley, Davies, Dell, King, McCabe and Purves, as well as official studies by Rose and by Simon and Weatheritt. There is yet further work outside the scope of this book such as the LSE Jury Project and the Oxford Shadow Jury Study.

Without any question this has been a most healthy development. Practising lawyers are apt to generalise, not to say pontificate, from a few cases they have handled; academic lawyers are too prone to armchair speculation about empirical reality. Both groups have found out from this spate of research that their presumed knowledge has sometimes not stood the hard test of adequate empirical evidence. Even more importantly, the climate of opinion has changed so that few if any are now to be heard (as once they were) decrying empirical research as unnecessary to legal study, and as leading at best to confirmation of the obvious.

So much is pure gain. Yet we need to stand back a little and question whether this particular phase, useful as it has been, may not need to be transcended.

Leaving on one side the official studies such as Rose's, two things stand out about the research done in English criminal justice to date. The first is that virtually all the studies have been carried out by individuals or groups primarily motivated by a liberal-reformist ideology. The second, and closely related, point is that the primary interest in the research has been the policy implications rather than explanations of the phenomena observed.

This seems likely to change very soon. The research to date has been carried out either by empirically minded lawyers or by social administration researchers with an interest in law. For both of these groups, the primacy of policy interest is natural. More recently, however, there has been a notable burgeoning of academic interest in the sociology of law; and although this has so far been more concerned with theoretical discussion than empirical study, the latter is certain to follow. When it does, it is natural that it should have a stronger explanatory interest than the existing body of literature: for a pioneering study, see Carlen's (1974) work in a London magistrates' court.

Our own research was conceived largely in the older traditions. As we have explained in chapter 1, we were originally motivated partly by an administrative or policy interest, and partly by a civil rights or 'liberal-reformist' ideology (though within these parameters, we were interested in psychologistic explanation). Quite by chance, however, we alighted on a particular interest—the defendant's perspective—which was partially compatible with certain strands in modern deviance theory, and which thus allowed us to graft an 'appreciative' perspective on to our earlier design. Although this grafting was only partial, and the appreciative element of our research is less than we would now have wished it to be, yet it did lead us to our 'appreciative typology' as developed in chapter 3. And that typology, as we said at the end of that chapter, directly raises major explanatory questions about the action of defendants in the 'survival crisis' which a criminal charge so often presents.

Yet that is not the end of the matter. Earlier in this chapter, we were able to consider the possible role of aspects of the criminal justice system itself in producing the various defendants' postures which we had earlier identified in the typology; and it seemed clear that links existed between some rules and procedures of the system and the passivity of many defendants. In developing this argument, we had to develop a new 'model' of a criminal justice system, which we called the 'Liberal Bureaucratic Model'. It seems a reasonable speculation, from our knowledge of the English system and our reading of American materials, that the Liberal Bureaucratic Model is far more fully developed in practice in this country than in the USA; conversely, of course, 'bargain' models of justice seem much more prevalent there.

Such observations raise problems at a deeper level of explanation. For adequate explanation of the individual defendant's action, we shall need in the last resort an explanation also of the strength of the Liberal Bureaucratic Model in the English context. Such an explanation can only come from a wide-ranging yet deep historio-sociological analysis of the development of the English system, including inter alia analyses of the ideology and organisation of the legal profession. This kind of explanation-in-depth is an important part of the explanatory task which is clearly apparent, but which has scarcely yet been even touched upon, in the context of the English criminal justice system.

A distinctive feature of our research has been its emphasis on the defendant's perspective. Other researchers have also considered this perspective (see Zander's studies of appellants), but none previously in England across such a wide range of topics as in this study. We think it can fairly be claimed that this has been a fruitful exercise; but we are conscious that our study has done no more than make an initial contribution in this area. For one thing, there were many possible areas of defendants' views which we did not fully investigate, such as their perception of the role of the judge or magistrates in the case, the role of the clerk, detailed exploration of solicitor-client contacts and so on. Second, we are aware that from a fully 'appreciative' perspective one would have required a deeper explication of what defendants said and meant in the areas where they did give us their views; and a study along these lines, less concerned with some of the factual and structural questions which we felt we needed to ask in a pioneering study, would be beneficial.

These wider and deeper explorations of the defendant's perspective, which we propose, would be of value for both policy and explanatory purposes. We have seen above how the defendant's view is a neglected element in policy discussion, and further work along these lines needs to be done. From an explanatory point of view also, we hope we have shown enough to indicate that the meaning of the court processes to the defendant is one of the very important aspects of explanation. But here we need to be cautious, for we have shown also (especially in the first part of this chapter) how crucial for explanation are the structures of the system. Hence we would be wary of a straightforwardly phenomenological extension of our view of the defendant's perspective, since this would run the danger of abandoning the importance of structure: rather we would favour a mode of explanation such as the Weberian which emphasised both structure and the defendant's meaning.

Essentially, then, we suggest a move towards more explanatory research in criminal justice arising out of this study, while retaining the importance of the defendant's perspective. That is not to say that we decry liberal-reformist administrative research, for we do not—especially as our own research is in large part of this nature! Nor does it mean that we think administrative 'fact-finding' research for policy ends should come to a halt at this point in time—there are clearly many aspects of the criminal justice system of which we need to know more, and research of this kind can help us to do so. But the continuation of this kind of research should be accompanied by a move towards explanatory research, for ultimately (as we have shown from our own study) administrative research raises important explanatory questions. Moreover, unless we know more of the answers to some of those explanatory questions, our efforts at policy-making will be hindered by operating to change the system in ignorance of the true nature of the system, and hence of the possible consequences of policy changes we might introduce into it.

Appendix: The press and the probation service

Readers may have been surprised to find very little reference to either the press or the probation service in the main text, even though members of both organisations were present in court when almost all our defendants were dealt with. In fact our research showed these institutions to be of relatively little importance to most defendants, so the apparent neglect is justified: but a short note on each should be included.

The press

Sheffield's nightly evening newspaper, the *Star*, carried short reports on the outcome of the vast majority of cases in our sample. Defendants given non-custodial sentences, or acquitted, had usually seen these reports: those in custody had not, unless a relative or friend had brought a cutting. But the great majority (76 per cent, as reweighted) of those interviewed had fully expected the case to be in the paper, since they knew that such cases are routinely reported. Only in two sub-sample groups, the SGUs and the SNs, did the proportion definitely not expecting publicity reach as high as one-fifth: significantly, these were the least criminally experienced sub-sample groups. Overall, the proportion not expecting publicity was 13 per cent, while the remaining 11 per cent said they had not thought about possible publicity before the hearing.

The original reason for our inclusion of questions about press reporting was that some legal books, and some practising lawyers, assert that defendants sometimes plead guilty rather than not guilty because of the greater publicity thought to be accorded to contested cases. If a not guilty plea is entered, much more court time is occupied, witnesses' statements are made in greater detail, prosecution and defence lawyers make longer speeches—and so the newspaperman gets more 'copy'. The defendant, frightened of this, may decide to go for minimum publicity and plead guilty.

This hypothesis depends on the view that defendants think there will be more publicity for not guilty pleas. Of those defendants who had thought about it at all in our sample, a clear majority did take this view. But a few did not, and we ought to point out that there is some justification for their view. We did not count column inches, but a previous study which did (Martin and Webster, 1971, p.67) failed to produce clear-cut differences by plea decision. Moreover in our sample at the lower court level, there was actually less chance of publicity for the not guilty cases, because the *Star* often did not send a reporter to the special afternoon court sessions set aside for hearing contested magistrates' court cases. Hence the SN group had a higher proportion (33 per cent) of unreported final appearances than any other sub-sample group: however, no case was found in the sample of anyone knowing about this and pleading not guilty to avoid publicity.

Five of our interviewees did follow the line of the 'lawyer's hypothesis' and said that they had been influenced to plead guilty by the fear of greater press coverage. However, these constitute only 2·2 per cent of all guilty pleas, and moreover only 2 of the 5 said that the question of publicity had been more than a peripheral consideration in deciding their plea. In short, any suggestion that large numbers of defendants are induced to plead guilty by the fear of greater publicity should—on the basis of our research—be discounted.

Since we were exploring this question of the press, we decided to ask all defendants who had seen reports about themselves what they felt about it. (Martin and Webster, though discussing 'the social consequences of conviction' and including a thorough study of the press coverage of their sample, had surprisingly failed to ask their men this question.) The replies we received range from total indifference to real shock and suffering at the unpleasant exposure. The answers, classified into broad categories, are shown in Table A.1.

When these categories were considered by sub-sample type, it was noticeable that the not guilty pleas were more likely to be worried by press publicity than the guilty pleaders: 22 per cent of the former were in the 'very upset' category, against 13 per cent for guilty pleaders.

A more dramatic result appeared when the data were considered by the defendants' typology. Not surprisingly, the 'respectable first-timers' were the group most upset by the publicity; but the difference between this group and the rest was enormous—76 per cent of respectable first-timers who had seen a report were very upset, as against 28 per cent for the next highest typology group

Table A.1 Defendants' reaction to press reports

Reaction	%
Not worried at all	36·4
Not worried for himself, but upset for sake of relatives, etc.	14·7
Somewhat disturbed	22·4
Very upset	14·2
Other reaction	2·4
Not relevant (not in paper or defendants had not seen report)	9·8
Total	100·0

(the 'other strategists', including many middle-class defendants).

The following are some examples of 'respectable first-timers'' reactions to press publicity:

> 'I feel awful—it's really very bad. The neighbours all know, and there's my job—I might lose my job.'

> 'I feel terrible. I'm well known round here, and to see it in the paper is just terrible. My wife is very ill, it would really upset her if she knew, I have to keep it away from her somehow.'

> 'I felt very upset about it. I didn't think it would be in the paper for a first offence.'

Thus, although overall at least half of all our defendants were not very worried about the press publicity from their own point of view, nevertheless for a minority press exposure is a very traumatic experience. Martin and Webster (1971, p.71) have pointed out that in some European countries it is unusual to give the names and addresses of defendants as is routinely done in the English press: it is worth considering whether there really are any social benefits in the English practice, to set against the undoubted distress to some defendants.

The probation service

In the Sheffield courts, it is customary for a probation officer's 'social inquiry report' to be considered at the sentencing stage in the

Crown Court; but at the magistrates' court level, social inquiry reports are relatively rare except in serious cases.

It is sometimes suggested that where social inquiry reports are available, the role of the defence lawyer is minimal, because the probation report will be a much more effective weapon in procuring a low sentence. There is some truth in this in some defendants' eyes:

> 'The probation officer came to court, he was very good, and stopped me from going down.'
>
> 'The probation officer helped me more than Mr X (defence lawyer) did.'
>
> 'The probation officer got me the conditional discharge by his report' (a represented case).
>
> 'The probation officer spoke for me in court and said probation was what I needed; the judge really listened to him, and then seemed as if he wanted to help me.'
>
> 'The probation officer was to make a report with all the details, there was no point in getting a lawyer' (an SGU case).

However, we must not exaggerate the influence of the probation service. Our results are less than complete, because we did not ask direct questions about probation officers' roles in the case, but only in 6·5 per cent of cases did defendants spontaneously mention the great help of the probation service, as in the extracts above; and in only one SGU case (the last-cited extract) was the probation officer's help given as a reason for not having a lawyer. Nor are these results entirely attributable to differential availability of social inquiry reports, for in Crown Court cases (where reports are commoner) probation officers' helpfulness was mentioned marginally less often than in lower court cases. Overall, it would seem from these results, incomplete as they are, that most defendants do not see the probation officer as a worthwhile substitute for a defence lawyer.

In recent years social workers have increasingly tended to move away from a quasi-psychotherapeutic role vis-à-vis their clients; and one possible substitute role which has been suggested is the 'advocate' role, whereby the worker acts as an advocate, pointing out to the client his rights, how he may fight threatened freedoms and so on. We were interested to find that in a very small number of cases (about 3 per cent in all), probation officers had been reported by defendants as strongly pressing the need for legal representation, or suggesting a not guilty plea, or advising an appeal, or advising application to the judge in chambers. Though this is a small proportion, it is probably larger than that to be found a few years ago.

Overall, however, as with the press, the main conclusion is that probation officers at present have little direct influence over the way that most defendants approach the court, or over the various decisions that have to be made by defendants in the criminal process.

Notes

Chapter 1 Birth of a research project

1 Actually this was a doubtful view; during the trial there was a technical dispute between counsel on a point of evidence, and the judge had given quite a strong hint about the possibility of an appeal: for details see note 2 to chapter 7.

2 Casper's work (1972) did not come to our attention until a late stage in drafting this report, and had no influence on our original research design. It covers a wider field than our own work, including defendants' comments on, e.g., prosecutors, judges, the nature of law and the causes of crime. It is restricted, however, to 71 respondents (almost half of them addicted to heroin: p.151) who were apparently chosen by less than perfect sampling methods and whose trials were not observed by the author (p.xii): rightly therefore Casper offers little quantitative evidence in his report. The utility of the book for comparison between English and American defendants is considerably reduced by the very different context of the legal systems of the two countries with, e.g., the American stress on 'bargain justice', the role of the public defender and so on.

3 In a very few cases juveniles were included because they were tried jointly with an adult and the court did not remit to the juvenile court for sentence.

4 When the grant for the project was made it was not clear when the date of changeover would be; once we had begun the research and completed the pilot period it would have been uneconomic to pay staff, etc. for two months just to wait for the inception of the new system.

5 These categories do not cover every possible eventuality, e.g. of a defendant at first in custody by court order, then granted bail, then committing a further offence while on bail and being recommitted to custody. In the very rare cases of this kind, we took along different parts of the interview schedule (in this case, IV B(f) and (g)) and applied them as well as was possible in the circumstances.

6 This conclusion would have been strengthened had we at that time read Martin and Webster (1971), where the careless and dangerous drivers were shown to be very different from ordinary indictable offenders on many aspects of the social consequences of conviction.

7 Defendants given custodial sentences were of course seen in the relevant institution, usually Leeds Prison. But to ensure comparability between custodial and non-custodial interviewees, we made no attempt to interview defendants with addresses outside Sheffield who were given custodial sentences.

8 On 'disproportionate stratified sampling', see Moser and Kalton (1971, pp. 93ff). Stratification itself usually causes an increase in accuracy of the sample: the effect of disproportionate stratification as against simple stratification (i.e. with a single sampling fraction) is complex and depends on the variability within strata, which in this case was unknown at the time of constructing the research design.

9 A seasonal factor may be involved: we found the highest proportion of defendants choosing higher court trial in our November magistrates' court cases (9 per cent), and the lowest (1½ per cent) in December. It is also

possible that fears about the (unknown) effect of the new Crown Court artificially reduced the number of 'D' cases in our research period, but nothing in our interviews directly suggested this. A further possibility is that lawyers' recommendations as to court of trial may have changed from 1970-2; we show in chapter 4 that these are often very important in venue decisions.

10 The letter was headed 'Survey of Sheffield Court Cases', a deliberately neutral form of words intended to suggest that the emphasis was to be on the legal process rather than on the defendant himself. The text of the letter is given below:

> The University Law Department is making a survey of some of the cases heard in the Sheffield Court. I was in court when your case was heard and I would like to come and talk to you about it. We are very interested to find out what you thought about the court and in hearing your opinions.
>
> I hope that it will be convenient for me to call on you in the next few days, and that you will be able to help with our survey. It will not take long and we hope that what you say will help other people appearing before the court in the future.
>
> Anything you say will be completely confidential, your name will not be given to anyone else and nobody will be told what you have said. My visit is made with the knowledge and approval of the court authorities.

Unlike Martin and Webster (1971, p.20), we experienced no difficulty about our university auspices, possibly because we were working from the local university which is centrally situated and well known to most Sheffield residents.

11 In Tables 1.5, 1.6 and 1.8, details are given for the complete court sample and the complete interview sample. In carrying out tests of significance, however, the measurement was always between the interview sample and one of two groups (made clear in the context)—either the full court sample less the interviewed cases, or the 'eligible for interview' (excluding non-Sheffield and sex cases) less the interviewed cases.

12 The rateable value measurement was found in an earlier Sheffield study to be a useful but incomplete measure of social class differential (Baldwin and Bottoms, 1975, chapter 2, esp. note 22). That study also found a slight tendency for convicted offenders from outside Sheffield to be of higher social class than Sheffield residents ($p < 0.05$, see Table 10), and thus be excluding such defendants we might have marginally weighted our interview sample towards the working class. There was however no way of providing a direct test of this in the present study.

13 Because the occupation data were contained on otherwise confidential records, police manpower had to be used to extract this information for us, and we did not feel justified in asking for any but the minimum necessary cases to obtain data for the interview sample only.

14 The 'DG' group was an exception in being of higher social class than the other guilty-plea groups, and almost equivalent to the not guilty groups. But this exception really does prove the rule, since the majority of DGs originally intended to plead not guilty (chs 4 and 5).

Chapter 2 Court business: legal and administrative considerations

1 A strict comparison would involve taking into account in the England and Wales figures those offences which though summary offences give the defendant the right to trial by jury. Almost certainly, no significant change in the distribution would appear.

2 Additionally, more information about the police case is available to the defendant tried on indictment. This may increase the likelihood of a not guilty plea: see case 7026, discussed at the end of chapter 5.

3 The post-war trend has been to reduce considerably the categories of offences which must be tried at a higher court: see especially the Criminal Justice Administration Act 1962. As more serious offences have become triable summarily, it could be that magistrates have made proportionately greater use of their power to refuse summary trial.

4 This policy is not followed slavishly: in one case, some youths had burgled the attic of an unoccupied house and taken stamps which, unknown to them, were rare and subsequently valued at £7,300—summary trial was agreed to. Reliance on value as a criterion has its dangers, as value is not always accurately assessed: in one case in our sample the magistrates ordered Crown Court trial on a charge of burgling a shop and theft of goods valued £2,574; in the Crown Court the defendant pleaded not guilty to this but said he would plead guilty to an amended charge valuing the goods at £100, which the prosecution accepted.

5 For those tried in the magistrates' courts, Gibson had a sample of remanded cases only, i.e. those not dealt with at one appearance. For this reason we make no direct comparisons of our summary trial data against hers.

6 Here, and throughout this section, it must be remembered that there can be more than one adjournment for the same reason in a particular case. The relationship between the number of adjournments and the resulting delay is complicated by the different lengths of adjournments. An adjournment coupled with a remand in custody cannot be for a period in excess of 8 days. Where there is remand on bail, or in the case of a convicted defendant remanded in custody or on bail for reports, longer adjournments are possible, and usual.

7 Table 2.4 actually slightly understates the guilty-not guilty distinction: in a small number of cases unrepresented defendants pleaded not guilty, were adjourned X weeks, and advised to get a lawyer; the lawyer's advice was to plead guilty, but the defendant still had to wait the full period for his final disposal.

8 We should record also that all but one committal cases were actually committed for trial; the exception was an intended 'section one' committal which was abandoned by the prosecution.

9 Gibson examined the period between committal and the commencement of the trial in the higher court; Rose that between committal and the final disposal of the case. We follow Rose's practice; it is this delay which concerns the defendant.

Chapter 3 Approaching the court: the defendant's perspective

1 In some cases 'bail' is omitted; where this is so, the defendant was on bail throughout the proceedings.

2 Casper (1972, p.55) independently indicated a 'passive' versus 'strategist' distinction in relation to two cases, but made no attempt to develop a full typology of defendants' responses.

Chapter 4 Venue

1 As we show more fully in chapter 6, the criminal legal aid system now ensures legal representation in almost all higher court cases. The report on which this system is based (Home Office, 1966) was clearly aware of the venue choice question (para. 145) but did not note the obvious implication that one sure way of obtaining legal aid under the system would be to insist on higher court trial

(even if pleading guilty). However, none of our defendants chose the higher court for this reason.

2 Lord Hailsham, the then Lord Chancellor, had said in speeches before this announcement that serious consideration must be given to restricting the right to trial by jury in order to relieve the pressure on the Crown Court. In announcing the formation of the Committee, to sit under Lord Justice James, the Home Secretary referred to the 'widespread view that the law allows too many cases to go for trial' at the Crown Court; but he acknowledged that fundamental issues were involved in any possible rearrangement of business (H.C. Deb. 859, col. 224). The terms of reference of the Committee are: 'to consider within the framework of the existing court structure what should be the distribution of business between the Crown Court and magistrates' court; and what changes in law and practice are desirable to that end.'

3 See also chapter 5, Table 5.2, where it is shown that sexual and aggressive offences have (taking summary and higher court cases together) the highest proportions of not guilty pleas of any offence types—and of course not guilty pleas are far more likely to result in defendants' election of higher court trial than are guilty pleas.

4 Astute readers will perceive some differences between the proportions with experience in previous criminal cases, as shown in Table 4.4, and the previous convictions data from the court sample (Table 1.7). In all sub-sample groups, the difference (if any) is in the direction of more previous experience being revealed in the interview sample; this is explained by defendants telling us in interview of motoring convictions or other minor convictions not known to or not revealed by the police in court.

5 Actually this is a doubtful view. There is no direct evidence, but indirect evidence may be adduced from the fate in the Crown Court of cases sent up for sentence by magistrates because (under s.29, Magistrates' Courts Act 1952) they considered their own sentencing powers inadequate. In 1972, 20 per cent of such cases received a non-custodial sentence in the Crown Court; 12 per cent received a suspended sentence of imprisonment; and 11 per cent received immediate imprisonment for 6 months or less, i.e. within the magistrates' sentencing powers for imprisonment (source: *Criminal Statistics 1972,* tables II(a) and III).

6 Willett's (1973, p.81) sample of serious motoring offenders gave 'expense' as a dominant reason for not choosing Crown Court trial (mentioned by one-third of those who had considered but rejected the possibility of such trial). This reason did not appear at all in our sample (see Table 4.8), presumably because our defendants were much more likely than Willett's to be financially eligible for legal aid in the Crown Court. The other reasons given by Willett's sample roughly accorded with our results.

7 The size of the 'other' category in Table 4.12 may occasion surprise: but because of the small numbers in the 'D' sub-sample groups, it actually amounts to six DGs and five DNs. The DGs are largely the 'real' DGs, who had special reasons for the decision (see the case histories at the end of this chapter); the rest often gave 'other' reasons in addition to main reasons as specified in the table. One pair of DN cases is worth recording as a classic case of shared misunderstanding; this concerned two co-employees charged with theft from their employers. They were separately represented and did not know or like each other; A, the younger man, was advised by his solicitor that B (the older) was going to the Crown Court and there was the danger of his being acquitted there while A was convicted by the magistrates, although (on A's version of the affair) he was much less involved in the matter. Thus A elected Crown Court trial; but actually B had been going to elect summary trial. After

A's election, B's solicitor advised him also to go to the Crown Court, although in B's own view 'it should have been in the magistrates' '!

8 One of these three is a woman; but we refer to her throughout the book in the masculine gender. This is not male chauvinism, it is the only available means to conceal her identity and preserve anonymity.

9 A further feature of Table 4.13 is that Mr A has a higher proportion of guilty pleas among his cases (77 per cent) than do either B or C (each 55 per cent). There is however no evidence from the interviews that Mr A presses harder for guilty pleas in borderline cases than do Messrs B and C.

10 The single exceptional case of an SN represented by Mr C is worth brief examination. The reason given by the defendant for the venue choice was that 'the amount of money involved in the case was less than the cost of lawyer's fees in the higher court' (the defendant was not legally aided as he had £3,000 capital); the matter was discussed with Mr C who 'thought it a good idea' to have summary trial. Perhaps significantly, this was a case where the defendant admitted in our interview that he was guilty of handling stolen goods as charged, and that the only reason he had pleaded not guilty was that 'the police said they had information to suggest I was a big-time fence; I knew I'd been dishonest but they weren't going to make me out to be a criminal, so I pleaded not guilty'.

11 The *Legal Action Group Bulletin,* August 1973, alleged that 'one reason why so many legally represented defendants elect trial by jury is the persistent refusal of prosecuting authorities to disclose their case to the defence before summary trials' (p.162). This may be part of the motivation of solicitor C, but if so, no hint of it was passed on to any defendant in the sample. In any case it is obvious from our data that not all solicitors hold the view expressed in the *LAG Bulletin.*

12 As we showed in chapter 1, there was a higher proportion of DGs in our preliminary three-month sample than in the final court sample. Because we have data from magistrates' courts' records only, we do not know how many of the DGs in the preliminary sample were plea-changes.

Chapter 5 Plea

1 The DG category are excluded from this section because of their special features: 12 of the 17 interviewed cases were late changes of plea, discussed later in this chapter, and the other 5 cases have already been set out in chapter 4. Readers may note that in chapter 4 we did not present a similar randomly selected list of cases on venue choice; the reason is that the answers were less interesting, being dominated for summary trials simply by the two reasons of 'getting it over' and 'lesser sentencing powers'.

2 This result should not be treated as necessarily typical of all American jurisdictions. Thus Casper (1972, p.33) reports that of his sample, 'only a few protested their innocence, most in an unconvincing manner'.

3 A further short study is by Clive Davies (1970). This contains interesting case material and general observations, but cannot be regarded as an adequate study of the problem: Davies's interview schedule asked only about bail, and no other information was sought, so data on 'innocent guilty pleas' is confined to those in the sample who volunteered such information without any prompting. From his general experience as a barrister in criminal courts, Davies guesses that the number of innocent guilty pleas 'may run into thousands—possibly tens of thousands—every year'.

4 It seems illogical to exclude this group since they may in fact have a better legal defence than some who believe themselves innocent. For example, in case 4027 (one of the 'true DGs' discussed in chapter 4), the defendant pleaded

guilty to theft of money which he had taken from a fellow-lodger's mantelpiece, believing that because the other man owed him money it was in order for him to take this sum. He was advised by a solicitor that this was theft, and accepted the advice; in fact the legal position is much less clear-cut, and the man's case in law was stronger than that of some others who thought themselves innocent.

Chapter 6 Legal representation

1 The other four headings are: (i) that the charge raises a substantial question of law; (ii) that (due to poor command of English, mental illness, etc.) the accused is unable to follow the proceedings and state his case; (iii) that the nature of the defence involves the tracing and interviewing of witnesses or expert cross-examination of a witness for the prosecution; (iv) that legal representation is desirable in the interest of someone other than the accused.

2 The delay from 1968 to 1972 in officially commending the Widgery criteria to courts seems to have been something of an oversight. The matter was raised during debates on the Criminal Justice Bill 1972, when attempts were made statutorily to enact the criteria; this the government successfully resisted but promised to issue the circular, which it did shortly thereafter.

3 Section 57 of the Criminal Justice Act 1967 allowed the Home Secretary to make rules prohibiting the passing of a custodial sentence in the absence of a social inquiry report. No such rules have been made, though the section has been commended to courts by Home Office Circular (HOC Nos 188-9/1968).

4 One amusing incident should be recorded. A defendant, H, applied for legal aid and did not specify any solicitor. To his horror he was allocated Mr X, whose office H had helped to burgle some years before, receiving 6 months' imprisonment for his trouble! Surprisingly, H did not seek to change the lawyer on this occasion; changing lawyers, although allowed under the legal aid scheme, is very rare and took place in only 4 cases in our sample (twice because of a conflict of interests between two codefendants previously represented by the same advocate, and twice because of the client's dissatisfaction with the lawyer's performance).

5 For the reasons stated in the preceding text, these extracts are taken only from 'D' and 'H' cases for barristers, and only from 'S' cases for solicitors. We have restricted the extracts to opinions on the leading practitioners: the three leading solicitors each have 5 cases quoted, and the five leading barristers each have 3 cases quoted.

6 In the Japanese criminal trial, such a system operates. After the closing statement by the defence counsel, the presiding judge says to the defendant: 'Defence counsel has made a favourable argument for you. Is there anything you wish to add to it?' See Dando (1965) at p.621.

7 The Widgery Committee did state that cases requiring 'expert' cross-examination should receive legal aid (see note 1 to this chapter); we do not consider this enough. It is recognised that there is a potential problem of the strategist who may plead not guilty just to get legal aid; however, such cases will be few and in any case a similar possibility as regards venue choice already exists under the Widgery rules (see note 1 to chapter 4).

Chapter 7 Appeal

1 One defendant who had been given a suspended prison sentence feared that the appeal court might give him a worse sentence, a fine. This is an interesting comment on the defendant's perception of a suspended sentence, and raises a

nice legal point. The courts cannot vary a sentence on appeal so as to deal 'more severely' with the defendant. Is a fine more or less severe than a suspended sentence? (See the cases discussed by Thomas, 1972a, at p.298.)

2 This case (no. 5013) has been fully summarised at the beginning of chapter 1. The technical point concerned the admissibility of the evidence of the recidivist (who at the time of the alleged offence had been a shop assistant in the shop, but by the trial was already in prison!): he said he could not remember which case this was as he had made 'so many statements at that time', and asked permission to refresh his memory of events by reading his signed statement. Defence counsel objected strongly to this, but the judge permitted it, while asking the recidivist witness to 'state whether the statement helped him genuinely to recollect'. The judge added that he was 'aware' that his ruling on this matter 'could be taken to a higher authority'.

3 As Zander pointed out, Prison Department establishments vary in the degree of special attention paid to appeals. During the course of our research, we were informed that one senior detention centre made a special feature of briefing all its inmates about appeals, and that all were given full details on arrival. As a result, 150 out of 700 youths received at the centre in 1971 had lodged applications for appeal, which in view of the short sentences involved (typically 2 months, allowing for remission) is a very high proportion. However, none of the detention centre inmates in our interview sample appealed.

Chapter 8 Bail or custody

1 Bottomley (1973, p.87) suggests that greater use should be made of summonses; he argues that the appearance of the defendant in response to the summons provides firm evidence about the likelihood of his appearing for a subsequent hearing without the need for a remand in custody. It is difficult to see the force of this argument, for the appearance of the defendant in response to police bail provides similar evidence. The use of summonses seems irrelevant: so, in Sheffield summonses are used in many fewer cases than in Bottomley's urban court area (see his 1970 research on which his 1973 comment is based) but remands in custody are also much fewer in Sheffield.

2 Here and elsewhere in this chapter, comparisons have been made with the Simon and Weatheritt sample excluding cases triable only summarily (which do not fall within our Sheffield sample). The bail rates given in the text are calculated from the totals in Simon and Weatheritt's Tables 3, 4 and 7; there is a slight element of inaccuracy (as their tables are based on patterns of decisions at certain stages, and do not count individual decisions) but the change over time is important.

3 Thus, Bottomley (1970, p.18) quotes the national figure of committal on bail in 62 per cent of such cases in 1965; his rural court granted bail in 54 per cent but his urban court in only 40 per cent (p.29). The Cobden Trust found a bail rate of 61 per cent (King, 1971, p.15; but p.97 gives 66 per cent).

4 A professor of law who is also a senior lay magistrate accepts the dominance of the police view as inevitable: 'the justices often cannot at that stage learn much about the case and must rely to a considerable extent on police statements' (Jackson, 1972, p.190). Simon and Weatheritt (1974) had no information about police opposition to bail in their cases; but they demonstrate (at p.15) the close relationship between police bail and court decisions.

5 The Cobden Trust (1971) report 61 per cent at p.15 for committals for trial, but 66·3 per cent for 'remand during committal proceedings after committal for trial' at p.97. Zander (1971, p.193) finds 74 per cent for 'remands during or after committal for trial proceedings' which appears to include remands at early appearances.

6 One case was brought of a man already serving a prison sentence for another offence, appearing in court on a Home Office production order—he has been excluded from this figure, although obviously he did not apply for bail.

Chapter 9 Conclusions and implications

1 Certain grave crimes could be excluded from this procedure and made the subject of automatic committal to the Crown Court if the defendant pleaded guilty.

Bibliography

Alschuler, A. W. (1968), 'The prosecutor's role in plea bargaining', *University of Chicago Law Review,* 36, pp. 50-112.

Arcuri, A. F. (1973), 'Police perceptions of plea-bargaining', *Journal of Police Science,* 1, pp. 93-101.

Association of Chief Police Officers (1966), 'Trial by jury', *New Law Journal,* 116, pp. 928-31.

Baldwin, J. and Bottoms, A. E. (1975), *The Urban Criminal,* Tavistock, London.

Beeching Report (1969), *Report of the Royal Commission on Assizes and Quarter Sessions* (Chairman, Lord Beeching), HMSO, London (Cmnd 4153). (See also Rose, 1971.)

Blumberg, A. S. (1967), *Criminal Justice,* Quadrangle Books, Chicago.

Borrie, G. J. and Varcoe, J. R. (1971), *Legal Aid in Criminal Proceedings,* University of Birmingham Institute of Judicial Administration.

Bottomley, A. K. (1968), 'The granting of bail: principles and practice', *Modern Law Review,* 31, pp. 40-54.

Bottomley, A. K. (1970), *Prison Before Trial,* Bell, London.

Bottomley, A. K. (1973), *Decisions in the Penal Process,* Martin Robertson, London.

Bottoms, A. E. (1973), 'Methodological aspects of classification in criminology', *Collected Studies in Criminological Research* (Council of Europe), 10, pp. 27-76.

Bottoms, A. E. and McClintock, F. H. (1973), *Criminals Coming of Age,* Heinemann Educational, London.

Carlen, P. (1974), 'Magistrates' Courts: an ethnography in the sociology of the absurd', unpublished Ph.D. thesis, University of London.

Casper, J. D. (1972), *American Criminal Justice: the Defendant's Perspective,* Prentice-Hall, Englewood Cliffs, New Jersey.

Cobden Trust: see Paterson, (1970), King, (1971).

Cohen, S. and Taylor, L. (1972), *Psychological Survival,* Penguin, Harmondsworth.

Criminal Appeal Office (1974), *Preparation for Proceedings in the Court of Appeal, Criminal Division,* June.

Criminal Law Revision Committee (1972), *Eleventh Report: Evidence [General],* HMSO, London (Cmnd 4991).

Cross, R. (1971), *The English Sentencing System,* Butterworth, London.

Cross, R. and Jones, P. A. (1972), *Introduction to Criminal Law,* 7th edn, Butterworth, London.

Dando, S. (1965), *The Japanese Law of Criminal Procedure* (trans. B. J. George), F. B. Rothman, South Hackensack, New Jersey.

Davies, C. (1970), 'The innocent who plead guilty', *Law Guardian,* March 1970, pp. 9-15.

Davies, C. (1971), 'Pre-trial imprisonment: a Liverpool study', *British Journal of Criminology,* 11, pp. 32-48.

Davis, A. (1971), 'Sentences for sale: a new look at plea-bargaining in England and America', *Criminal Law Review,* pp. 150-61, 218-28.

Dell, S. (1971), *Silent in Court,* Bell, London.

Downes, D. M. (1965), *The Delinquent Solution,* Routledge & Kegan Paul, London.

Durant, M., Thomas, M. and Willcock, H. D. (1972), *Crime, Criminals and the Law,* Office of Population Censuses and Surveys, London.

Foote, C., Markle, J. P. and Wolley, E. (1954), 'Compelling appearance in court: administration of bail in Philadelphia', *University of Pennsylvania Law Review,* pp. 1031-79.

Friedland, M. L. (1965), *Detention before Trial,* University of Toronto Press.

Gibson, E. (1960), *Time Spent Awaiting Trial,* HMSO, London.

Goldberg, E. M. (1970), *Helping the Aged,* Allen & Unwin, London.

Griffiths, J. (1970), 'Ideology in criminal procedure, or a third "model" of the Criminal Process', *Yale Law Journal,* 79, pp. 359-417.

Hogarth, J. (1971), *Sentencing as a Human Process,* University of Toronto Press.

Home Office (1966), *Report of the Departmental Committee on Legal Aid in Criminal Proceedings* (Chairman, Lord Widgery), HMSO, London (Cmnd 2934).

Home Office (1974), *Report of the Working Party on Bail in Magistrates' Courts,* HMSO, London.

Home Office: see also Gibson, (1960); Simon and Weatheritt, (1974); Home Office Research Studies.

Hood, R. (1972), *Sentencing the Motoring Offender,* Heinemann Educational, London.

Institute on the Operation of Pretrial Release Projects (1965), *Bail and Summons 1965,* New York.

Jackson, R. M. (1972), *The Machinery of Justice in England,* 6th edn, Cambridge University Press.

JUSTICE (1971), *The Unrepresented Defendant in Magistrates' Courts,* Stevens, London.

Katz, L., Litwin, L. and Bamberger, R. (1972), *Justice is the Crime: Pretrial Delay in Felony Cases,* Case Western Reserve University Press, Cleveland, Ohio.

King, M. (1971), *Bail or Custody,* Cobden Trust, London.

LaFave, W. (1965), *Arrest,* Little, Brown, Boston.

Legal Action Group (1974), 'Duty solicitor schemes: a LAG report', *Legal Advice Group Bulletin,* pp. 207-10.

Lord Chancellor's Office (1965), *Report of the Interdepartmental Committee on the Court of Criminal Appeal* (Chairman, Lord Donovan), HMSO, London (Cmnd 2755).

McCabe, S. and Purves, R. (1972), *By-passing the Jury,* Basil Blackwell, Oxford.

Martin, J. P. and Webster, D. (1971), *The Social Consequences of Conviction,* Heinemann Educational, London.

Matza, D. (1969), *Becoming Deviant,* Prentice-Hall, Englewood Cliffs, New Jersey.

Mayer, J. E. and Timms, N. (1970), *The Client Speaks,* Routledge & Kegan Paul, London.

Moser, C. A. and Kalton, G. (1971), *Survey Methods in Social Investigation,* 2nd edn, Heinemann Educational, London.

Napley, D. (1966a), 'Problems of effecting the preparation of the case for the defense', *Columbia Law Review,* 66, pp. 94-108.

Napley, D. (1966b), 'The case for preliminary inquiries', *Criminal Law Review,* pp. 490-8, 556-7.

Newman, D. J. (1966), *Conviction: the Determination of Guilt or Innocence without Trial,* Little, Brown, Boston.

OPCS: see Durant et al. (1972).

Packer, H. L. (1969), *The Limits of the Criminal Sanction,* Stanford University Press.

Paterson, A. (1970), *Legal Aid as a Social Service,* Cobden Trust, London.

Phillipson, M. (1971), *Sociological Aspects of Crime and Delinquency,* Routledge & Kegan Paul, London.

Phillipson, M. (1972), 'Theory, methodology and conceptualization', chapter 5 in P. Filmer et al., *New Directions in Sociological Theory,* Collier-Macmillan, London.

Phillipson, M. and Roche, M. (1974), 'Phenomenology, sociology and the study of deviance', pp. 125-62 in P. Rock and M. McIntosh, eds, *Deviance and Social Control,* Tavistock, London.

Rose, G. N. G. (1971), *Royal Commission on Assizes and Quarter Sessions 1966-69: Special Statistical Survey,* HMSO, London.

Simon, F. and Weatheritt, M. (1974), *The Use of Bail and Custody by London Magistrates' Courts Before and After the Criminal Justice Act 1967,* HMSO, London.

Sparks, R. F. (1971), *Local Prisons: the Crisis in the English Penal System,* Heinemann Educational, London.

Steer, D. J. and Carr-Hill, R. A. (1967), 'The motoring offender—who is he?', *Criminal Law Review,* pp. 214-24.

Streatfeild Report (1961), *Report of the Interdepartmental Committee on the Business of the Criminal Courts* (Chairman, Mr Justice Streatfeild), HMSO, London (Cmnd 1289).

Sudnow, D. (1965), 'Normal crimes: sociological features of the penal code', *Social Problems,* 12, pp. 255-70.

Thomas, D. A. (1970), *Principles of Sentencing,* Heinemann Educational, London.

Thomas, D. A. (1972a), 'Increasing sentences on appeal—a re-examination', *Criminal Law Review,* pp. 288-306.

Thomas, D. A. (1972b), 'Committals for trial and sentence—the case for simplification', *Criminal Law Review,* pp. 477-94.

Timms, N. (1973), *The Receiving End,* Routledge & Kegan Paul, London.

West, D. J. (1963), *The Habitual Prisoner,* Macmillan, London.

Wice, P. B. (1974), *Freedom for Sale: A National Study of Pre-trial Release,* Lexington Books, D. C. Heath, Lexington, Mass.

Willett, T. C. (1973), *Drivers after Sentence,* Heinemann Educational, London.

Zander, M. (1967), 'Bail—a re-appraisal', *Criminal Law Review,* pp. 25-39, 100-10, 128-42.

Zander, M. (1969), 'Unrepresented defendants in the criminal courts', *Criminal Law Review,* pp. 632-45.

Zander, M. (1971), 'A study of bail/custody decisions in London magistrates' courts', *Criminal Law Review,* pp. 191-211.

Zander, M. (1972a), 'Legal advice and criminal appeals: a survey of prisoners, prisons and lawyers', *Criminal Law Review,* pp. 132-73.

Zander, M. (1972b), 'Access to a solicitor in the police station', *Criminal Law Review,* pp. 342-50.

Zander, M. (1973), *Cases and Materials on the English Legal System,* Weidenfeld & Nicolson, London.

Zander, M. (1974), 'Are too many professional criminals avoiding conviction?—a study in Britain's two busiest courts', *Modern Law Review,* 37, pp. 28-61.

Index of names

Index of subjects

Routledge Social Science Series

Routledge & Kegan Paul London and Boston

68–74 Carter Lane London EC4V 5EL

9 Park Street Boston Mass 02108

Contents

Authors wishing to submit manuscripts for any series in this catalogue should send them to the Social Science Editor, Routledge & Kegan Paul Ltd, 68–74 Carter Lane, London EC4V 5EL

● *Books so marked are available in paperback*
All books are in Metric Demy 8vo format (216 × 138mm approx.)

International Library of Sociology

General Editor John Rex

GENERAL SOCIOLOGY

Barnsley, J. H. The Social Reality of Ethics. *464 pp.*

Belshaw, Cyril. The Conditions of Social Performance. *An Exploratory Theory. 144 pp.*

Brown, Robert. Explanation in Social Science. *208 pp.*

● Rules and Laws in Sociology. *192 pp.*

Bruford, W. H. Chekhov and His Russia. *A Sociological Study. 244 pp.*

Cain, Maureen E. Society and the Policeman's Role. *326 pp.*

●**Fletcher, Colin.** Beneath the Surface. *An Account of Three Styles of Sociological Research. 221 pp.*

Gibson, Quentin. The Logic of Social Enquiry. *240 pp.*

Glucksmann, M. Structuralist Analysis in Contemporary Social Thought. *212 pp.*

Gurvitch, Georges. Sociology of Law. *Preface by Roscoe Pound. 264 pp.*

Hodge, H. A. Wilhelm Dilthey. *An Introduction. 184 pp.*

Homans, George C. Sentiments and Activities. *336 pp.*

Johnson, Harry M. Sociology: *a Systematic Introduction. Foreword by Robert K. Merton. 710 pp.*

●**Keat, Russell,** and **Urry, John.** Social Theory as Science. *278 pp.*

Mannheim, Karl. Essays on Sociology and Social Psychology. *Edited by Paul Keckskemeti. With Editorial Note by Adolph Lowe. 344 pp.*

Systematic Sociology: *An Introduction to the Study of Society. Edited by J. S. Erös and Professor W. A. C. Stewart. 220 pp.*

Martindale, Don. The Nature and Types of Sociological Theory. *292 pp.*

●**Maus, Heinz.** A Short History of Sociology. *234 pp.*

Mey, Harald. Field-Theory. *A Study of its Application in the Social Sciences. 352 pp.*

Myrdal, Gunnar. Value in Social Theory: *A Collection of Essays on Methodology. Edited by Paul Streeten. 332 pp.*

Ogburn, William F., and **Nimkoff, Meyer F.** A Handbook of Sociology. *Preface by Karl Mannheim. 656 pp. 46 figures. 35 tables.*

Parsons, Talcott, and **Smelser, Neil J.** Economy and Society: *A Study in the Integration of Economic and Social Theory. 362 pp.*

Podgórecki, Adam. Practical Social Sciences. *About 200 pp.*

●**Rex, John.** Key Problems of Sociological Theory. *220 pp.*

Discovering Sociology. *278 pp.*

Sociology and the Demystification of the Modern World. *282 pp.*

●**Rex, John** (Ed.) Approaches to Sociology. *Contributions by Peter Abell, Frank Bechhofer, Basil Bernstein, Ronald Fletcher, David Frisby, Miriam Glucksmann, Peter Lassman, Herminio Martins, John Rex, Roland Robertson, John Westergaard and Jock Young. 302 pp.*

Rigby, A. Alternative Realities. *352 pp.*

Roche, M. Phenomenology, Language and the Social Sciences. *374 pp.*

Sahay, A. Sociological Analysis. *220 pp.*

Strasser, Hermann. The Normative Structure of Sociology. *Conservative and Emancipatory Themes in Social Thought. About 340 pp.*

Urry, John. Reference Groups and the Theory of Revolution. *244 pp.*

Weinberg, E. Development of Sociology in the Soviet Union. *173 pp.*

FOREIGN CLASSICS OF SOCIOLOGY

●**Durkheim, Emile.** Suicide. *A Study in Sociology. Edited and with an Introduction by George Simpson. 404 pp.*

Professional Ethics and Civic Morals. *Translated by Cornelia Brookfield. 288 pp.*

●**Gerth, H. H.,** and **Mills, C. Wright.** From Max Weber: *Essays in Sociology. 502 pp.*

●**Tönnies, Ferdinand.** Community and Association. (*Gemeinschaft und Gesellschaft.*) *Translated and Supplemented by Charles P. Loomis. Foreword by Pitirim A. Sorokin. 334 pp.*

SOCIAL STRUCTURE

Andreski, Stanislav. Military Organization and Society. *Foreword by Professor A. R. Radcliffe-Brown. 226 pp. 1 folder.*

Coontz, Sydney H. Population Theories and the Economic Interpretation. *202 pp.*

Coser, Lewis. The Functions of Social Conflict. *204 pp.*

Dickie-Clark, H. F. Marginal Situation: *A Sociological Study of a Coloured Group. 240 pp. 11 tables.*

Glaser, Barney, and **Strauss, Anselm L.** Status Passage. *A Formal Theory. 208 pp.*

Glass, D. V. (Ed.) Social Mobility in Britain. *Contributions by J. Berent, T. Bottomore, R. C. Chambers, J. Floud, D. V. Glass, J. R. Hall, H. T. Himmelweit, R. K. Kelsall, F. M. Martin, C. A. Moser, R. Mukherjee, and W. Ziegel. 420 pp.*

Jones, Garth N. Planned Organizational Change: *An Exploratory Study Using an Empirical Approach. 268 pp.*

Kelsall, R. K. Higher Civil Servants in Britain: *From 1870 to the Present Day. 268 pp. 31 tables.*

König, René. The Community. *232 pp. Illustrated.*

●**Lawton, Denis.** Social Class, Language and Education. *192 pp.*

McLeish, John. The Theory of Social Change: *Four Views Considered. 128 pp.*

Marsh, David C. The Changing Social Structure of England and Wales, 1871-1961. *288 pp.*

●**Mouzelis, Nicos.** Organization and Bureaucracy. *An Analysis of Modern Theories. 240 pp.*

Mulkay, M. J. Functionalism, Exchange and Theoretical Strategy. *272 pp.*

Ossowski, Stanislaw. Class Structure in the Social Consciousness. *210 pp.*

●**Podgórecki, Adam.** Law and Society. *302 pp.*

SOCIOLOGY AND POLITICS

Acton, T. A. Gypsy Politics and Social Change. *316 pp.*

Clegg, Stuart. Power, Rule and Domination. *A Critical and Empirical Understanding of Power in Sociological Theory and Organisational Life. About 300 pp.*

Hechter, Michael. Internal Colonialism. *The Celtic Fringe in British National Development, 1536–1966. 361 pp.*

Hertz, Frederick. Nationality in History and Politics: *A Psychology and Sociology of National Sentiment and Nationalism. 432 pp.*

Kornhauser, William. The Politics of Mass Society. *272 pp. 20 tables.*

● **Kroes, R.** Soldiers and Students. *A Study of Right- and Left-wing Students. 174 pp.*

Laidler, Harry W. History of Socialism. *Social-Economic Movements: An Historical and Comparative Survey of Socialism, Communism, Co-operation, Utopianism; and other Systems of Reform and Reconstruction. 992 pp.*

Lasswell, H. D. Analysis of Political Behaviour. *324 pp.*

Mannheim, Karl. Freedom, Power and Democratic Planning. *Edited by Hans Gerth and Ernest K. Bramstedt. 424 pp.*

Mansur, Fatma. Process of Independence. *Foreword by A. H. Hanson. 208 pp.*

Martin, David A. Pacifism: *an Historical and Sociological Study. 262 pp.*

Myrdal, Gunnar. The Political Element in the Development of Economic Theory. *Translated from the German by Paul Streeten. 282 pp.*

Wootton, Graham. Workers, Unions and the State. *188 pp.*

FOREIGN AFFAIRS: THEIR SOCIAL, POLITICAL AND ECONOMIC FOUNDATIONS

Mayer, J. P. Political Thought in France from the Revolution to the Fifth Republic. *164 pp.*

CRIMINOLOGY

Ancel, Marc. Social Defence: *A Modern Approach to Criminal Problems. Foreword by Leon Radzinowicz. 240 pp.*

Cain, Maureen E. Society and the Policeman's Role. *326 pp.*

Cloward, Richard A., and **Ohlin, Lloyd E.** Delinquency and Opportunity: *A Theory of Delinquent Gangs. 248 pp.*

Downes, David M. The Delinquent Solution. *A Study in Subcultural Theory. 296 pp.*

Dunlop, A. B., and **McCabe, S.** Young Men in Detention Centres. *192 pp.*

Friedlander, Kate. The Psycho-Analytical Approach to Juvenile Delinquency: *Theory, Case Studies, Treatment. 320 pp.*

Glueck, Sheldon, and **Eleanor.** Family Environment and Delinquency. *With the statistical assistance of Rose W. Kneznek. 340 pp.*

Lopez-Rey, Manuel. Crime. *An Analytical Appraisal. 288 pp.*

Mannheim, Hermann. Comparative Criminology: *a Text Book. Two volumes. 442 pp. and 380 pp.*

Morris, Terence. The Criminal Area: *A Study in Social Ecology. Foreword by Hermann Mannheim. 232 pp. 25 tables. 4 maps.*

Rock, Paul. Making People Pay. *338 pp.*

● **Taylor, Ian, Walton, Paul,** and **Young, Jock.** The New Criminology. *For a Social Theory of Deviance. 325 pp.*

● **Taylor, Ian, Walton, Paul,** and **Young, Jock** (Eds). Critical Criminology. *268 pp.*

SOCIAL PSYCHOLOGY

Bagley, Christopher. The Social Psychology of the Epileptic Child. *320 pp.*

Barbu, Zevedei. Problems of Historical Psychology. *248 pp.*

Blackburn, Julian. Psychology and the Social Pattern. *184 pp.*

● **Brittan, Arthur.** Meanings and Situations. *224 pp.*

Carroll, J. Break-Out from the Crystal Palace. *200 pp.*

● **Fleming, C. M.** Adolescence: Its Social Psychology. *With an Introduction to recent findings from the fields of Anthropology, Physiology, Medicine, Psychometrics and Sociometry. 288 pp.*

● The Social Psychology of Education: *An Introduction and Guide to Its Study. 136 pp.*

● **Homans, George C.** The Human Group. *Foreword by Bernard DeVoto. Introduction by Robert K. Merton. 526 pp.*

● Social Behaviour: *its Elementary Forms. 416 pp.*

● **Klein, Josephine.** The Study of Groups. *226 pp. 31 figures. 5 tables.*

Linton, Ralph. The Cultural Background of Personality. *132 pp.*

● **Mayo, Elton.** The Social Problems of an Industrial Civilization. *With an appendix on the Political Problem. 180 pp.*

Ottaway, A. K. C. Learning Through Group Experience. *176 pp.*

Plummer, Ken. Sexual Stigma. *An Interactionist Account. 254 pp.*

Ridder, J. C. de. The Personality of the Urban African in South Africa. *A Thermatic Apperception Test Study. 196 pp. 12 plates.*

● **Rose, Arnold M.** (Ed.) Human Behaviour and Social Processes: *an Interactionist Approach. Contributions by Arnold M. Rose, Ralph H. Turner, Anselm Strauss, Everett C. Hughes, E. Franklin Frazier, Howard S. Becker, et al. 696 pp.*

Smelser, Neil J. Theory of Collective Behaviour. *448 pp.*

Stephenson, Geoffrey M. The Development of Conscience. *128 pp.*

Young, Kimball. Handbook of Social Psychology. *658 pp. 16 figures. 10 tables.*

SOCIOLOGY OF THE FAMILY

Banks, J. A. Prosperity and Parenthood: *A Study of Family Planning among The Victorian Middle Classes. 262 pp.*

Bell, Colin R. Middle Class Families: *Social and Geographical Mobility. 224 pp.*

Burton, Lindy. Vulnerable Children. *272 pp.*

Gavron, Hannah. The Captive Wife: *Conflicts of Household Mothers. 190 pp.*

George, Victor, and **Wilding, Paul.** Motherless Families. *248 pp.*

Klein, Josephine. Samples from English Cultures.

1. Three Preliminary Studies and Aspects of Adult Life in England. *447 pp.*
2. Child-Rearing Practices and Index. *247 pp.*

Klein, Viola. Britain's Married Women Workers. *180 pp.*

The Feminine Character. *History of an Ideology. 244 pp.*

McWhinnie, Alexina M. Adopted Children. *How They Grow Up. 304 pp.*

● **Morgan, D. H. J.** Social Theory and the Family. *About 320 pp.*

● **Myrdal, Alva,** and **Klein, Viola.** Women's Two Roles: *Home and Work. 238 pp. 27 tables.*

Parsons, Talcott, and **Bales, Robert F.** Family: Socialization and Interaction Process. *In collaboration with James Olds, Morris Zelditch and Philip E. Slater. 456 pp. 50 figures and tables.*

SOCIAL SERVICES

Bastide, Roger. The Sociology of Mental Disorder. *Translated from the French by Jean McNeil. 260 pp.*

Carlebach, Julius. Caring For Children in Trouble. *266 pp.*

George, Victor. Foster Care. *Theory and Practice. 234 pp.*

Social Security: *Beveridge and After. 258 pp.*

George, V., and **Wilding, P.** Motherless Families. *248 pp.*

● **Goetschius, George W.** Working with Community Groups. *256 pp.*

Goetschius, George W., and **Tash, Joan.** Working with Unattached Youth. *416 pp.*

Hall, M. P., and **Howes, I. V.** The Church in Social Work. *A Study of Moral Welfare Work undertaken by the Church of England. 320 pp.*

Heywood, Jean S. Children in Care: *the Development of the Service for the Deprived Child. 264 pp.*

Hoenig, J., and **Hamilton, Marian W.** The De-Segregation of the Mentally Ill. *284 pp.*

Jones, Kathleen. Mental Health and Social Policy, 1845-1959. *264 pp.*

King, Roy D., Raynes, Norma V., and **Tizard, Jack.** Patterns of Residential Care. *356 pp.*

Leigh, John. Young People and Leisure. *256 pp.*

● **Mays, John.** (Ed.) Penelope Hall's Social Services of England and Wales. *About 324 pp.*

Morris, Mary. Voluntary Work and the Welfare State. *300 pp.*

Morris, Pauline. Put Away: *A Sociological Study of Institutions for the Mentally Retarded. 364 pp.*

Nokes, P. L. The Professional Task in Welfare Practice. *152 pp.*

Timms, Noel. Psychiatric Social Work in Great Britain (1939-1962). *280 pp.*

● Social Casework: *Principles and Practice. 256 pp.*

Young, A. F. Social Services in British Industry. *272 pp.*

Young, A. F., and **Ashton, E. T.** British Social Work in the Nineteenth Century. *288 pp.*

SOCIOLOGY OF EDUCATION

Banks, Olive. Parity and Prestige in English Secondary Education: a Study in Educational Sociology. *272 pp.*

Bentwich, Joseph. Education in Israel. *224 pp. 8 pp. plates.*

●**Blyth, W. A. L.** English Primary Education. *A Sociological Description.*
1. Schools. *232 pp.*
2. Background. *168 pp.*

Collier, K. G. The Social Purposes of Education: *Personal and Social Values in Education. 268 pp.*

Dale, R. R., and **Griffith, S.** Down Stream: *Failure in the Grammar School. 108 pp.*

Dore, R. P. Education in Tokugawa Japan. *356 pp. 9 pp. plates.*

Evans, K. M. Sociometry and Education. *158 pp.*

●**Ford, Julienne.** Social Class and the Comprehensive School. *192 pp.*

Foster, P. J. Education and Social Change in Ghana. *336 pp. 3 maps.*

Fraser, W. R. Education and Society in Modern France. *150 pp.*

Grace, Gerald R. Role Conflict and the Teacher. *150 pp.*

Hans, Nicholas. New Trends in Education in the Eighteenth Century. *278 pp. 19 tables.*

● Comparative Education: *A Study of Educational Factors and Traditions. 360 pp.*

●**Hargreaves, David.** Interpersonal Relations and Education. *432 pp.*

● Social Relations in a Secondary School. *240 pp.*

Holmes, Brian. Problems in Education. *A Comparative Approach. 336 pp.*

King, Ronald. Values and Involvement in a Grammar School. *164 pp.*

School Organization and Pupil Involvement. *A Study of Secondary Schools.*

●**Mannheim, Karl,** and **Stewart, W. A. C.** An Introduction to the Sociology of Education. *206 pp.*

Morris, Raymond N. The Sixth Form and College Entrance. *231 pp.*

●**Musgrove, F.** Youth and the Social Order. *176 pp.*

●**Ottaway, A. K. C.** Education and Society: An Introduction to the Sociology of Education. *With an Introduction by W. O. Lester Smith. 212 pp.*

Peers, Robert. Adult Education: *A Comparative Study. 398 pp.*

Pritchard, D. G. Education and the Handicapped: *1760 to 1960. 258 pp.*

Richardson, Helen. Adolescent Girls in Approved Schools. *308 pp.*

Stratta, Erica. The Education of Borstal Boys. *A Study of their Educational Experiences prior to, and during, Borstal Training. 256 pp.*

Taylor, P. H., Reid, W. A., and **Holley, B. J.** The English Sixth Form. *A Case Study in Curriculum Research. 200 pp.*

SOCIOLOGY OF CULTURE

Eppel, E. M., and **M.** Adolescents and Morality: *A Study of some Moral Values and Dilemmas of Working Adolescents in the Context of a changing Climate of Opinion. Foreword by W. J. H. Sprott. 268 pp. 39 tables.*

●**Fromm, Erich.** The Fear of Freedom. *286 pp.*
● The Sane Society. *400 pp.*
Mannheim, Karl. Essays on the Sociology of Culture. *Edited by Ernst Mannheim in co-operation with Paul Kecskemeti. Editorial Note by Adolph Lowe. 280 pp.*
Weber, Alfred. Farewell to European History: *or The Conquest of Nihilism. Translated from the German by R. F. C. Hull. 224 pp.*

SOCIOLOGY OF RELIGION

Argyle, Michael and **Beit-Hallahmi, Benjamin.** The Social Psychology of Religion. *About 256 pp.*
Nelson, G. K. Spiritualism and Society. *313 pp.*
Stark, Werner. The Sociology of Religion. *A Study of Christendom.*
Volume I. *Established Religion. 248 pp.*
Volume II. *Sectarian Religion. 368 pp.*
Volume III. *The Universal Church. 464 pp.*
Volume IV. *Types of Religious Man. 352 pp.*
Volume V. *Types of Religious Culture. 464 pp.*
Turner, B. S. Weber and Islam. *216 pp.*
Watt, W. Montgomery. Islam and the Integration of Society. *320 pp.*

SOCIOLOGY OF ART AND LITERATURE

Jarvie, Ian C. Towards a Sociology of the Cinema. *A Comparative Essay on the Structure and Functioning of a Major Entertainment Industry. 405 pp.*
Rust, Frances S. Dance in Society. *An Analysis of the Relationships between the Social Dance and Society in England from the Middle Ages to the Present Day. 256 pp. 8 pp. of plates.*
Schücking, L. L. The Sociology of Literary Taste. *112 pp.*
Wolff, Janet. Hermeneutic Philosophy and the Sociology of Art. *150 pp.*

SOCIOLOGY OF KNOWLEDGE

Diesing, P. Patterns of Discovery in the Social Sciences. *262 pp.*
●**Douglas, J. D.** (Ed.) Understanding Everyday Life. *370 pp.*
●**Hamilton, P.** Knowledge and Social Structure. *174 pp.*
Jarvie, I. C. Concepts and Society. *232 pp.*
Mannheim, Karl. Essays on the Sociology of Knowledge. *Edited by Paul Kecskemeti. Editorial Note by Adolph Lowe. 353 pp.*
Remmling, Gunter W. The Sociology of Karl Mannheim. *With a Bibliographical Guide to the Sociology of Knowledge, Ideological Analysis, and Social Planning. 255 pp.*

Remmling, Gunter W. (Ed.) Towards the Sociology of Knowledge. *Origin and Development of a Sociological Thought Style. 463 pp.*

Stark, Werner. The Sociology of Knowledge: *An Essay in Aid of a Deeper Understanding of the History of Ideas. 384 pp.*

URBAN SOCIOLOGY

Ashworth, William. The Genesis of Modern British Town Planning: *A Study in Economic and Social History of the Nineteenth and Twentieth Centuries. 288 pp.*

Cullingworth, J. B. Housing Needs and Planning Policy: *A Restatement of the Problems of Housing Need and 'Overspill' in England and Wales. 232 pp. 44 tables. 8 maps.*

Dickinson, Robert E. City and Region: *A Geographical Interpretation 608 pp. 125 figures.*

The West European City: *A Geographical Interpretation. 600 pp. 129 maps. 29 plates.*

● The City Region in Western Europe. *320 pp. Maps.*

Humphreys, Alexander J. New Dubliners: *Urbanization and the Irish Family. Foreword by George C. Homans. 304 pp.*

Jackson, Brian. Working Class Community: *Some General Notions raised by a Series of Studies in Northern England. 192 pp.*

Jennings, Hilda. Societies in the Making: *a Study of Development and Redevelopment within a County Borough. Foreword by D. A. Clark. 286 pp.*

●**Mann, P. H.** An Approach to Urban Sociology. *240 pp.*

Morris, R. N., and **Mogey, J.** The Sociology of Housing. *Studies at Berinsfield. 232 pp. 4 pp. plates.*

Rosser, C., and **Harris, C.** The Family and Social Change. *A Study of Family and Kinship in a South Wales Town. 352 pp. 8 maps.*

●**Stacey, Margaret, Batsone, Eric, Bell, Colin,** and **Thurcott, Anne.** Power, Persistence and Change. *A Second Study of Banbury. 196 pp.*

RURAL SOCIOLOGY

Chambers, R. J. H. Settlement Schemes in Tropical Africa: *A Selective Study. 268 pp.*

Haswell, M. R. The Economics of Development in Village India. *120 pp.*

Littlejohn, James. Westrigg: *the Sociology of a Cheviot Parish. 172 pp. 5 figures.*

Mayer, Adrian C. Peasants in the Pacific. *A Study of Fiji Indian Rural Society. 248 pp. 20 plates.*

Williams, W. M. The Sociology of an English Village: *Gosforth. 272 pp. 12 figures. 13 tables.*

SOCIOLOGY OF INDUSTRY AND DISTRIBUTION

Anderson, Nels. Work and Leisure. *280 pp.*

●**Blau, Peter M.,** and **Scott, W. Richard.** Formal Organizations: *a Comparative approach. Introduction and Additional Bibliography by J. H. Smith. 326 pp.*

Dunkerley, David. The Foreman. *Aspects of Task and Structure. 192 pp.*

Eldridge, J. E. T. Industrial Disputes. *Essays in the Sociology of Industrial Relations. 288 pp.*

Hetzler, Stanley. Applied Measures for Promoting Technological Growth. *352 pp.*

Technological Growth and Social Change. *Achieving Modernization. 269 pp.*

Hollowell, Peter G. The Lorry Driver. *272 pp.*

Jefferys, Margot, *with the assistance of Winifred Moss.* Mobility in the Labour Market: *Employment Changes in Battersea and Dagenham. Preface by Barbara Wootton. 186 pp. 51 tables.*

Millerson, Geoffrey. The Qualifying Associations: *a Study in Professionalization. 320 pp.*

●**Oxaal, I., Barnett, T.,** and **Booth, D.** (Eds). Beyond the Sociology of Development. *Economy and Society in Latin America and Africa. 295 pp.*

Smelser, Neil J. Social Change in the Industrial Revolution: *An Application of Theory to the Lancashire Cotton Industry, 1770–1840. 468 pp. 12 figures. 14 tables.*

Williams, Gertrude. Recruitment to Skilled Trades. *240 pp.*

Young, A. F. Industrial Injuries Insurance: *an Examination of British Policy. 192 pp.*

DOCUMENTARY

Schlesinger, Rudolf (Ed.) Changing Attitudes in Soviet Russia.

2. The Nationalities Problem and Soviet Administration. *Selected Readings on the Development of Soviet Nationalities Policies. Introduced by the editor. Translated by W. W. Gottlieb. 324 pp.*

ANTHROPOLOGY

Ammar, Hamed. Growing up in an Egyptian Village: *Silwa, Province of Aswan. 336 pp.*

Brandel-Syrier, Mia. Reeftown Elite. *A Study of Social Mobility in a Modern African Community on the Reef. 376 pp.*

Crook, David, and **Isabel.** Revolution in a Chinese Village: *Ten Mile Inn. 230 pp. 8 plates. 1 map.*

Dickie-Clark, H. F. The Marginal Situation. *A Sociological Study of a Coloured Group. 236 pp.*

Dube, S. C. Indian Village. *Foreword by Morris Edward Opler. 276 pp. 4 plates.*

India's Changing Villages: *Human Factors in Community Development. 260 pp. 8 plates. 1 map.*

Firth, Raymond. Malay Fishermen. *Their Peasant Economy. 420 pp. 17 pp. plates.*

Firth, R., Hubert, J., and **Forge, A.** Families and their Relatives. *Kinship in a Middle-Class Sector of London: An Anthropological Study. 456 pp.*

Gulliver, P. H. Social Control in an African Society: a Study of the Arusha, Agricultural Masai of Northern Tanganyika. *320 pp. 8 plates. 10 figures.*

Family Herds. *288 pp.*

Ishwaran, K. Shivapur. *A South Indian Village. 216 pp.*

Tradition and Economy in Village India: *An Interactionist Approach. Foreword by Conrad Arensburg. 176 pp.*

Jarvie, Ian C. The Revolution in Anthropology. *268 pp.*

Little, Kenneth L. Mende of Sierra Leone. *308 pp. and folder.*

Negroes in Britain. *With a New Introduction and Contemporary Study by Leonard Bloom. 320 pp.*

Lowie, Robert H. Social Organization. *494 pp.*

Peasants in the Pacific. *A Study of Fiji Indian Rural Society. 248 pp.*

Smith, Raymond T. The Negro Family in British Guiana: *Family Structure and Social Status in the Villages. With a Foreword by Meyer Fortes. 314 pp. 8 plates. 1 figure. 4 maps.*

SOCIOLOGY AND PHILOSOPHY

Barnsley, John H. The Social Reality of Ethics. *A Comparative Analysis of Moral Codes. 448 pp.*

Diesing, Paul. Patterns of Discovery in the Social Sciences. *362 pp.*

●**Douglas, Jack D.** (Ed.) Understanding Everyday Life. *Toward the Reconstruction of Sociological Knowledge. Contributions by Alan F. Blum. Aaron W. Cicourel, Norman K. Denzin, Jack D. Douglas, John Heeren, Peter McHugh, Peter K. Manning, Melvin Power, Matthew Speier, Roy Turner, D. Lawrence Wieder, Thomas P. Wilson and Don H. Zimmerman. 370 pp.*

Jarvie, Ian C. Concepts and Society. *216 pp.*

●**Pelz, Werner.** The Scope of Understanding in Sociology. *Towards a more radical reorientation in the social humanistic sciences. 283 pp.*

Roche, Maurice. Phenomenology, Language and the Social Sciences. *371 pp.*

Sahay, Arun. Sociological Analysis. *212 pp.*

Sklair, Leslie. The Sociology of Progress. *320 pp.*

International Library of Anthropology

General Editor Adam Kuper

Brown, Paula. The Chimbu. *A Study of Change in the New Guinea Highlands. 151 pp.*

Hamnett, Ian. Chieftainship and Legitimacy. *An Anthropological Study of Executive Law in Lesotho. 163 pp.*

Hanson, F. Allan. Meaning in Culture. *127 pp.*

Lloyd, P. C. Power and Independence. *Urban Africans' Perception of Social Inequality. 264 pp.*

Pettigrew, Joyce. Robber Noblemen. *A Study of the Political System of the Sikh Jats. 284 pp.*

Street, Brian V. The Savage in Literature. *Representations of 'Primitive' Society in English Fiction, 1858–1920. 207 pp.*

Van Den Berghe, Pierre L. Power and Privilege at an African University. *278 pp.*

International Library of Social Policy

General Editor Kathleen Jones

Bayley, M. Mental Handicap and Community Care. *426 pp.*

Butler, J. R. Family Doctors and Public Policy. *208 pp.*

Davies, Martin. Prisoners of Society. *Attitudes and Aftercare. 204 pp.*

Holman, Robert. Trading in Children. *A Study of Private Fostering. 355 pp.*

Jones, Kathleen. History of the Mental Health Service. *428 pp.*

Opening the Door. *A Study of New Policies for the Mentally Handicapped. 260 pp.*

Thomas, J. E. The English Prison Officer since 1850: *A Study in Conflict. 258 pp.*

Walton, R. G. Women in Social Work. *303 pp.*

Woodward, J. To Do the Sick No Harm. *A Study of the British Voluntary Hospital System to 1875. 221 pp.*

International Library of Welfare and Philosophy

General Editors Noel Timms and David Watson

● **Plant, Raymond.** Community and Ideology. *104 pp.*

Primary Socialization, Language and Education

General Editor Basil Bernstein

Bernstein, Basil. Class, Codes and Control. *3 volumes.*

1. *Theoretical Studies Towards a Sociology of Language. 254 pp.*
2. *Applied Studies Towards a Sociology of Language. 377 pp.*
3. *Towards a Theory of Educational Transmission. 167 pp.*

Brandis, W., and **Bernstein, B.** Selection and Control. *176 pp.*

Brandis, Walter, and **Henderson, Dorothy.** Social Class, Language and Communication. *288 pp.*

Cook-Gumperz, Jenny. Social Control and Socialization. *A Study of Class Differences in the Language of Maternal Control. 290 pp.*

● **Gahagan, D. M.,** and **G. A.** Talk Reform. *Exploration in Language for Infant School Children. 160 pp.*

Robinson, W. P., and **Rackstraw, Susan D. A.** A Question of Answers. *2 volumes. 192 pp. and 180 pp.*

Turner, Geoffrey J., and **Mohan, Bernard A.** A Linguistic Description and Computer Programme for Children's Speech. *208 pp.*

Reports of the Institute of Community Studies

Cartwright, Ann. Human Relations and Hospital Care. *272 pp.*

● Parents and Family Planning Services. *306 pp.*

Patients and their Doctors. *A Study of General Practice. 304 pp.*

Dench, Geoff. Maltese in London. *A Case-study in the Erosion of Ethnic Consciousness. 302 pp.*

● **Jackson, Brian.** Streaming: *an Education System in Miniature. 168 pp.*

Jackson, Brian, and **Marsden, Dennis.** Education and the Working Class: *Some General Themes raised by a Study of 88 Working-class Children in a Northern Industrial City. 268 pp. 2 folders.*

Marris, Peter. The Experience of Higher Education. *232 pp. 27 tables.*

Loss and Change. *192 pp.*

Marris, Peter, and **Rein, Martin.** Dilemmas of Social Reform. *Poverty and Community Action in the United States. 256 pp.*

Marris, Peter, and **Somerset, Anthony.** African Businessmen. *A Study of Entrepreneurship and Development in Kenya. 256 pp.*

Mills, Richard. Young Outsiders: *a Study in Alternative Communities. 216 pp.*

Runciman, W. G. Relative Deprivation and Social Justice. *A Study of Attitudes to Social Inequality in Twentieth-Century England. 352 pp.*

Willmott, Peter. Adolescent Boys in East London. *230 pp.*

Willmott, Peter, and **Young, Michael.** Family and Class in a London Suburb. *202 pp. 47 tables.*

Young, Michael. Innovation and Research in Education. *192 pp.*

● **Young, Michael,** and **McGeeney, Patrick.** Learning Begins at Home. *A Study of a Junior School and its Parents. 128 pp.*

Young, Michael, and **Willmott, Peter.** Family and Kinship in East London. *Foreword by Richard M. Titmuss. 252 pp. 39 tables.*

The Symmetrical Family. *410 pp.*

Reports of the Institute for Social Studies in Medical Care

Cartwright, Ann, Hockey, Lisbeth, and **Anderson, John L.** Life Before Death. *310 pp.*

Dunnell, Karen, and **Cartwright, Ann.** Medicine Takers, Prescribers and Hoarders. *190 pp.*

Medicine, Illness and Society

General Editor W. M. Williams

Robinson, David. The Process of Becoming Ill. *142 pp.*
Stacey, Margaret, *et al.* Hospitals, Children and Their Families. *The Report of a Pilot Study. 202 pp.*

Stimson, G. V., and **Webb, B.** Going to See the Doctor. *The Consultation Process in General Practice. 155 pp.*

Monographs in Social Theory

General Editor Arthur Brittan

●**Barnes, B.** Scientific Knowledge and Sociological Theory. *192 pp.*
Bauman, Zygmunt. Culture as Praxis. *204 pp.*
●**Dixon, Keith.** Sociological Theory. *Pretence and Possibility. 142 pp.*
Meltzer, B. N., Petras, J. W., and **Reynolds, L. T.** Symbolic Interactionism. *Genesis, Varieties and Criticisms. 144 pp.*
●**Smith, Anthony D.** The Concept of Social Change. *A Critique of the Functionalist Theory of Social Change. 208 pp.*

Routledge Social Science Journals

The British Journal of Sociology. *Managing Editor – Angus Stewart; Associate Editor – Michael Hill. Vol. 1, No. 1 – March 1950 and Quarterly. Roy. 8vo. All back issues available. An international journal publishing original papers in the field of sociology and related areas.*
Community Work. *Edited by David Jones and Marjorie Mayo. 1973. Published annually.*
Economy and Society. *Vol. 1, No. 1. February 1972 and Quarterly. Metric Roy. 8vo. A journal for all social scientists covering sociology, philosophy, anthropology, economics and history. Back numbers available.*
Religion. Journal of Religion and Religions. *Chairman of Editorial Board, Ninian Smart. Vol. 1, No. 1, Spring 1971. A journal with an interdisciplinary approach to the study of the phenomena of religion.*
Year Book of Social Policy in Britain, The. *Edited by Kathleen Jones. 1971. Published annually.*

Printed in Great Britain by Unwin Brothers Limited
The Gresham Press Old Woking Surrey
A member of the Staples Printing Group

June 1975